THE
FACES
OF THE
GODS

LESLIE G. DESMANGLES

THE
FACES
OF THE
GODS

VODOU AND ROMAN

CATHOLICISM IN HAITI

THE UNIVERSITY OF NORTH CAROLINA PRESS

CHAPEL HILL & LONDON

The paper in this book meets the guidelines for
permanence and durability of the Committee on
Production Guidelines for Book Longevity of the
Council on Library Resources.

99   98   97   6   5   4   3

Library of Congress Cataloging-in-Publication Data
Desmangles, Leslie Gérald.
   The Faces of the Gods: Vodou and Roman
Catholicism in Haiti / Leslie G. Desmangles.
      p.   cm.
   Includes bibliographical references and index.
   ISBN 0-8078-2059-8 (hard : alk. paper).—
ISBN 0-8078-4393-8 (pbk. : alk. paper)
   1. Voodooism—Haiti.   2. Catholic Church—Haiti.
3. Haiti—Religion.   I. Title.
BL2530.H3D48   1992
299'.67—dc20   92-53625
                                            CIP

In loving memory of my mother,
Irène "Miche" Hippolyte-Desmangles

CONTENTS

....

ILLUSTRATIONS

....

FIGURES

PREFACE   *Mountains cannot meet, people can.*

Written on a plaque in front of a *taptap* (street bus) in the city of Port-au-Prince, this proverb summarizes the nature of Haitian culture, which historically is a by-product of the meeting between peoples from three different regions: Europe, Africa, and the New World. Like Haitian culture, the traditions of Vodou, the folk religion of Haiti (an inextricable part of Haitian life), manifest beliefs and practices from these three regions. The characteristic ethos of Vodou reveals what the Haitian writer Jean Price-Mars recognized many years ago about negritude: that black cultures everywhere in the New World are unique expressions of African-American peoples' historical journey from slavery to freedom. In this journey, they have affronted sociopolitical circumstances in which they have learned to blend widely divergent cultural and religious traditions.

Written in connection with research in West Africa (Benin, Togo, Nigeria, and Zaïre) and throughout Haiti, this book explores the mythology surrounding the envisaged personae or faces of the Vodou gods, and describes the ritual practices tendered in their honor. More precisely, it examines the ways in which historically the West African, European Christian, and Amerindian New World beliefs and practices have combined to shape Vodou's theology as we know it today. This book also describes the role of Vodou in Haitian personal and public life.

There is much academic disagreement among scholars about the name of Haiti's folk religion, and about the orthography of the word *vodou*. The common term *voodoo*, a distortion of the Dahomean (or Beninois) word *vodu* (meaning "god" or "spirit"), has been used by many scholars (Deren, Laguerre). But unfortunately, in popular literature and films the term *voodoo* has been misconstrued as sorcery, witchcraft, and in some cases cannibalistic practices, all of which are false and have kindled many foreigners' prejudices not only about Vodou, but about Haitian culture in general. Other scholars have used the term *vodun* or *vodoun* (Leyburn, Mintz, Davis, Courlander) in order to dispel popular misconceptions about the religion. Although I have used *vodun* in the past, I adopt *Vodou* for this book because it is phonetically more correct, and because it corresponds to the nomenclature used by the Haitians themselves for their religion. Until 1986, Haitian Creole had no official orthography. Hence, both Haitian and foreign writers were left to their own devices in developing their systems of phonetic transcriptions. Many (Price-Mars and Paul, among others) have been influenced heavily by French orthography, using the francophone form *vaudou* in their writings. But the current method of phonetic transcription developed by Yves Dejean—the method most widely accepted by Haitians and used in elementary schools in Haiti since 1986—suggests that the correct spelling of the term is the one I have adopted. Likewise, because Haitian Creole possesses no *complete* dictionary, there is no official orthography for all the words in its vocabulary. Hence, the phonetic transcriptions of unwritten (or unrecorded) Creole words used throughout this book approximate the orthographic method suggested by Dejean.

No project of any magnitude can be undertaken without the cooperation of others, and I owe profound gratitude to many persons without whose support this book could not have become a reality. Many thanks go to my Vodouisants and West African friends with whom I spent many months during the field research that preceded this writing; they showed courtesy and friendliness toward me, introduced me to members of their communities, and patiently answered my numerous, naive questions about their religious beliefs and practices. I would like to extend my heartfelt appreciation and respect to them. I am also indebted to the National Endowment for the Humanities and to Trinity College in Hartford, Connecticut, for grants that made possible my field research in West Africa and Haiti, and my research at the Archives Nationales de Paris in France. To the Catholic brothers and fathers at the Catholic school of St. Louis de Gonzague and the Collège St. Martial in Port-au-Prince goes my profound gratitude for the use of their archival materials included in the historical details described in this study, and also to the Catholic Archevêché of Port-au-Prince and to the Haitian government's Department of Cults for providing the vital statistics related to the work of the Catholic Church in Haiti.

Finally, my work through the years has led me to "meet" a number of people without whose inspiration this book could not have been written. These include, among many others, Maya Deren, Roger Bastide, Sidney Mintz, James Leyburn, George Eaton Simpson, Robert Farris Thompson, Jean Price-Mars, Rémy Bastien, Harold Courlander, Leonard Barrett, Michel Laguerre, Alfred Métraux, and Melville Herskovits. I also wish to acknowledge particularly Dr. Jan Cohn, Dean of the Faculty of Trinity College, for her support and for making special funds available for the final preparation of this manuscript. My sincere gratitude goes also to Richard Hinman of North Carolina State University, Stephen Glazier of Kearney College, and Noel Erskine of Emory University for reading earlier versions of this manuscript; to André Craan of the Université du Québec à Montréal, and Louis Mars and Emmanuel Paul in Haiti, for reading portions of the present text; to McKim Steele, my esteemed colleague on the faculty of the Department of History at Trinity College, for making valuable suggestions about the history of Haiti included in Chapter 2; and to Gay Weidlich for typing and Julia McVaugh and Karlee Etter for editing this manuscript.

Most of all, I am indebted to my wife, Gertrude Chassagne, without whose patience and cooperation my field research would not have been possible; and to the children, Michelle, Tanya, and Micaël. They all sacrificed my presence and many of life's basic necessities to make this study possible.

L.G.D.

THE
FACES
OF THE
GODS

Republic of Haiti

Me

• Jérémie

Bahama Islands

Les Cayes •

Cuba

Dominican
Republic

Virgin
Islands

Jamaica   **HAITI**   Puerto Rico •

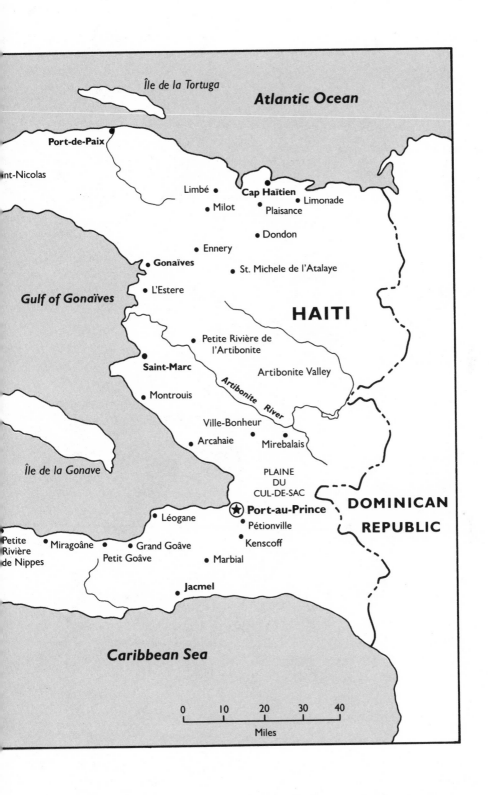

CULTURAL
....
SETTING:
....
RELIGIOUS
....
PARADOX OR
....
SYMBIOSIS

1

Anyone who has visited Haiti at least once is likely to have heard the maxim that Haitians are 100 percent Catholics and 90 percent Vodouisants. What seems to be a paradox here is no error, for the Roman Catholicism of Haiti is typically Haitian: in its institutional forms, its colorful and formal rituals, and its strict doctrinal emphases, it represents an extensive effort on the part of the clergy to respond to the religious, social, and cultural needs of Haitians. Concurrently, Vodou is the folk religion of Haiti that pervades the framework of Haitian culture.

Thanks to Hollywood and the film industry,[1] what average persons conjure up in their minds when they think of *Voodoo* is a picture of witches and sorcerers who, filled with hatred, attempt to inflict diseases or even death on other persons by making wax or wooden representations of them, and perforating them with pins. Another popular image of *Voodoo* or *Hoodoo* is that of a conglomeration of exotic spells celebrated clandestinely by blacks inebriated with blood: stunned by the invasion of their persons by supernatural forces, they enter into ecstatic and frenzied states of consciousness while performing magical rituals accompanied by occult incantations (Verschueren 1948, 276, 279).

The questionable reputation of Vodou today is due partly to a fictional incident that was said to have occurred in Bizoton, a section of the city of Port-au-Prince, during the latter half of the nineteenth century. On December 27, 1863, Claircine, a little girl, disappeared. The story is told that Haitians from all parts of the country conducted an extensive but futile search for her, with dwindling hope of ever finding her. It was then discovered that she had been killed and eaten by religious fanatics as part of a diabolic Vodou ceremony. An inquest into the matter revealed that fifteen people were responsible for the incident, all of whom were arrested, tried, and subsequently charged with cruelty, sorcery, and murder. Six weeks after the crime, amidst an angry mob that wanted revenge in exchange for Claircine's life, the accused villains were shot to death.

Whether this incident actually transpired remains a mystery; there are no legal records to substantiate its occurrence. But the publicity surrounding the report captured the imagination of journalists and novelists who, gifted with a flair for the exotic, dramatized the story and added to it details that appealed to a readership with an unquenchable thirst for the macabre and sinister. Their readers assumed that this fictional incident was true, and it reconfirmed in the minds of many what they already knew: that such atrocities were the result of the inherent and untamed savagery of blacks, not only in Haiti but throughout the world.

The intrigue that surrounded this incident both at home and abroad would have passed into oblivion within a few years after its publication, had it not been revived near the end of the century by Spenser St. John, a retired member of the British diplomatic corps in Haiti. Writing at the end of the Victorian era, when pioneers were discovering the interior of "dark Africa" and Christian missionaries were proselytizing its people, St. John described the culture of "primitive" Haitians whom he met during his tour of duty in the country. His book, entitled *Haiti and the Black Republic* and published in 1884, reflects the Europeans' widespread notions at that time about the "heathen practices" of unenlightened blacks whose moral laxity could only be redressed by the saving message of Christianity.

Whatever the motives may have been in popularizing such notions about Vodou, a scholarly examination reveals that in practice, none of its rituals confirms these popular views. As a religion, Vodou is practiced by nearly six million Haitians whose lives are shaped by the beliefs and practices of a complex religion with a rich historical tradition. It was brought largely by slaves from the Kongo and Dahomean regions (as well as many other parts) of West Africa to Santo Domingo or Saint-Domingue—as Haiti was called during its colonial period (1492–1804)—and the term *Voodoo* is a deterioration of the Dahomean term *vodu* or *vodun*, meaning "deity" or "spirit." Hence, Vodou in Haiti is a religion that, through a complex system of myths and rituals, relates the life of the devotee to the deities who govern that life. Like many religions of the world, Vodou is a system of beliefs and practices that gives meaning to life: it uplifts the spirits of the downtrodden who experience life's misfortunes, instills in its devotees a need for solace and self-examination, and relates the profane world of humans to that of incommensurable mythological divine entities, called lwas, who govern the cosmos. It also provides an explanation for death, which is treated as a spiritual transformation, a portal to the sacred world beyond, where productive and morally upright individuals, perceived by devotees to be powerful ancestral figures, can exercise significant influence on their progeny. In short, it is an expression of a people's longing for meaning and purpose in their lives. By extension, the use of the term Vodou in Haiti is also generic, referring to a whole assortment of cultural elements: personal creeds and practices, including an elaborate system of folk medical practices; a system of ethics transmitted across generations, which encompasses numerous proverbs and stories, songs and folklore; and various other forms of artistic expression.

As it exists in Haiti, Vodou contains some paradoxes that invite far-reaching speculations, for although it is West African in its form, it has also borrowed much from Roman Catholicism. The connection between the two religions may not be apparent at first glance because Catholicism is visible and official, whereas Vodou is unofficial and, until recently, largely secretive. Historically, Catholics have constituted the bulk of the elite, and they have upheld their religion's strict traditions and official order. Their churches are large, spacious, and architecturally the most elegant buildings in every town and city. Catholic priests and sisters staff many of the public schools as well as church-related schools, which provide the best available education in the country. Moreover, Catholicism is always represented by its dignitaries in all of the public and official governmental functions. In contrast, Vodouisants, who constitute the bulk of the lower classes and the peasantry, worship in temples that, viewed from any distance, bear few distinguishing marks that would identify them as places of worship; nor do the Vodou priests or priestesses (oungans or mambos) wear distinctive garb.

In the roles that the oungans and Catholic priests play in the performance of their respective rituals, too, one sees the differences between the two religions. In the Mass, the priest serves as the only conduit through which one can gain access to the sacred world; in his role as the sole dispenser of grace, he stands at the crossroads between the sacred and profane worlds. Conversely, the oungan does not control his flock's contact with the world of the gods, for Vodou is indeed a democratic religion (Davis 1988, 46; Courlander 1960, 9). In Vodou ceremonies, each believer has direct access to the spirit world through spirit possession. Possession is an altered state of consciousness during which a person is believed to be "mounted" like a horse by a lwa (Mars 1955; Bourguignon 1973; Métraux 1958, 118). This invasion of one's person by a lwa results in the temporary displacement of one's own personality by the envisaged mythological personality of the lwa. Possession is therefore considered a quintessential spiritual achievement in a believer's religious life, because it represents a direct engagement with the spirit world. It is also a public commitment to the religion that heightens one's exercise of religious authority in the community. For these reasons, Haitians would wish to have possession conferred on them, not once, but several times in their lives. In short, the Haitian view of the nature of the rituals of both religions can be summarized by the frequent remark that one goes to Catholic Mass to talk about God, but one goes to a Vodou ceremony to *become* God (Davis 1988, 48).

Another difference is that, while the Catholic church, in Haiti's history, has been supported economically by the state, Vodou has enjoyed no such privilege. Further, it maintains no theological or ecumenical centers for the training of its clerics, no formal religious communities, no presses, no editorial staff, and no publications. Nor is there even any formal creed: unlike the content of Roman Catholic theology, that of Vodou varies from one locality to another; it is not unusual to find that within an area of one square mile, two *ounfòs* (temples) maintain differing myths and rituals regarding divergent pantheons of lwas. Moreover, unlike Catholics, and similar to the devotees of African traditional religions, Vodouisants' names are not listed in the membership roll of a local temple. Their worldview does not allow them to consider religion as a formal organization with a list of members with whom they may or may not identify. Their religion is a way of life. Vodouisants' worldview is constructed from certain factual observations of their environment which they hold to be self-evident. Their subjective apprehension of these observations rests upon the immediate understanding that all phenomena are manifestations of supernatural, and yet observable, powers. These powers have two natures. First, they are manifestations of the complex persona of the Godhead (Bondye),[2] the creator of the universe. Bondye is beyond the individual's scrutiny and transcends the objective world. The phenomenal world is a posteriori to numerous incommensurable deities whose characteristics and mythological attributes render them ineffable and awesome. Second, Vodouisants conceive of these deities also as immanent; they believe that all existent things in the world are manifestations of these deities, and that their power is forever active in their devotees' lives.

The concept of *belief* in Haiti does not have the same connotation that it does in English (Deren 1972). The English word *belief* suggests an intellectual activity by which one may or may not choose to identify with a system of thought. Vodouisants never think of believing in something in the sense of identifying with a system of thought—or, by extension, with a community that affirms such a system (Deren 1972). Spiritual reality cannot be the object of academic investigation, nor can it be an issue of casual scrutiny for skeptics. Vodouisants have no room in their worldview for skepticism; they regard it as the consequence of an ambivalent attempt to establish rationally the design in the cycle of successive events, to debate the relationships between their parts, and to question the divine hand in their purpose. Skepticism is the outcome of an improper or otherwise faulty apprehension of what should admittedly be self-evident: that the world harbors powerful entities (lwas) that are forever active in human lives, and that such entities are the cause of all occurrences in the mechanical operation of the world.

Asked if they believe in the Vodou deities, notes Maya Deren, Vodouisants never reply that they believe in the gods; rather, they answer, "I serve the lwas," or "I obey the Mysteries of the world" (1972, 73–74). The significance of their statements lies in their outlook on the nature of belief in general, for they do not think of religion in abstract terms, but in practical ones. Because the lwas are the fount of all wisdom and the cause of all of life's circumstances, Vodouisants effect the lwas' volitions merely by the living of life itself. Concurrently, they expect the lwas to respond to their needs and to offer their assistance in practical matters of life. Vodouisants cannot afford the self-surrender of mysticism, nor can they permit themselves the luxury of an idealism that seeks to mask the miseries and frustrations of their existence. Their needs are too immediate for that. Their religion must satisfy actual needs rather than merely invite them to high-flown intellectual exercises of theology. Deren observes that they have neither the time, the energy, or the means for inconsequential activity. She notes that in Haiti, religion "must do more than give moral sustenance; it must do more than rationalize [the Vodouisant's] instinct for survival when survival is no longer a reasonable activity. It must do more than provide a reason for living; it must provide the means of living. It must serve the organism as well as the psyche. It must serve as a practical methodology, not an individual hope. In consequence, the Haitian thinks of his religion in working terms" (1972, 73).

Although the religious life of the Vodouisants marks one of the overt differences between Catholicism and Vodou, these differences do not prevent them from practicing both religions simultaneously with no attempt to resolve whatever paradoxes may exist between them. These paradoxes can be seen particularly in the details of the cultural and religious life of Haitians, the outcome of which have contributed to a strange intermixture of attitudes, of creeds and rituals, of patriotic pride, and of mental struggles.

Religiously, they venerate the saints of the church and the Vodou lwas simultaneously. They will attend a Vodou meeting that begins on a Saturday evening and lasts throughout the night; and while their clothes are still wet with the perspiration caused by the exhausting contortions of their sacred dances, they will walk directly from the ounfò to the four o'clock Mass on Sunday morning. Often the church and the ounfò share the same city block, and the tolling of the bell that announces the beginning of the Mass may be the signal for the Vodou ceremony to end. The priest in his performance of the Mass functions as a point of contact with an impersonal Godhead who maintains the universe, including its mechanical, biological, and stellar operations. In contrast, the oungan in his performance of the Vodou ceremony facilitates the devotees' contact with minor deities and ancestral spirits who are personifications of Bondye, the Godhead. The lwas are also identified with a variety of cosmological principles of order, and are divine mediators between Bondye and human beings. But the paradox in the Vodouisants' religious life can be seen particularly when the priest, attempting to keep his parishioners on the straight and narrow, inveighs in his sermon against their participation in the Vodou rituals the night before and against their service to the lwas.

Traditionally, the Haitian elite has comprised approximately 15 percent of the population. They have been ambivalent toward Vodou; many know little about it, most drawing their information from popular books and reports, such as the one mentioned earlier, written on the subject around the turn of the century. Many refer to its morbid nature and regard it as the remnant of "primitive" religious practices that are deleterious to Haitian society, give the country an undesirable international reputation, and impede literacy and socioeconomic development. Yet many members of this same elite are intensely drawn to Vodou, adhering to its teachings and secretly consulting oungans on occasion. They must acknowledge Vodou's continual presence in Haitian society, and the enduring sustenance it has provided to its devotees for centuries. They are also forced to recognize the historical fact that without Vodou, Haiti could not have become an independent nation as early as the nineteenth century, for its rituals provided the spirit of kinship that fueled the slaves' revolts against their masters (Desmangles 1990).

As will be described in a later chapter, the church, embarrassed by the encroachment of what it has regarded as "superstitious practices" on its theology, and using the arm of the government, has conducted a number of so-called Antisuperstitious Campaigns in which it has seized, burned, and destroyed a large number of ounfòs and ritual paraphernalia throughout the country. These campaigns have left indelible marks on Haitian society, for they have resulted not only in the secretive nature of the religion, but also in Vodouisants' ambivalence toward both religions. Vodouisants have traditionally been reluctant to admit openly to their service to the lwas, for fear of grave legal consequences. On the one hand, they have felt the need to participate in the country's official culture by claiming their unquestionable allegiance to Catholicism, and almost never to Vodou. On the other hand, because it is essential to participate in the sociocultural and religious life of their community, they have felt the need to serve the lwas as well.

But if Vodou as a religion has been able to survive such suppression, it is not only because it is part of the cultural fabric of Haitian life but also, ironically, because it has so frequently been suppressed. Very often, suppression attempts to destroy something that many see as harmful to society—but it also engenders the very sustenance of the precise thing it is attempting to destroy, for the threat of the total eradication of religious values among the oppressed can cause a sudden reawakening of those values. Vodou in Haiti today is a religion whose theology has attempted to sustain many of the religious and cultural African values in Haitian society. Its continued existence in Haitian culture is symbolic of the Vodouisants' resistance to renouncing their African traditions and acclimating themselves, by force if necessary, to European Catholicism. Hence, Vodou in effect is a reaction to the oppression caused by the intransigent hostility of the Roman clergy. Moreover, the present content of its theology, which includes both Catholic and African religious traditions, derives from the contact between the cultures of two continents on Haitian soil.

Because Vodou is in part a by-product of Catholicism and traditional religions from various regions of Africa, any discussion of it necessitates an analysis of the contact between these two religious sources. Hence, this book has three principal goals:

(1) My first aim is to describe the historical events in Haiti that have caused Vodou to incorporate ethnic religious traditions from diverse regions of Africa into its theology. The historical events will also shed light on the processes by which Catholic doctrines were similarly incorporated. This incorporation of elements from Africa and Europe has often been referred to by scholars as syncretistic, as the fusion of Catholic and African religious traditions (Deren 1972; Herskovits 1972; Métraux 1958). The present study describes the nature of this syncretism—that is, the relation between these

religious elements—as a symbiosis.[3] As used in this book, *symbiosis* has a different meaning from that in the biological sciences, where it refers to the living together of dissimilar organisms in a mutually beneficial relationship. Etymologically, symbiosis—from the Greek *sún*, "with," and *biós*, "life"—means "life together with." In its ethnological sense, symbiosis refers to the spatial juxtaposition of diverse religious traditions from two continents, which coexist without fusing with one another. Just as tiny parts of a stained-glass window are juxtaposed to form a whole, so too parts of the Vodou and Catholic traditions are juxtaposed in space and in time to constitute the whole of Vodou.

As it exists in Vodou, symbiosis takes two forms: symbiosis by ecology, and by identification. The first suggests the juxtaposition of religious elements necessitated by environmental and geographical adaptation, and the second suggests specifically the system by which, on the basis of similarity, Catholic saints were identified with or "transfigured into" Vodou gods. A brief examination of several examples may make the nature of each of these forms of symbiosis clearer.

Symbiosis by ecology refers to Roger Bastide's notion of syncretism in mosaic (1978, 153), which manifests itself in two paradigms: on the one hand, in the spatial juxtaposition of Vodou (or diverse African-derived) elements and Catholic symbols in the ounfò, as well as in the temporal use of these symbols in the ounfò; and on the other hand, in the prescribed ritualistic observances for the lwas on the Catholic holy days reserved for the saints in the Christian liturgical calendar.

In the first paradigm, the geographical proximity of a church to a ounfò constitutes the spatial juxtaposition of the two traditions. This juxtaposition also exists within the ounfò. A ounfò consists of two main sections, a holy of holies which contains the *pe* (altar), and the *peristil*, a terrace-like enclosure in which ritual ceremonies and sacred dances are performed. When one faces the pe, all distance between Vodou and Catholicism seems abolished: crucifixes, lithographs of saints, missals, and other Catholic ritual objects coexist on the same altar with sacred rattles and decorated jars believed to harbor ancestral spirits. Moreover, in many ounfòs the walls of the peristil are richly decorated with paintings representing various scenes from Vodou mythology and Catholic hagiology, as well as the symbols associated with both religious traditions.

The ritualistic use of objects from both religions, too, constitutes a temporal juxtaposition of these traditions. Vodou ceremonies contain fragments of the Catholic liturgy. These fragments, or infrastructures in these cere-

Vodou altar showing lithographs of saints, as well as bottles and jars said to contain ancestral gwo-bon-anjs

monies, are performed at the beginning of the ritual by a figure known as the prèt savann or bush priest. A discussion of the role of this figure and the historical events that led to his emergence cannot be attempted here, but must be deferred until later. Suffice it to say that he is part of the hierarchical structure of the ounfò, although his power is by no means analogous to that of the oungan. He holds no independent power and exercises little authority over those attending a ceremony. His role is by and large perfunctory: he recites the prayers, chants the hymns, and uses makeshift symbols of the church in Vodou ceremonies. Although Vodouisants see him as the representative of the church in their rituals, in reality he is not.[4] He can be seen as the symbolic embodiment of the contact between Catholicism and Vodou. The coexistence of the observance of fragments of the Catholic ritual by the prèt savann, and of traditional Vodou rites performed by the oungan in the same temple, constitutes the spatial and temporal juxtaposition of the two religions. At the same time, Vodouisants have learned to separate the functions of each of these persons as well as their use of ritual paraphernalia in Vodou ceremonies. The Vodou and Catholic objects possess their own power related to different aspects of reality: those of the church represent the power of the Godhead, and those of the ounfò, the power of the gods of Africa.

In the second paradigm, the conflict of two calendars led to the temporal juxtaposition of two cultures. The gods of Africa are related to calendrical events and are identified with natural phenomena, such as the spring new year festivals. Under the intense missionary activity that accompanied slavery in colonial Haiti, the African priests transported as slaves to Saint-Domingue were torn between two irreconcilable chronological systems—the Christian cycle of holy days, and the recurring cycle of mythical deeds performed *ab origine* in honor of their African deities. In the face of oppression, they were undoubtedly forced to observe their special African rituals on the days on which work was not required of them. This meant that they had to adapt their traditional calendar to the Gregorian calendar.

Symbiosis by ecology meant that African religious elements were cast in a European mold. While this process may have caused discrepancies in adjustment initially, the difficulties were later resolved. For example, in the Nigerian traditional calendar, the year began with the ceremony known as the "water of Oshala," in which various religious objects were washed in water and purified of the accumulated impurities that they had gathered during the course of the previous year. Since the Christian and Nigerian calendars did not coincide, the slaves in Saint-Domingue took the major Catholic feast days to perform their African ceremonies: the Christmas cycle up to Epiphany for the rituals of purification, the Feast of All Souls (November 1) as an occasion to honor the spirits of their departed ancestors, and so on.

The second form of symbiosis in Vodou has been termed a *symbiosis by identity*—that is, a system of identification or transfiguration by which, on the basis of the similarities between African and Catholic myths and symbols, the saints were identified with African gods. This pattern of identity operates according to the methods elucidated by Melville Herskovits (1972, 281–82). Thus Ezili, the beautiful water goddess of love in Vodou, whose originals exist both in the African goddess of the same name in Whydah in Dahomey (or Benin) and in Oshun in Nigeria, becomes the Virgin Mary; Benin's python god Damballah becomes Saint Patrick, because of the story of the triumph of Patrick over the snakes of Ireland in Catholic hagiology; Legba, the guardian of destiny who holds the keys to the doors of the underworld, becomes Saint Peter; and so forth.

Symbiosis by identification is basic to an understanding of the cultural and religious juxtaposition of Catholicism and Vodou in Haiti today. The reasons for such a symbiosis date back to the Haitian colonial period. As Bastide (1978) noted in the case of Brazil, Catholic missionaries probably used lithographs showing the various symbols associated with the lives of the saints in Christian hagiology, and it is possible that the slaves learned to associate these symbols with those related to the African gods. Moreover, in colonial Haiti as in Brazil, colonial authorities and the church forbade the slaves to practice Vodou; therefore the slaves danced before the Catholic altars and strictly observed the feast days of the saints. Although their masters may have found their behavior bizarre, it probably did not occur to them that the slaves were honoring the African gods, and that their behavior was a mask over black faces (Bastide 1978), a veil behind which they could practice their African religions. As Jean Price-Mars noted, "choked by oppression, the slaves were obliged to hide their secret adoration of obscure forces to which they felt themselves tied by long ancestral traditions" (1928, 44).

Price-Mars's observations in no way contradict the information gathered during my field research. In the city of Port-au-Prince, where Vodou's close association with Catholicism could have created theological fusion, the two religious systems represented in the minds of their adherents two disparate "objects" juxtaposed to one another. I found that many conceived of the interplay between the two religions as a necessary form of social integration. Thus, the paradox in the Haitians' religious life consisted of two strong social and cultural forces: on the one hand, they perceived their membership in the church as a means of social recognition and social stability; and on the other, they sensed the need to reaffirm their African heritage, as well as to join those in their immediate communities by participating in the rituals of the local ounfòs. In the case of the slaves, they needed to survive the hardships of plantation life and they found solace in their African religious traditions. Because Vodou was not allowed in the colony, they learned to conceal their practice of these traditions behind the veil of Catholicism.

(2) Although Vodou has assimilated much of Catholic theology, it is also continuous with African religious traditions. Continuity and change are cultural processes present in every society and will endure whether or not they

are studied by scholars. No study of continuity can be made without an examination of the factors that have engendered it. Hence, the second purpose of this study is to examine the sociohistorical and other factors that have caused Vodouisants to look toward their past and to maintain so much of their African heritage.

In his analysis of continuity and change in African traditional religions, J. N. K. Mugambi noted that every culture has made an impact on world history, and has done so only after it has discovered and affirmed "its roots" and traced them to antiquity (1989, 111). But the rediscovery of a culture's heritage does not consist of a blind leap into the past—or into the future, for that matter. Rather, it consists of a cultural renaissance in which the past is reincarnated into the present and provides a vision for the future (Mugambi 1989, 111).

The rediscovery by a people of their past is not unique to Haiti: in the anthropological literature, students of culture have recorded similar reactions to acculturation in "primal" religions in other parts of the world. Ralph Linton noted that in situations of contact between cultures where one dominates the other, and where the dominated culture's existence and indigenous development are threatened by the dominant culture, the dominated group may give rise to what he called *nativism*—religious movements that consciously attempt to revive or perpetuate selected elements of their culture. The threat felt by the members of a dominated culture may result from the extensive diffusion into it of cultural elements from the dominant culture. Consequently, members of the dominated culture may feel the need to emphasize cultural elements fallen into desuetude, stressing their uniqueness and practicality in order to reduce individual stress created by the situation of contact. Hence, as Georges Balandier observed, a nativistic movement can also be viewed as "contra-acculturative," wherein a people come to emphasize the values in their original way of life, and move aggressively to restore those past values, even in the face of their apparent impotence to throw off the power that restricts them (Balandier 1963, 496–97; Linton 1979, 414).

In the case of Haiti, as will be shown in Chapter 2, the imposition of European culture on African cultures through force and police control helped to fuel a series of slave revolts throughout the colonial period, revolts that resulted in the independence of Haiti in 1804. The role of Vodou in these revolutions was one of providing a channel through which ancestral African traditions could be re-created. The emphasis on past religious traditions became vital in inspiring the slaves to revolt against their masters. Subversive activity was often preceded by religious ceremonies that included sacrifices to gods originating in diverse regions of Africa.

Anthony F. C. Wallace, who broadened Linton's theories, included in his analysis all social movements of a radical type, referring to them as "revitalization movements" (1979, 422). These movements, he said, arise in situations of extreme "stress" that, according to many scholars, occur particularly in settings in which dominated societies experience relative deprivation—that is, the reduction of their expectations of ameliorating their present situation either immediately or in the future (Barkun 1986, 35; Aberle 1962). Despite objections in the anthropological literature to Wallace's Gestaltian psychosocial approach to culture change, and despite his lack of a definition of stress (Barkun 1986, 34–40), his descriptions of these movements deserve attention. He noted that such movements may be prophetic or millenarian or both, for messianism and millenarianism are not mutually exclusive categories. Although the ideologies of millenarian movements take different adaptive cultural forms as they are shaped by the situations in which they arise, scholars agree that, by and large, they share many common characteristics:

(a) They promise their members redemption from oppression; they rely heavily on the supernatural in that the "golden age" that they await will be ushered in by divine figures (Talmon 1965, 526).

(b) The metahistorical future envisaged by millenarian movements is based on the teachings of prophets—or charismatic figures who are often viewed by their followers as messiahs—who promise that the new era will be a re-creation and reestablishment of the situation of their ancestors. In such cases, the remembered ancestral traditions that are selected and given emphasis are endowed with symbolic value, and are considered to be formulae designed to achieve a favorable modification of a society's frustrations, both present and future. The revivified past and the situation of the ancestors thus provide the model for the world to come (Balandier 1963, 496; Talmon 1965, 524).

(c) The emphasis on ancestral traditions entails a people's selection of what appears to them as desirable in the situation of their progenitors. Hence, a reconstructed past is never identical to the real past, but is modified to conform to the present and to future situations as the people conceive of them (Cohn 1961). Moreover, as Maurice Halbwachs noted, this emphasis on the past on the part of the dominated is based upon "collective memories"—that is, those elements that are remembered or selected for emphasis are those that can integrate themselves into the current socioeconomic and political contexts of the dominated (Halbwachs 1975, 401). In the case of Haiti, collective memory meant that many of the past cultural elements selected for emphasis or reconstruction were those that related contextually to the African slaves' struggle for social dignity and liberation. Thus, for example, the Nigerian god of war Ogou was remembered and became a major lwa in Haiti because of the slaves' confrontation with colonial rule and because, as will be noted in Chapter 2, later political and social strife occasioned the emphasis of his envisaged persona, and many of the myths associated with that persona.

(d) The desire to "fly" from the brutal reality of oppression has often inspired members of such movements to believe that the new dispensation will only come through unprecedented cataclysms, disastrous calamities including war and bloody human confrontations, generally brought about by supernatural intervention. The prophets of these movements not only are viewed as signs of the impending final event, but also announce the destruction of the present order and the imminent advent of the new order (Barkun 1986, 91ff.).

(e) Millenarianism often assumes characteristics common to movements of nationalism and can be prepolitical in nature (Balandier 1963, 33). Societies that either appear to be stateless, or have rudimentary political institutions, or lack any specialized institutions tend to give rise to millenarian movements of a political nature, due to the lack of an efficient political institution that can bear the grievances and the pressing claims of a frustrated segment of the population. The deprived members may seek an adequate solution to their problems through millenarianism (Barkun 1986, 68ff.; Talmon 1965, 531).

In the case of Haiti, the slaves revolted against slavery because the French colonial administration provided no channel through which they could air their complaints. As will be discussed in Chapter 2, the removal of the rights of the mulattoes known as "free slaves" (a decision made by the Assemblée Nationale in France toward the end of the eighteenth century) not only caused them to emphasize their ancestral traditions, but sparked the vividness of the millennium in the minds of those who actively participated in the final revolution in 1804.[5] Furthermore, the Haitian Revolution had political overtones: many religious leaders during the revolution assumed political office once independence had been achieved.

(3) The third aim of this study is to describe Vodou as a *tertium quid*, part of which is a "creole" phenomenon that owes little to Africa or Europe (Smith 1960, 36) but is indigenous to Haiti, born out of the difficult and oppressive conditions of slavery and the necessary adaptation to a new environment. This corresponds to Sidney Mintz's suggestion (1972) that the ubiquity of African elements in Vodou may have caused scholars to search for resemblances with the religions of Africa and Europe at the expense of the indigenous characteristics unique to Vodou. Traditionally, Vodou may have been largely a religion of the peasants in Haiti—but those peasants, like other peasant societies of the world, are by no means static, nor are their institutions "diachronically stable" (Davis 1988, 32; Thomas and Znaniecki 1971). Mintz and others have shown that peasant societies throughout the world have moved aggressively toward social change and have engendered radical transformations of societal norms. As already noted, social change can often occur through revitalization (or millenarian) movements that threaten to destroy the present order that suppresses them.

Among the religious elements indigenous to Haiti is the fact that Vodou maintains several sects, known as *nanchons*, each of which bears the name of one of the pantheons most prevalent in the sect's location. These pantheons will be discussed at some length in Chapter 4; it suffices here to note that, for historical reasons, their names are derived from the names of the different African ethnic religious traditions represented in Haiti during the colonial period. One such sect is the Petro nanchon, which is typically Haitian. The names of its lwas, their ascribed personae in Vodou mythology, and the rituals performed in their honor are woven into the fabric of Haitian history and culture, and bear little resemblance to European or African religious traditions. They derive from the oppressive conditions of slavery and are associated with the Haitian Revolution; they are said to inspire violence and are associated with the rage of the slaves against their masters. In Haiti today the Petro lwas still become prevalent in religious and political thinking from time to time, as witnessed by the recent retribution of the masses against former government officials after President Jean-Claude Duvalier's fall from power.

Moreover, the identification of the lwas with the saints of the church, the spatial juxtaposition of Catholic practices in Vodou rites, the use of both Catholic and Vodou objects in these rites, the attitudes of Vodouisants toward both religions, and the calendrical adjustments achieved in their observances of the two traditions, are neither African nor European in form, but creole phenomena emerging out of the contact of the two cultures on Haitian soil.

In order to achieve the above purposes, the present study will focus on the Vodou pantheons—more specifically, on the mythology and folklore that surround the personae of the Vodou lwas, on the private rites and public ceremonies tendered to these lwas by their devotees, and on the bases for their symbiotic identity with particular Catholic saints.

Hence, this book is not about some exotic religion; its descriptions of Vodou rituals have nothing to do with the macabre characterizations of the religion found in popular films and Western literature. It is concerned with a viable religion, the theology of which has woven itself into the fabric of Haitian life. It also differs from earlier scholarly studies on Vodou because it focuses on the nature of Vodou's pantheons, and emphasizes the cultural, historical, political, and social contexts in which various ethnic African religious traditions came into contact with Catholic theology.

Finally, the overall purpose of this book is to make an original contribution to Caribbean studies—an area of research in which there is currently a scarcity of field work, but also one that, in recent years, has gained much importance in the field of anthropology of religion. Of late, religion has become a peripheral field of study in the departments of anthropology of many colleges and universities in Europe and the United States. It is hoped that this study will make a contribution to the anthropological approach to the study of religion, and will help validate the significance of the theoretical and ethnographic study of religion for cultural studies.

Moreover, the contact between African and European religions is not unique to Haiti, but is characteristic of so-called Third World countries. As with Haiti, these countries' post-colonial status as emerging nation-states derives from historical circumstances that entailed many periods of hardship in adverse situations of domination—situations that were well beyond their peoples' control. Most of these nations are currently confronted with a new spirit of national consciousness, a yearning for political and socioeconomic self-determination among their peoples. In this spirit, they have not only sought to recognize their rich historical traditions, but have learned to appreciate the significance of their indigenous cultural and religious values as well. Like Haitians, most have had to deal with substantive paradoxes between imported and indigenous cultural and religious values.

HISTORICAL

....

SETTING:

....

THE SHAPING

....

OF TWO

....

RELIGIONS IN

....

SYMBIOSIS

2

The story of a people is one told to express that people's fulfillment and its frustrations. No study of the Vodou lwas can begin without relating the successes and failures in the life of a nation whose people's religious sentiments have been shaped by historical circumstances and a pressing need for survival. The study of the Vodou pantheons is the study of such circumstances, for the mythological personae or faces of their lwas mirror Haitians' brave encounter with life's crises, their common sentiments and efforts, and their hopes for the future.

Because space does not allow a complete examination of the history of the contact between Catholicism and Vodou in Haiti, this chapter will merely include the details that relate to the subject of this study. The religious history of Haiti will be divided into four periods:

1492–1790: The birth of the colony of Saint-Domingue and the beginning of slavery.

1790–1804: The period of political turmoil, and the stresses placed on religion amidst the intensity of revolts for independence.

1804–1860: The shaping of the Haitian republic, the birth of the peasantry, the suppression of Vodou, and the adoption of Catholicism as a state religion.

1860 to the present: The spread of Vodou in Haitian life, and the emergence of the religion's present forms.

....

RELIGION IN THE COLONY: 1492–1790

When Christopher Columbus set foot on Haitian soil on December 6, 1492, he arrived by way of San Salvador. Despite the climatic and environmental differences between Europe and the West Indies, some of the landscape must have reminded him of Spain, for he named the island Hispañola, meaning "little Spain." Of the three ships used for his long voyage, the *Santa Maria* ran aground near Môle St. Nicolas on the northwest peninsula of the island. Unable to accommodate its entire crew for the rest of his voyage on the two remaining ships, he left behind a small contingent of about forty and hoped to return with additional cargo the following year. This small group built the first European settlement on the island with the dismantled wood and hardware from what was left of their battered ship. Their settlement was called La Navidad. When Columbus returned to the Môle a year later, he found the tiny settlement destroyed and its inhabitants vanished, presumably killed by the island's native Indian population. Another colony was started by the newcomers and joined later by other explorers, and this colony proved successful.

Little is known about the Indians of Hispañola. They seem to have descended from the Taino of South America (Courlander and Bastien 1966, 1), and had migrated to the island a few hundred years before Columbus's arrival (Rouse 1964, 499–513). They were primarily a horticultural society, engaged in tilling small garden plots in the mountainous regions of the interior of the island (Oexquemelin [1674] 1681).

The first Europeans to settle on the island became known as the "buccaneers," a word that derives from the French *boucan*, meaning smoking fire. The word was appropriately applied to them, stemming from their practice of lighting fires to smoke the meat procured in their hunts. The buccaneers settled along the coast of Tortuga, an island a few miles north of Hispañola. From their safe refuge they sailed to Hispañola to hunt wild cattle, returning home to escape harm from the Indians. Their presence had a profound effect on these Indians. Consumed by their determination to find the gold that was reputed to exist on Hispañola, the Spanish subjected the Indians to hard labor, forcing them to search for the precious metal, and to till the new settlers' fields. Their cruelty toward the Indians caused some to flee to the mountains in the interior of the island; others are said to have poisoned themselves in despair (Courlander and Bastien 1966, 1; Peytraux 1897).

The settlers' cruel mistreatment of the Indians did not go unnoticed. Early in the sixteenth century, Bartolomé de las Casas went to Santo Domingo and later to Cuba as a *conquistador*.[1] After a conversion experience in Cuba that caused him, as he later reported in his letters, to dedicate his life to Christian service, he became a Catholic missionary and took up the cause of the Indians before the Spanish Crown. The initial progress of his mission was slow, and angered the Spanish government, for Spain was only interested in expanding its territories in the New World, and gave little consideration to the native population. Las Casas's proposed reforms did not really begin to take root until the middle of the sixteenth century (Ferguson 1989, 2). They had come too late, however, for the tyranny of the Spanish had already caused the death of thousands of Indians, as revealed by the few statistics available for that period. A mere fifteen years after the settlers' arrival, four-fifths of the Indian population had perished. Various diseases imported by the new settlers, diseases that were common in Europe but against which the Indians were not immune, also took their toll; statistics at the end of the seventeenth century showed that their number had been reduced drastically, from approximately half a million to sixty thousand (Davis 1988, 16).

Las Casas's efforts actually were not as laudable as many historians would have us believe, for although he worked to improve the Indians' lot, he was also one of the first to endorse plans to replace Indian laborers with African slaves.[2] While no one is sure of the exact date, Africans probably began to arrive on the island around 1512, twenty years after Columbus's first trip. They came from a variety of ethnic nations covering a wide geographical area of West Africa, from the northwest coast of sub-Sahara to the Bakongo regions, for the slave traders were not selective about the location of their human cargo, but acquired them wherever they could (M. Campbell 1988, 16). The slaves brought with them their cultural and religious traditions, which they poured into the fabric of the island's colonial life. Although many of them were highly trained tradesmen, priests, and members of royal families, the Spanish were as cruel to them as they had been to the Indians (Courlander and Bastien 1966, 2). They forced them to work on their small plantations, cultivating primarily cash crops for local and limited international markets (Moreau de Saint-Méry [1797] 1958, vol. 1).

Throughout the sixteenth and seventeenth centuries the Spanish struggled to keep these islands under their control, but offered little support to their settlements. France's covetous interest in the gold discovered on the island had already lured small contingents of French, who settled along the western shores of Hispañola as early as the end of the sixteenth century. The steady growth in their numbers was soon to overwhelm the Spanish and enable French hegemony; the end of the Spanish reign came in 1697 with the signing of the Treaty of Ryswick in Europe, by which the Spanish ceded the western part of the island to the French.

Throughout the period of Spanish rule, religion was one of the most important aspects of life on the island. Indeed, zealous Catholic priests and missionaries followed Spanish explorers wherever they went. Rome considered Europe's discovery of the New World a challenge to her missionary spirit, and encouraged young men and women within her fold to devote their lives to Christian service. That many young people enthusiastically responded to Rome's challenge is apparent, for by 1511 Pope Julian II had formed three bishoprics on the island, and in 1547 Clement VII added to the dignity of the Santo Domingo mission by declaring it the seat of ecclesiastical power for the area of the West Indies, extending its jurisdiction eastward to Trinidad and westward to the isthmus of Panama, including the southern tip of Florida (Gayot 1956, 45–46).

The enthusiasm for missionary activity did not fluctuate from 1510 to 1685. Numerous congregations were invited to send missionaries to the island (Moreau de Saint-Méry [1797] 1958, 1:83), and no doubt the clergy worked tenaciously in the performance of their often unrewarding tasks. But the heat of the scorching sun, the environmental adjustments to a new tropical habitat, and the long distances to be traveled on foot or on horseback made the priests' work extremely difficult. Yellow fever and malaria also took their toll and made the work even more discouraging. And to these difficulties can be added another: the execrable morality among the early French colonists with whom the priests had to cope. After the Treaty of Ryswick, both the religious zeal of the missionaries and public morality began to wane; economic prosperity and luxurious living supplanted spiritual growth and development in the colony throughout the seventeenth century (Gisler 1965, 61).

By 1730 a new breed of businessmen had begun to migrate to the island, and soon seven maritime companies were contracted to transport slaves from Africa. From 1730 to 1790, the French colony of Saint-Domingue demonstrated that high profits could be made with the sale of indigo, coffee, sugar, and cocoa to the European market. Large plantations were staked out in the valleys and small hills near the northern coast at Cap-Français, and a European market awaited the arrival of shiploads of native crops. The French built complex irrigation canals that increased the amount of arable land, and a new system of roads that gave access to previously unexploited territories. In short, what had been a subsistence economy during the Spanish and early French rule had given way to an economy oriented toward mass export.

So significant was the agricultural yield of the colony that, by the latter half of the eighteenth century, it was exporting 163 million pounds of sugar annually, a figure representing nearly 60 percent of the world's sugar consumption (Davis 1988, 18; James 1949, 41). It also produced three times more indigo than the two Carolinas combined, and coffee and cotton crops that equaled in value the annual tobacco crops of both Maryland and Virginia (d'Auberteuil 1782, 1:168). Moreover, by 1740 the mixed cargo of Saint-Domingue filled the hulls of 500 ships annually (ANP, File C9) and comprised two-thirds of France's tropical produce (Rotberg 1971, 27–28); by 1789, its 8,000 plantations were producing more than 40 percent of France's foreign trade, and more than four thousand ships anchored at its ports annually to ensure the exportation of goods to France and to the rest of the world.[3] Such a concentration of wealth undoubtedly made the colony most valuable to France and at the same time highly coveted by her European neighbors, precisely because France's revenues from foreign trade made it possible for her to maintain an efficient and potent military force.

The increasing exploitation of native resources and the demand for crops by France's widening European market required the expansion of the plantations, as well as a large labor force which Africa alone could not provide. Around the middle of the eighteenth century, shiploads of more than 500 Natchez Indians arrived from Nouvelle France (Louisiana), in addition to some Renards from the coast of Newfoundland in Canada, and others from Guiana and other parts of the world (Moreau de Saint-Méry [1797] 1958, 1:83). European *engagés* (bondsmen) were also contracted to work on the plantations, pledging their services for a period of three years. Most of them were French criminals, discharged soldiers, and army deserters who, lacking the financial resources to pay their passage to the New World, were given plots of land as remuneration for their services.

As the number of plantations and the agricultural yields increased, many succumbed under the weight of strenuous labor, considerably reducing the labor force and threatening the economy of the colony. This precipitated the expansion of the slave trade, thus causing a significant increase in the black population, which by 1791 far outnumbered the white population. Statistics of the period indicate that during the first hundred years of French rule (1697–1797) the slave population increased severalfold. In 1681, the ratio of blacks to whites was 2:1 (Ott 1973, 14); in 1697, 3:1; and by 1790, 11:1 (Davis 1988, 18). On the plantations themselves, the blacks outnumbered whites 100:1 in 1790 (Thompson 1983). Shortly before the revolution there were 700 ships carrying some 20,000 slaves into the colony annually (Moreau de Saint-Méry [1797] 1958, 1:111), rendering Saint-Domingue the colony with the largest number of slaves in the Caribbean (Geggus 1989, 23). The 1780 census, reputed to be the first official one and the most accurate, revealed the following demographic figures:

French Europeans	40,000
Africans	452,000
Affranchis (mulattoes)	28,000
Ratio of black slaves to whites	11³⁄₁₀ to 1
Ratio of whites to affranchis	10 to 7
Ratio of slaves to affranchis	16 to 1
Total population	520,000

Source: Gisler 1965, 34; Moreau de Saint-Méry [1797] 1958, 1:28–29.

The figures for manufactures and places of business for the same year read as follows:

Sugar manufactures	793
Indigo manufactures	3,150
Cotton processing plants	789
Coffee processing plants	3,117
Distilleries	182
Tanneries	6
Pottery manufactures	29
Cacao processing plants	50

Source: Moreau de Saint-Méry [1797] 1958, 1:111.

These numbers do not include lumber processing plants. Lumber, especially oak and mahogany, was an important export of the colony, and a large quantity of it was transported to Canada and New England (Frostin 1975, 151).

Personal wealth often engenders the rise of social classes. Early in Saint-Domingue's history, a developing class system produced discords whose repercussions were to fuel the Haitian Revolution, and whose beginnings could already be seen in sporadic slave insurrections as early as the sixteenth century. The rigid class structure of present-day Haiti traces its roots to the beginning of the eighteenth century. Three social groups were formed in the colony: the *grands blancs*, the *petits blancs*, and the *gens de couleur*. The first two were degrees within the same class and included wealthy plantation owners, white merchants, and various civil servants. The gens de couleur were also called *affranchis*, people of "mixed blood," or mulattoes. They were the result of miscegenation between white masters and African slave women and they were divided into various subcategories related to their proportion of white ancestry (Moreau de Saint-Méry [1797] 1958, 1:86–89; James 1949, 33). They were also referred to as "free slaves," for slave labor was not required of them. (The slaves did not figure in this class system, being generally considered beneath the colonial social structure.)

The importance of the affranchis lay in their sudden multiplication. Between 1703 and 1715 their numbers increased from 500 to 1,400, and in the next thirty years, to 3,000. By 1770 there were 6,000; by 1780, 10,000; and by 1790, 28,000 (Frostin 1975, 28; Moreau de Saint-Méry [1797] 1958, 1:84). This rapid increase was partly due to the legislation known as the Code Noir. Adopted by the French parliament in Paris in 1685, the Code regulated the social, political, and religious life of all the French colonies throughout the world. The fifty-ninth of the sixty articles of this legal document guaranteed to affranchis the same rights of liberty and ownership of property that it did to whites: "Let us grant to the affranchis the same rights, privileges, and immunities that are enjoyed by all persons born free; let us wish that the merit of their earned liberty produce in them, both in their persons and in their estate, similar effects as in persons and other subjects with natural liberty" (ANP, File F3). The remaining portion of this article gave affranchis the right to dispose of their wealth as they pleased, to bear testimony in legal cases (even against whites), to travel freely, and to own slaves.

It is all too easy for wealth to occasion a lack of self-discipline and moral laxity in a people. The French who came to the island led a deplorable life with such execrable morals that Saint-Domingue came to be known as the "Babylon of the New World" (Girod-Chantrans 1785, 180–83). Although most were perhaps more sophisticated than their Spanish predecessors, intemperance and greed were the "worst of their vices" (Frostin 1975, 387). They were quick-tempered and imperious, and when "their sex drives stirred," they took whatever slave servants pleased them, "living a life tormented by the thoughts of possible infidelity to their spouses" (Cabon 1930, 13–15).

These debauched Frenchmen regarded the clergy with hostility and antagonism, and with good reason: not only did the clergy continuously admonish them for their immorality and exhort them to return to the straight and narrow, but the church had been largely responsible for the content of the Code Noir, which the planters did not like. Their hostility rested on two basic issues. First, articles 2 and 6 of the Code required every slave to be baptized and stipulated that each slave's acceptance into the church be preceded by a period of religious instruction in the "Catholic, Apostolic, and Roman faith" (ANP, File F52; File F3, 90:110–21). These requirements generated the resentment of the planters toward the clergy, because most felt that these sections of the Code conflicted with their economic interests.

The valuable time that the slaves spent at Mass and at catechism hampered the efficiency of crop production and diminished the planters' annual revenues. They felt that production and export were more important to France's flourishing economy and international reputation than the Christianization of slaves. Second, the church made it possible for many affranchis to study in French universities, and the rise of an educated "middle class" of free slaves displeased the whites. This displeasure was noted in a letter written to the Minister of Colonies in Paris from Saint-Domingue in 1764, which expressed the sentiments of most planters. It reported that educated affranchis returning from tours of study in France were "inundating" the colony. They returned with "ideas of equality," popular in academic circles on the eve of the French Revolution, "which were dangerous to the citizens living in the colony" and threatened to destroy "the need for subordination" that was so vital to social order and economic growth. The letter continues: "The Negroes who return from France are insolent because of the familiarity that they have contracted with the whites, they have acquired certain forms of knowledge which might be used dangerously.... It would be better for them if they had never gone or never returned to the colonies.... I have always stressed, my Lord the Duke, that they must be kept in the most profound ignorance" (ANP, File F3, 90:106–7).

Unaffected by the overt piety of the pastors who might have served as their models, the planters indulged in self-gratification and immoderation. Immorality and cruelty were commonplace; to make a fortune and to seek the pleasures of luxurious living also became the order of the day (Moreau de Saint-Méry [1797] 1958, 1:35–39; Leyburn 1972, 117). Administrative agents used their public offices for their own economic gains; judges sold their judicial responsibilities to the highest bidder; planters disregarded the articles of the Code as well as a ruling of 1785 (ANP, File G1) that dealt with the social and public health of their slaves, and drove their human chattels to their death. The eye-witness account of a man who visited the island around 1790 puts it this way:

> The crowing of the rooster: the cracking of the whip, the choking of screams, the deafening groans of the Negroes who experience the beginning of the day only to curse it, who are reminded of their feeling for existence only by painful sensations, these are the sounds that replace the crowing of the rooster in the morning. It is with the harmony of this infernal melody that I was awakened from my sleep in Saint-Domingue. I was startled.... I thought that I was being awakened at the bottom of

Tartarus, between Ixion and Prometheus, but I was among Christians. (Gisler 1965, 35; Wimpffen 1911, 60)

Under such conditions the continuation of African traditions was not easy. Nevertheless, while the slaves, especially in the presence of the affranchis, may have adopted European language, code of dress, and, to a certain degree, housing, other cultural characteristics remained African. Pierre de Vaissière reported in the seventeenth century that slaves carried on communal hoeing, timing their strokes in the rhythm of African songs which would delight any visitor. He also noted certain ways of preparing meals, of eating, and of fixing the time for their meals, the respect that they had for their elders, their attitudes toward death, their rituals of burial, their dances, their songs, and above all, their characteristically non-Christian religious beliefs (de Vaissière 1909, 1:201–2).

The domain of religion exhibited the strongest forms of continuity with Africa. In the eighteenth century M. L. E. Moreau de Saint-Méry, who, as a white, was fortunate to witness a Vodou ceremony, provided an excellent description of it. He reported that it consisted of the veneration of "a non-venomous snake . . . under whose auspices are gathered all those who profess the same doctrine. Knowledge of the past, the science of the present, the foreknowledge of the future, all of this belongs to the snake, which consents to communicate its power through the medium of a high priest whom the adherents choose" ([1797] 1958, 1:64). These high priests were the predecessors of the contemporary Vodou oungan and mambo (priestess). As the "chieftains of the large Vodou family," they possessed unlimited powers over those who composed that family. They were the ones who decided whether the gods would or would not receive a neophyte in their midst. They also held the right to prescribe the duties that the convert must perform; they received all gifts and offerings presented to the snake; and they offered the sacrifices that it demanded of the community. To disobey or to resist them was to disobey God himself; it was to make oneself liable to misfortune, illness, or death (Moreau de Saint-Méry [1797] 1958, 1:64).

Moreau de Saint-Méry also mentions that Vodou ceremonies took place in the secrecy of the night, in an enclosed area hidden from all "profane eyes"—presumably because the Code Noir prohibited the practice of Vodou in the colony, and because the slaves feared the possible harsh punishments of local authorities. The high priest stood before a makeshift altar upon which was placed a wooden box containing the sacred snake. An animal was then sacrificed and its blood, collected in a large bowl, went to seal the lips of all the members of the snake's family, who promised to suffer death rather than reveal the secret ties that bound the "family of the snake." Spirit possession occurred during the ceremonies. One of the high priests was usually the first to be possessed; the initiates usually followed suit during the dances that followed. The ceremony ended with a collective delirium involving "nervous trembling, violent agitation, and a sort of fury" (Moreau de Saint-Méry [1797] 1958, 1:64).

The church worked assiduously toward the eradication of these African "superstitious" practices in the colony. In addition to capitalizing on the royal edicts of the Code, which made baptism compulsory, missionaries were responsible for a series of police rulings that curtailed the movement of the slaves and controlled the use of objects that might be of use in Vodou rituals (Gisler 1965, 78–79). The Police Rulings of 1758 and 1777 prohibited the slaves, "under penalty of death," from meeting "during the night or day," especially in the absence of a Catholic priest, under the pretext of celebrating weddings or grieving over the body of a departed friend. Furthermore, the Ruling of 1758 stipulated that slaves were not to congregate either "near the house of their master or anywhere else, and even less in and around remote places." Article 16 decreed: "Let us enjoin upon our subjects that offenders must be reported in order that they may be arrested and imprisoned, even though these might be officers and no decree might as yet be enacted against them" (ANP, File F3, 5). This edict reconfirms Moreau de Saint-Méry's report that Vodou ceremonies had to be held in the secrecy of the night. Drums could not be sounded, nor was singing allowed save for field-labor. A letter written by M. Blaru states that once, when he was sick, slaves "danced silently" around him in order to obtain the healing power from their spirits (de Vaissière 1909, 1:204).

Other articles dealt with the prohibition of the sale of goats, or fetishes that could be used for magic (ANP, File F3, 90). The same Ruling of 1758 forbade the absence of slaves from their plantations at any time: "Nothing is more important for the security of the inhabitants of the islands, and to prevent the revolt of the Negroes, than to stress the [poor excuses] that have been made and [the error of] letting the Negroes wander without a note from their masters" (Moreau de Saint-Méry 1784, 1:348).

One striking aspect of Vodou during the colonial period is the syncretistic process by which Roman Catholic elements were included in its practices (Moreau de Saint-Méry 1784, 1:348; Le Ruzic 1912, 153). In 1722, Father Jean-Baptiste Labat observed that "Vodou meetings or ceremonies mix often the sacred things of our religion with profane objects of an idolatrous cult":

The Negroes have no scruples. . . . They intermix Dagon's ark and secretly keep all the superstitions of their ancient idolatrous cult with
the ceremonies of the Christian religion. All the Negroes have much
devotion for the communion wafer. They eat it only when they are ill,
or when they are afraid of some danger. In regard to the holy water,
the little bit of water that is consecrated during the Sunday Mass, it is
rare that one finds one drop of it when the ceremony has ended; they
carry it in little calabashes and drink some drops when they rise (in the
morning) and pretend that it will guarantee their welfare against all the
witchcraft that might befall them. (Labat 1722, 4:330–31)

This syncretistic nature of Vodou was disturbing to the church. Vodou assemblies were a cause for alarm among the colonists, for not only were
they profane in their use of objects stolen from the church, but the planters
feared that they would serve as catalysts for slave insurrections. Throughout
the sixteenth century, Vodou meetings had often been converted into offensive mechanisms for violent raids against the planters, some costly in human
lives and materials.

Writings of the period comment on the discouragement of the Catholic missionaries who took their task seriously, for all too often the baptism
of converts was followed by "their return . . . to their superstitions" (ANP,
File B, 186–87). Such lapses were unavoidable, since the slaves embraced
Christianity only nominally. In 1790 Moreau de Saint-Méry attested to this
phenomenon when he noted that African slaves used their Catholic faith as
a scheme under which "primitive" religious practices could be performed.
Baptism was only an occasion for feasting, and many slaves sought to have
it conferred on them as many as seven or eight times with the intention of
mimicking the work of the priest (Moreau de Saint-Méry [1797] 1958, 1:55).
Others sought baptism when they were ill, and sent for the Catholic priest,
thinking that his performance of the sacrament would cure their illnesses
(ANP, File F3, 117–18). Their demeanor at Sunday Mass too prompted the
concern of the clergy, for, as Moreau de Saint-Méry observed, "If they go to
Church, they recite prayers which they know badly or they sleep. . . . [Their]
grimaces would be envied by certain European devotees, who would not be
capable of teaching them anything about hypocrisy" (Moreau de Saint-Méry
[1797] 1958, 1:55).[4]

Many other testimonies and descriptions of the colonial period in Saint-
Domingue concur with Moreau de Saint-Méry's observations (e.g., de Vaissière 1909, 3:367). On the one hand, the evangelization of the slaves resulted

in the syncretism between Catholicism and African religious practices. On the other hand, the Christianity that the slaves embraced was one that Jean Price-Mars recognized as an "apparent Christianity" which provided religious continuity with Africa (1928, 44). Furthermore, Vodou meetings permitted Africans to establish a communal spirit and a basis for common identity under difficult conditions of slave labor. The meetings also engendered a social solidarity among the slaves, which not only fueled the Haitian Revolution, but also shaped the succeeding events in Haitian history.

....

RELIGION AND THE REVOLTS FOR INDEPENDENCE: 1790–1804

Politics

The fears of the colonists regarding Vodou were well grounded, for between 1791 and 1804 developments took place that tore the political and economic stability of the tiny colony. The number of affranchis had increased, and their relationship with the grands blancs had grown closer. Like the grands blancs, some were prosperous and had acquired large and handsome plantations. One source noted that in 1791 they owned approximately one-third of the plantations in the colony and one-fourth of the slaves (Leyburn 1972, 18).

The affranchis' wealth stirred the resentment of the petits blancs. From the early colonial days on, many affranchis had attempted to dissociate themselves from their African ancestries by publicly denying their African background and making reference to obscure Indian ancestors. Some even secured letters from government officials in order to establish their freedom legally on that basis. Having entered white society and having diluted their African ancestry through successive generations of concubinage with whites, these social climbers often passed for whites and "snubbed" the petits blancs (Leyburn 1972). The consequent resentment of the affranchis by the petits blancs led to the enactment of discriminatory laws in the latter part of the eighteenth century that prohibited the affranchis from traveling, bearing arms, filling certain political and governmental offices, and assuming certain careers, such as medicine and law. They were also barred from participating in Catholic masses because of the public and honorific nature of these celebrations. In 1768, they were forbidden to marry whites and were forced to be endogamous; by 1779, they were not allowed to wear shoes and their clothes were not to be as handsomely cut as those of whites (*Adresse de la Société*). A curfew required them to be indoors by nine o'clock so that they could not attend the evening functions of the white *haute société* (*Du Morier à l'Assemblée Nationale*).

As discrimination reached its apex, the French Revolution broke out in France in 1789; the passage of the Declaration of the Rights of Man, the recent rise of the humanitarian liberal group in France called *Amis des Noirs* (Friends of the Blacks) who advocated the end of slavery, the inherent dissatisfaction of the affranchis, and the inhumane treatment of slaves engendered a series of revolts in Saint-Domingue. Vincent Ogé, a young affranchi studying in France, was encouraged and given funds by the Amis to return to the colony and campaign for the political rights of all people of color. He and a friend, Jean-Baptiste Chavannes, led a demonstration with twenty other companions at Cap-Français that brought about their arrest and notably brutal death (Geggus 1989, 28). The harshness and racial antagonism inflicted upon the affranchis were even more intense toward the inarticulate slaves who had no rights at all. Floggings became more frequent as discrimination deepened. Many slaves, judged to be disrespectful to their masters, were forced to eat their own excrement or to drink the saliva of other slaves; others, their bodies covered with molasses, were tied to active beehives (James 1949, 11); blazing irons and hot beeswax applied to the heads, arms, and shoulders of slaves were common punishments; pregnant women were convicted to such hard labor that often miscarriages resulted (James 1949, 11, 93).[5] Atrocities and brutal treatment mounted until August 14, 1791, when a maroon rebellion broke out, led by a runaway slave called Boukman. The 1791 Revolution began with a Vodou ceremony at Bois Caïman in the northern part of the island. After sacrificing a pig, the participants went into the towns and cities of the north and indiscriminately slaughtered every white man, woman, and child (James 1949, 79–82).

Amidst the ensuing slave rebellions that occurred between 1792 and 1804, Toussaint Louverture and Jean-Jacques Dessalines emerged as the leaders of a large-scale revolution in 1797. The mounting threat posed by the powerful affranchis and the subversive activities of the slaves led Napoleon to send his brother-in-law, Charles Leclerc, with a contingent of 20,000 highly trained French troops. These made two landings, the first in February 1801 with 12,000 men, and the second on January 2, 1802 (James 1949, 273, 301). Leclerc arrived at Cap-Français in 1802, a city which by this time was under the leadership of Toussaint's black general Henri Christophe. On February 8 of the same year, Christophe set the city afire and retreated to the adjacent mountains. The final stages of the war of independence had begun. Leclerc's orders were clear: he was to rid the colony of all the "gilded Africans" who were generating the insurrection (Leyburn 1972, 29) and then proceed to Louisiana to take control of the Mississippi Delta, to prevent the expansion of the United States in that region. The expedition was to be a long and complex one, intended to reestablish France's hegemony in these areas. He understood his mission well and set out to carry it through meticulously. Wanting to decapitate the slaves' leadership, and thereby paralyze their military strength, he persuaded Toussaint to dine with him at his headquarters under the pretext of wishing to negotiate certain mitigating terms regarding the insurrection in the colony. During the meal, French soldiers seized Toussaint and rushed him aboard a waiting vessel. He was brought to France where he remained in exile, unable to counsel his generals or to participate in the insurrection; he died of cold and starvation a year later (1803), at the Fort de Joux in the Juras mountains. Leclerc himself succumbed (reportedly of yellow fever) in November 1802, the year of his landing at Cap-Français; his troops never reached Louisiana but died in Saint-Domingue.

France's dominion over Saint-Domingue was nearing its end. General Donatien Rochambeau, who replaced Leclerc, hunted every black maroon and affranchi actively involved in the revolution with fifteen hundred dogs imported from Jamaica—but to no avail, for by the end of 1803 he was forced to concede defeat (Leyburn 1972, 30). His battalion of nearly 17,000 men had been decimated. On January 1, 1804, Dessalines proclaimed the colony's independence and chose the aboriginal Indian name "Haiti," meaning mountainous country, for the new republic. What had begun as a peaceful demonstration by the Amis in Cap-Français in 1790 had swelled to a comprehensive war by 1803. Moreover, the turbulence during these years had caused the death of some 70,000 French soldiers, and probably an equal number of blacks (Geggus 1989, 47).

An important question that transcends the scope of this book, but one to which historians and students of the revolution have alluded, deserves mention: Why did France lose the war against the slaves in Saint-Domingue? Scholars and historians have suggested that the revolution was successful primarily because Napoleon had so overextended his troops in Europe during the early 1800s that he was unable to send the additional reinforcements necessary to ensure Leclerc's efforts in the colony. From historical evidence, however, it would appear that Saint-Domingue was much too important economically to have been overlooked by the French leader, for his military victories and his hopes for France's successful expansion in Europe depended substantially on the revenues from the colony. Scholars have also suggested that a plague of yellow fever was responsible for the decimation of the French army in Saint-Domingue, facilitating the success of the revolutionary slaves (Geggus 1989, 46; James 1949). Yet yellow fever in Haiti, Wade Davis suggests, would have corresponded to the first rainy season of the year—that is, between late April and the end of June (Davis 1988, 20)—and as already noted, Leclerc's troops made two separate landings at Cap-Français, the first in February 1801 and the second under his personal supervision in January 1802, several months before the rains, and well before the accumulation of pools of stagnant water essential to the incubation of the fever's carrier mosquito. Between the time of the first landing and the beginning of the rainy season, Leclerc's own testimony indicates that his forces had already diminished by at least 10,000 men: 5,000 were killed in battle, and 5,000 others were hospitalized.[6] He noted in a letter of early April 1802 that as many as 250 to 300 men were admitted to hospitals daily (James 1949, 301). Blinded by their apparent parochialism, and ignoring the ethnocentrism of many of their sources, eyewitnesses and historians of the revolution have failed to recognize that the war was won by the remarkable leadership and valor of the blacks who succeeded in subduing two of Napoleon's mightiest battalions.

Religion

If the war of independence had been won, it had been primarily due to the indefatigable efforts of the maroons hiding in the forests and hills of the island. Although few signs of their struggles survive today, their resistance against white domination has been well documented by many sources (M. Campbell 1988; Fouchard 1981; Mintz 1971a; Genovese 1967). These sources all agree that the maroons hold a special significance for the study of slave societies in the New World, for their presence symbolizes the longing of enslaved people for freedom. In Saint-Domingue, their resistance to white domination lasted more than two hundred and fifty years and their aggressiveness became a nightmare for both the Spanish and French colonists (ANP, File C90; F3, 90).

The word maroon derives from the Spanish cimarron, a word used to designate a domesticated animal that had reverted to a wild state (Price 1973, 1). The term soon came to be applied to runaway slaves, and by 1530 it had gained strong connotations of violence and bloody confrontation. Indeed, the intermittent maroon raids throughout the sixteenth and seventeenth centuries not only destroyed large numbers of plantations but were costly in human lives as well.

Generally, there were few opportunities for the maroons to cooperate with the slaves on the plantations in these raids, for the plantations, as Moreau de Saint-Méry observed, were well guarded and their penetration was rendered difficult by efficient militias. But this same observer recognized Vodou as a powerful unifying agent and a "terrible weapon" in the hands of the maroon leaders, a serious threat to life in the colony (Moreau de Saint-Méry [1797] 1958, 1:69). That there was real danger everywhere was made clear by letters and other documents written during that period.[7] A report to the Minister of Colonies in Paris noted that the maroons represented a "formidable domestic enemy" to the safety of the colony's residents (de Vaissière 1909, 1:229–30). It was in the north that their activities were the most violent and destructive. Amidst the Montagnes Noires and the Montagnes Rouges, the final struggle for liberation began, led by powerful leaders who exercised absolute authority over their followers.

The cause for these rebellions can be examined in the light of studies made by sociologists and students of social change. According to them, when a more or less serious damage has occurred to the structure of a culture, as was the case in colonial Saint-Domingue with the uprooting of the slaves' African religious traditions, social stress sets in and the culture or "mazeway" deteriorates (Wallace 1979, 421). Its subsequent restructuring is often led by prophets or leaders who, with stringent criticism, point out the downfall of the existing culture. As Charles Gloch has noted, these leaders are "concatenations of cultural forces without which . . . they would live and die unnoticed"; furthermore, they are part of a complicated nexus intertwined with their culture, and their leadership is grounded in past experience as well as in their own psychological conditions of stress. Gloch adds that their roles cannot be understood without recognizing the social and cultural environments to which they belong (1959, 120).

Prophets are vital parts of social change and the reformulation of cultural traditions. The success of such reformulations depends upon the charisma of the leaders. According to Max Weber, charisma characterizes persons who are recognized as having exceptional, superhuman qualities, and who hold unquestionable authority over communities of true believers (1964, 353). Despite the different forms of charismatic authority in societies throughout the world, by and large they have many characteristics in common. For our purposes we may summarize some of these in the following way:

1. The authority of charismatic leaders is one that must be self-assumed, in that it stems from the leaders' sense of mission, or duty toward those whom they are serving (Weber 1964).

2. Charismatic leaders' authority must be recognized by those to whom their supernatural powers are displayed. They must show proof of power by various manifestations, among which is their courage to put personal gain aside, even in the face of eventual death, for the sake of the community. These manifestations are interpreted by the community as qualities uncommon in ordinary persons (Weber 1964).

3. The authority of charismatic leaders is not based on competence, social privilege, election, or judicial action; these constitute rational bureaucratic spheres, for they bind an individual's power to an office, subject to analyzable rules, geographical areas, and historical traditions. A leader's authority is based, rather, on a "call" believed to originate from a supernatural power (Weber 1964).

4. According to the suggestions of Ralph Linton and Michael Barkun described in Chapter 1, charismatic leaders sometimes proclaim, in situations of extreme stress, a violent millenarianism that can be troublesome to colonial administrators. As we have seen, such millenarian movements frequently arise in societies lacking formal political structure, and they can be prepolitical in nature. Charismatic leaders often conjure up vivid images of the world to come and appoint themselves to lead their followers to the "promised land" (Barkun 1986; Talmon 1965). The details of such images are generally selective re-creations of ancestral traditions that serve as models for the future (Linton 1979; Cohn 1961).

From 1748 to 1804, Saint-Domingue witnessed the emergence of many folk heroes who conducted slave revolts in the northern parish.[8] These revolts were inspired by the Petro lwas who, as noted in Chapter 1, were identified with violence and were born out of the resistance and the rage of the Africans against slavery; these lwas emerged out of Africans' brutal displacement from their fatherland. Nurtured in secret, the lwas provided the moral force and the solidarity necessary for those plotting against the Napoleonic forces.

The first of these charismatic leaders was Macandal. Little concrete information about him survives, but oral tradition has it that he was born in Guinea, and had been brought to the colony a few years before he rose to prominence in 1748. Called by the African gods to be a *papalwa* (high priest) to lead his people (James 1949, 78–79), he envisioned the coming of a new day in which his people would return to their African fatherland (Brutus [n.d.], 1:145). The vividness of his millenarian dream led him to gather around him a large following of maroons. He became convinced that they would bring about their own liberation by reviving many African ancestral traditions. Ritualistic dances offered to the African deities preceded the raids on plantations—a procedure that Macandal felt was a good way to instill a sense of solidarity among his followers. He also led an extensive recruitment campaign that encouraged many slaves from the plantations to join the struggle for liberation. So successful was his campaign between 1748 and 1758 that a report noted that planters who bought fifty slaves often lost as many as forty of them in a matter of three weeks (de Vaissière 1909, 1:229). The terror that the maroons caused in the north during these years was so intense that a letter written during that period by one planter to the Minister of Colonies in Paris noted, "a colony of slaves is a city under constant threat of assault; there one walks on barrels of gun powder" (quoted in de Vaissière 1909, 1:229–30).

The year 1758 brought an end to the terror. Macandal was hunted by the French militia with police dogs, was captured at the Habitation Dufresnes on January 20, 1758, and was burnt at the stake in the northern city of Limbé. After his death, his followers believed that he would be reincarnated in the body of new leader who would undertake the final struggle for liberation.

The messianic hope of Macandal's followers did not die, for two decades later another leader emerged. His name was Boukman. Under his leadership, the maroons conducted numerous destructive raids in the north, which were soon echoed by similar rebellions throughout the colony. Vodou was again used as a catalyst for these insurrections. After officiating at a Vodou ceremony in the forest at Bois Caïman, near Cap-Français, on August 14, 1791, Boukman led the most devastating assaults in the history of the colony so far. His indiscriminate slaughter of whites, and the burning of nearly a thousand plantations in the northern parish alone (Geggus 1989, 29), spurred the formation of a powerful militia that combined the military, the police, and a significant number of civilian volunteers. Boukman was captured and decapitated publicly in 1791; his head was displayed at the public park at Cap-Français. At the time of his death, he is said to have had a following of six thousand slaves and maroons (James 1949, 79).

Marronnage, then, was an important part of the Haitian Revolution. The vivid millenarian message of the leaders gave the maroons and slaves a more than ephemeral hope of escaping servitude—a hope that kept them from falling into despair. In the context of the nature of Vodou belief today, marronnage also played a significant role in preserving whole enclaves of religious tradition from different regions of Africa. Such preservation was made possible largely by the formation of confréries or secret societies (Bastide 1971, 51) from early on in the colony. Although these societies probably existed among the slaves on the plantations, they were especially predominant in the maroon communities on the remote hills in the interior of the island, where they were geographically isolated from the European cultural influences of the plantations (Bastide 1971, 53).

During the early period of the formation of these communities, in the sixteenth century, the plantations were small and required only a moderate labor force. The masters' treatment of their slaves was not as cruel as it would later become, and relatively few slaves escaped from the plantations to join the maroon communities (Laguerre 1974a). Hence, these communities were small, formed initially by Africans who congregated along ethnic lines. As the plantations increased in size and required a larger labor force, the number of maroons increased proportionately, so that by the end of the eighteenth century representatives of other ethnic groups joined the communities; soon, they federated to form what Roger Bastide called "maroon republics" (1971, 51). By and large, the various ethnic groups represented within each republic formed separate secret societies or fraternities based on ethnic origins. Each secret society possessed its own ancestral traditions, which it poured into the religious and cultural fabric of its republic; in the contact between these different ethnic cultures, the maroons hammered out for themselves new religious beliefs and practices based on the old (Bastide 1971, 53). Hence, marronnage can be seen as a phenomenon that bears witness not only to the slaves' political and social resistance to slavery, but also to the preservation and maintenance of widely divergent ethnic religious traditions from different parts of Africa.

Although religion in these republics was shaped by a blending of African beliefs and practices, the forms that it took depended upon a number of contingent variables that left indelible marks on Vodou as it exists today in Haiti. First, as seen in the ounfòs throughout Haiti, the practices of the religious leaders in each of the republics had a profound influence on the theology of that republic. Consequently, Michel Laguerre (1974a) is right when he assumes that the degree to which Vodou incorporated particular beliefs and practices in its theology depended upon the ethnic identity of the leaders of each of the republics. Second, the uneven distribution of ethnic groups within each republic caused the prominence of the theology of some over others. Hence, the practice of Vodou in each republic was shaped largely by its ethnic composition (Laguerre 1974a), the particular ethnic groups represented in each republic, and the demographic composition of these secret societies. This significant diversity in beliefs and practices among the various republics most certainly contributed to the marked geographical divergence in beliefs and practices found in Vodou today (Laguerre 1974a).

Finally, the republics' ethnic diversity was by far the most significant difference between religion in the New World and its counterpart in West Africa. As Sidney Mintz rightly observes, every maroon band could not have been a duplication of African culture in microcosmic form (Mintz 1971b). Environmental conditions, the mixture of African religious traditions represented in each republic, the ethnic identity of the leaders of each republic, and the need for the maroons to structure their societies according to new circumstances to preserve the safety of their members, would all have differed from the situation of their fatherland. These differences would have caused the maroons to transform the African traditions and to adapt them to a new milieu (Laguerre 1974a; Bastide 1971). As already noted, the maroon leaders attempted to revive their ancestral traditions, but only selectively, in that they espoused those that related to their apocalyptic visions of freedom. They modified these visions to conform to the present and future situations as they conceived them. The selective re-creation of their ancestral traditions would have contributed to the formation of the theology of Vodou as it exists today in Haiti.

This diversity in Vodou did not go unnoticed by writers of the colonial period. Around the end of the eighteenth century, Michel Descourtilz alluded to two prominent Vodou sects in the colony: the Rada, whose pantheons and religious traditions derived from the region of Arada in Dahomey—a form of Vodou that Moreau de Saint-Méry erroneously interpreted as ophiolatry because of the presence of a sacred snake in the rituals he attended; and the Petro (or Dompete), whose "creole" deities were a *tertium quid*, New World creations born out of the slaves' rage against the cruelty of their masters (Descourtilz 1809, 116–79; Moreau de Saint-Méry [1797] 1958, 1:64–69). In the days of the colony, as in the present day, the Petro lwas were known to be bitter, aggressive, and forceful, inspiring revolution. In contrast, the Rada lwas have been identified traditionally with benevolent forces.[9] The mythology surrounding the Petro lwas is not African but Haitian, for its stories tell about the slaves' struggle for liberation.

In short, the maroon republics were vital to the development of Vodou. While providing their inhabitants with a millenarian hope for repatriation to Africa, they fostered the maintenance of African religious traditions in Vodou theology. They also fostered the creation of a whole assortment of creole traditions that derived from historical and socioeconomic circumstances, as well as environmental adaptations.

As for Roman Catholicism, it almost disappeared during the time of the revolution. The indiscriminate killing by the maroons and the fear of black reprisals drove many priests to flee the colony or go into hiding with other whites, leaving many of the rural churches with no clergy. The celebration of the Mass and the work of missionaries was done by affranchis or by rene-gade priests, most of whom had been elevated to the priesthood by the colonial government, but whose ordination had not been sanctioned by Rome. In 1801, Toussaint Louverture attempted to revive the church and re-store the position of dignity it had held in the earlier days of the colony. In the face of economic disorganization, social chaos, and the religious void in the lives of the inhabitants of Saint-Domingue, he felt that the church was perhaps the only institution that could provide social solidarity and cohe-sion in a troubled land. He urged many of the white priests who had left to return to the island and to take charge of their former parishes. He also pleaded with those who were hiding to attend to their ecclesiastical duties (Beauvoir-Dominique 1991, 57).

Toussaint's efforts failed, for French priests were not inclined to return to an island under black rule, especially one that Napoleon was planning to suppress at all costs. In a moment of desperation, Toussaint sought help from Abbé Grégoire, who was then living in the colony, and appealed to his influence in the hierarchy of the European church to attract local curates to Haitian parishes (Beauvoir-Dominique 1991, 58). It is not clear whether Grégoire remained in the country long enough after its independence to reestablish Catholicism in Haitian life. Amidst the last phases of the bloody revolution in 1802, and afterwards amidst the considerable destruction that it had caused, tending the wounded and rebuilding society took precedence over religious concerns.

....

RELIGION AND THE SHAPING OF THE REPUBLIC: 1804–1860

Politics

During the first three years after independence (1804–7), under Jean-Jacques Dessalines's administration, Haiti was united economically and politically. But in 1807, the year of Dessalines's death, the country became divided between north and south, and between two rival political factions led by two ambitious men—tyrants who maintained political power solely by military force. Henri Christophe crowned himself king of the northern kingdom of Haiti in 1807 and ruled until 1820; his political rival Alexandre Pétion served as president of the south between 1807 and 1818. Haiti was reunited politically in 1822 during the presidency of Jean-Pierre Boyer (1818–43), Pétion's former personal secretary and minister.

In both the south and, particularly, the north, the first part of the history of independent Haiti is a story of servitude supported by a militarized agriculture whose government was drawn from the mulatto class. Their despotic rule early in the republic paved the way for the emergence of a rigid new social structure in which former affranchis were to become an elite distinctly separated from the black masses. At the outset of his administration, Dessalines, the first president of Haiti, divided the citizens of the country into two categories, the laborers and the soldiers. Fearing the return of the French army, Dessalines, and his successor Christophe in the north, organized all those who had actively participated in the war of independence into an army of 25,000 men (Bellegarde 1938, 86–94). Those who had been on the plantations during the war continued as laborers and cultivated the large acreages the government had annexed from the white planters.

The socioeconomic structures created by Dessalines, and later endorsed by Christophe, provided the roots of the peasantry that exists in Haiti today (Moral 1978, 1). For our purposes, "peasantry" can be defined as a life-style based upon an economic imbalance in which part of a rigidly structured society falls between the aristocracy and the great landholder. The characteristic of peasantry presupposes the existence of a powerful urban elite, which is placed in a direct "asymmetrical power relationship" with peasants (Wolf 1966, 3). The asymmetry consists in the fact that the peasants have an enduring dependence upon the city, where powerful landholders outside their social stratum exercise certain socioeconomic sanctions on the proletariat who cultivate the land. One of those sanctions can be the requirement of rent monies in the form of currency or cash crops, which are transferred from a lower to a higher level in the social stratification (Moral 1978; Wolf 1966; Shanin 1971). A broader definition of peasantry connotes the cultivation of the land by uneducated persons whose families have occupied a low status in a highly structured society in which it is difficult for them to climb the social ladder. They live and work on their land, for they are generally immobile and their subsistence depends upon the crop that they raise on their fields. A people is described as a peasant society when at least half its population fulfills these criteria (Moral 1978).

A census taken in 1805 revealed that the population of Haiti was 380,000 (a drop of 150,000 since the beginning of the war in 1790), and that more than half of that population provided the labor force on the plantations. The newly militarized agriculture, in which the state annexed all available land, produced largely sugar, cotton, and coffee, which mulatto overseers divided according to certain state-established criteria (Moral 1978, 29–33). The overseers were to transmit one-half of the crops to the state: one half of this was used for export, and the other half paid the rent on the land. Another quarter of the total crop yield was retained for the workers' salaries, and the remaining quarter paid the salary of the plantation overseers. The laws regulating life on the plantations were severe (Moral 1978, 38). In cases where the state agricultural inspectors had ordered plantation overseers to hand over a large amount of crops as rent for the land, rigid work schedules were established that required intense work in order to produce crops sufficient to meet these demands. Knowing no persuading power other than force, the plantation overseers subjected their field hands to forced labor and often backed up their commands by whipping the dawdlers with pliable vines which could be gathered in areas of dense vegetation. The law was inexorable, and the plantation overseers were praised by their superiors for successfully meeting the required quotas of crop production. A new form of slavery had been established (Rotberg 1971, 56); many lowly folk who had once been in bondage found themselves, to their chagrin, again in bondage. Because of these oppressive conditions, many became maroons, some for the second time. They escaped to the hills surrounding the large urban areas, where they settled on small plots of unclaimed land. By the middle of the nineteenth century, Haiti had become largely a land of peasants (Moral 1978, 40–41).

Simultaneously with these developments, a new elite class emerged. The mulattoes who had lost their lands through state annexation were now employed by the state as agricultural inspectors and plantation overseers. Moreover, the maintenance of such an extensive economic machinery necessitated a large bureaucracy, and due to the high rate of illiteracy among blacks, Dessalines and Christophe were forced to depend upon the assistance of the educated mulattoes to govern the country. It may be that this new bureaucracy used economic pressures to precipitate what Dessalines and Christophe vehemently resisted in Haiti: the creation of social classes on the basis of skin color. Also, it was perhaps inevitable that the slave mentality of the earlier colonial days carried into the new era: an affranchi whose rights had been taken away during the latter days of the colony was performing the duties of the slave master, and his children were liberated from field labor to direct the work of others. Out of this group arose a few ambitious men and women who later became Haiti's elite.

Between 1807 and 1842, the class system clearly emerged. After Christophe's death in 1820 Boyer, dissatisfied with Dessalines's and Christophe's militarized economy, reunited the country and undertook the task of parceling out the state-owned land. Under the Code Rural that he signed into law in 1826, land that had belonged to the mulattoes during the colonial period was restored to them, along with cash payments drawn from public funds to pay for the full estimated value of crops for one year. To finalize this restoration of land, deeds were issued to the landholders confirming the ownership of land in perpetuity (Code Rural 1826; Saint-Rémy 1854–57, vol. 1). The Code also created a judicial court with the responsibility of settling disputes over rented lands, and established that the "proof of death of the testators was to be forthcoming before wills could be probated" (Leyburn 1972).

The reasons for apportioning the land were many. First, after the war, France had negotiated a sizable financial settlement with Haiti in which her former colony was to pay to her 150 million francs in gold in reparation for damages incurred during the war,[10] in exchange for her recognition of Haiti as an independent nation (Delbeau 1990, 38; Geggus 1989, 48). In addition to the cost of maintaining a ready army in case France returned to invade the tiny nation, crop production was also crucial to Haiti in order to meet the steep demands of this agreement. Although Boyer, who had negotiated the accord, considered it a political tour de force,[11] the steep payments that Haiti continued dutifully to send for many decades caused irreversible damages to the country's economy. One might venture to say that to this day, Haiti's economy has not completely recovered from these damages. Second, apart from the reward that Haiti owed to those who had so ably defended her during the war, Pétion and Boyer knew that the wealth of a country was contained in its land, and that with a renewed production of coffee, sugar, and cotton, they could build the state treasury with the revenues from the exportation of these crops, as had been done earlier during the days of the colony. Third, they felt that the private ownership of land not only would instill pride among the citizens, but also (according to Adam Smith's theory of free enterprise) would yield more crop production. In pursuing his own self-interest, the landholder would unintentionally bring high profits to the state. Fourth, the fear of the return of the French necessitated the maintenance of a strong standing army, and the meager salaries of the officers could be complemented by annual gains from crop revenues, thus alleviating the pressures on the state treasury.

This system of land democratization proved effective at the outset. Mulatto landholders possessed large plantations on which a large labor force, operating under strict laws, cultivated sugar cane, cotton, and coffee. State revenues were high. By 1822, as much as twenty million francs flowed from the international market into the treasury, and practically every acre of land was under cultivation (Dalencourt 1923, 8).

Amidst a booming economy, Pétion took certain measures that were to cause irreparable damage to his meticulously planned economy. Pleased by the success of private enterprise, and hoping to further relieve the pressures on the state treasury, he began to distribute land among the black labor force, as well as among lesser officers and soldiers, in order to complement many more salaries. These grants consisted of unclaimed land that had previously been owned by planters during the colonial period. The effects of such grants were disastrous. First, the members of the black labor force who now owned small portions of land withdrew their services from the plantations, so that the labor force atrophied; production decreased, and the state revenues sank to an all-time low. By 1843, the state's annual revenues had fallen from the twenty million francs of 1822 to twelve million (Leyburn 1972, 85). Second, these grants took the form of small plots, which new owners converted into small-scale gardens devoted to the cultivation of staple foods for their immediate consumption. Third, when Pétion abolished the hundreds of agricultural inspectors whose salaries drained the national economy, he gave them large acreages of land to compensate for their lack of income. They further apportioned these lands into small plots, renting to peasants who no longer labored under the watchful eye of agricultural inspectors charged with keeping their crop production up to schedule. Both points two and three led to the peasants' subsistence economy that persists in Haiti to this day. It had become impossible to control the type of crop planted by the small farmer, since the depleted state treasury would not have permitted the rehiring of the agricultural inspectors. The once successful Code Rural had now failed, and Haiti had largely become a land of peasants. Eyewitness accounts of the economic conditions in Haiti in the first half of the nineteenth century noted that no governmental measures, save for military force, could have restored the economy. Land values had declined greatly (Franklin 1828, 313; Candler 1842, 37), and Boyer's administration was forced to take steps to control the prices of food and land.

In short, the first forty years after independence witnessed the emergence of an elite class in the cities and towns. That same period also witnessed the rise of the peasantry, which was to persist throughout Haiti's history. This peasant class was the result of carefully planned but unpredictable policies whose circumstantial outcome differed widely from their intent. The economy of the country had moved from large plantations to tiny plots, from carefully tilled fields to tiny gardens, from financial prosperity to national debt, from directed enterprise to sloth, and from strong determination for growth to an attitude of tolerance toward an existing decadence.

Religion

As soon as he assumed ascendancy, Dessalines proclaimed himself head of the church in Haiti, with the right not only to supervise the limits of the jurisdiction of each priest, but also to appoint men to vacant parishes. His indiscriminate slaughter of the white colonists during the period of the revolution had resulted in the assassination of a large number of the missionaries, and only a few of those who had fled had been persuaded by Toussaint to return to the island. Lacking an adequate number of priests to fill all the vacancies, Dessalines appointed ex-slaves with whom he had been allied during the war (Leyburn 1972, 119). He further sought to regulate the life of the church in his 1805 constitution, which liberalized marriage as a merely "civil act authorized only by the government" (Leyburn 1972, 119). The separation of husband and wife was proclaimed illegal except by divorce, and the reasons for which the state could sanction a divorce varied widely—from mutual consent from both partners, to application from one of the partners for simple reasons of incompatibility.

The provisions of the 1805 constitution did not go unnoticed. The Vatican refused to recognize Haiti as a republic and declined to send priests into the country, resulting in an open schism between the Haitian state and

Rome which lasted for fifty-six years. The longer this schism lasted, the further Haitians parted from the teachings of the church. By the time the break was healed in 1860, it was too late: Haitian religion had become a strange assortment of Catholic and Vodou beliefs.

Under the leadership of Henri Christophe, Catholicism was made the state religion. Christophe sought to restore the status of the church to what it had been during the colony. As the first king of Haiti, he created a nobility, and he wanted to revive the church in order to dignify his northern kingdom and his aristocracy. In 1811 and in 1814, therefore, he recognized the clergy with the formation of an archbishopric and three bishoprics. He also sent a small delegation of young black Haitian aspirants to the priesthood to Rome to be ordained, hoping that they would return to their homeland to train and ordain curates to fill the country's various parishes. In all of these instances he sought Rome's approval but was denied any cooperation. He then turned to a Spanish Capuchin named Corneille Brelle who had come to the island under Toussaint's persuasion. Christophe made Brelle "archbishop of Haiti and Grand Almoner to the king," giving him a palace and a substantial salary drawn from state revenues. The grand monarch then turned again to Rome for approval, but later announced to his subjects that the "king of Haiti did not even receive a response from his Majesty, the Pope" (Leyburn 1972, 121–22).

During the years of the presidencies of Pétion (1807–18) and Boyer (1818–43) Roman Catholicism remained the state religion, and both leaders made an effort to close the breach between Rome and the Haitian state. The few priests who had survived the war were dying, and no new priests were being sent to the republic. Many priests fleeing revolutions in South America sought refuge in Haiti, but their lack of a command of French limited their clerical effectiveness. France, not wishing to counter the will of the pope, refused to send sympathetic priests to Haiti. Deprived of support from the Vatican and badly in need of young priests, the state was again forced to make new regulations regarding the church. Young Haitian men were elevated to the priesthood and were ordained by the state—a step that the Vatican would not recognize as legitimate.

Toward the middle of the nineteenth century, orthodoxy declined rapidly in Haiti. Two generations of Haitians had received no religious instruction and knew little about the rituals of the church. They continued to adhere to Vodou, using the rituals of the church to mask the practices of their native traditions. The long separation with Rome had permitted Vodou to disseminate and to anchor itself solidly within the framework of Haitian society.

With no bishops and no titled dignitaries, only the seventy or so priests who had been ordained by the state labored to turn their parishioners to Catholicism—but to no avail.

The moral conduct of the clergy also left much to be desired, which did little to advance the cause of Catholicism in Haiti. In this connection, James Leyburn noted that many priests were renegades and adventurers, "who knew just enough of the ritual and theology to use the priestly garb as a cover for easy graft" (1972, 123). They collected set fees for baptizing houses, boats, and doorposts; they blessed fetishes, charms, amulets, and whatever other objects were brought to them by their parishioners (Le Ruzic 1912). They sold "scapularies and printed orations that were hung on chains or put around children's necks, occasionally adding a key to them to guard [these children] from whooping cough," and they received "ten gourdes [two dollars U.S.] for offering prayers that would cause rainfalls which a farmer needed" (Schoelcher 1843, 293). They also received five gourdes (one dollar U.S.) for exorcizing female parishioners known to harbor harmful spirits. These parishioners were women accused of being werewolves by members of their communities (Schoelcher 1843, 1:292–94). So avaricious were the priests in their dubious pastoral duties that when Victor Schoelcher, an eye-witness to Haitian spiritual life during the nineteenth century, questioned a priest about one such exorcism, the priest replied imperturbably, " 'but sir, one is saved merely by one's faith. This woman would still think of herself as a werewolf if I did not take her money' " (1843, 1:293–94).

Debauchery too became prevalent among many priests; a large number took women as concubines who bore children to them. Their licentiousness caused such embarrassment to the state that on numerous occasions Boyer's Secretary-General Balthasar Inginac was forced to deport priests from the country. As open-minded an observer of Haitian religious conditions during Boyer's administration as the Quaker John Candler remarked that the clergy's main interest was to seek gold and the worldly pleasures that life could give. Save for a few, they were fond of gambling and invested large sums of money in the European market. Candler stated: "With regard to the ecclesiastical institutions of the republic we may safely say . . . that if the standing army be one cause of the degradation of the people, the Church is surely another, and the sooner it can be reformed, the better for religion, for morals, and for the physical well-being of the community" (Candler 1842, 98).

The situation of Catholicism was desperate. Although historical circumstances had impelled the rulers of independent Haiti to seek approval of the pope, this was not so much for religious as for political reasons. They thought that Haitian public order would benefit by an educated priesthood, which would add to the prestige of the new state. Moreover, the Vatican's recognition of Haiti as an independent black nation would have encouraged the similar recognition of her as an independent state by other nations as well. For these reasons, recognition by the Vatican was important. Boyer attempted again and again to end the schism between Haiti and the Vatican by sending emissaries to Rome to seek approval for the state church. The Vatican considered Boyer's proposal and finally appointed the primate of the West Indies and Archbishop of Santo Domingo (now the Dominican Republic) as Archbishop of Haiti—but despite Boyer's efforts, he could not be lured, as Rome's new ambassador, to move to Port-au-Prince. From 1834 to 1860, the Haitian government's determination to obtain foreign priests caused Rome to send few representatives to Haiti, and most of these were Spaniards who spoke neither French nor Creole and consequently did little for Roman Catholicism among the Haitians (Cabon 1930, 186–87).

During the forty years following independence (1804–44), the first three black presidents set themselves against Vodou and attempted vigorously to suppress it (Verschueren 1948, 333). The military agriculture in the early life of the republic drove the Haitian people to hard labor and, as leaders of the revolution, Dessalines and Christophe were well aware of the revolutionary potential of the Vodou ceremonies. This was no time for political instability and rebellion, for the country had been debilitated by the ailments of a costly revolution. They therefore attempted to subdue the nocturnal dances and gatherings with police force. All offenders reported by the police were shot if they could be caught. No doubt, Dessalines and Christophe feared not only the latent potential of Vodou as a catalyst for revolution, but also the effects of magic done against them. It would seem that, while they practiced Roman Catholicism outwardly, their faith in the native folk beliefs persisted.[12] As for the mulatto president Boyer, his attitude toward Vodou has not been recorded, except that he was not proud of its existence in the republic. Indeed, no law from the twenty-five years of his presidency mentions it, or makes provision for its practice. The writings of Zachary Macaulay from 1835 give the impression that Boyer regarded Vodou as a primitive aberration with no significant content, deserving little attention. But it is also possible that he was reluctant to acknowledge the widespread practice of Vodou in the country, fearing the adverse effect of such an admission on his administration's ongoing negotiations with the Vatican to recognize Haiti as the first black republic in the world and to end its schism with the church. Macaulay noted that Vodou thoroughly permeated the Haitian peasantry and that although it claimed to be Catholic, it "intermix[ed] the legitimate ritual of the Catholic faith with the mysterious adoration paid to their national fetishes, and the African obi and the Catholic priest both [came] in for a share of their respect and homage" (1835, 90).

The practice of Vodou among Haitians expanded after the emergence of Faustin Soulouque as president in 1847. In Soulouque's twelve years in office, the future for Catholicism became darker than ever (Bonneau 1862, 24ff.). Unlike his predecessors, Soulouque revived Vodou and allowed the traditional respect for orthodoxy in Haitian society to die. He permitted ceremonies in which animals were sacrificed in the streets, and for the first time in Haitian history, state officials openly admitted their adherence to Vodou (Verschueren 1948, 333–34).

The abysmal state that Catholicism had reached under the rule of Soulouque made his successor's task rather simple. In 1858, the year of his ascendancy, President Fabre Nicolas Geffrard sought negotiations with Rome once more, depicting the sorry state of the Haitian church. Following the visit of special emissaries from Rome, a resolution to the conflict between the Haitian government and the Vatican was finally reached and the Concordat was signed in Rome on March 28, 1860. The conditions provided by the eighteen articles of this document can be summarized as follows (Duvalier 1969, 190–93; Cabon 1930, 475–89; Concordat, Archives de la Bibliothèque des Frères de l'Institution Chrétienne Saint Louis de Gonzague [ABFI]):

1. Port-au-Prince was declared the seat of ecclesiastical power in Haiti, and an archbishop was to be named by the president of the republic.

2. Roman Catholicism was declared the official religion of the republic and was to be protected and supported by state funds.

3. In collaboration with the Vatican, church officials were to reserve the right to reorganize the sizes of the various dioceses; they were to appoint bishops to these dioceses and pastors to local churches; and they were also to found a seminary responsible for training Haitian priests.

The archbishop and a delegation of forty priests began their missionary work in Haiti. The church edifices, nearly collapsing after more than fifty years of neglect, had to be refurbished, and the Haitian government committed itself financially to the renovation of a large number of them. So effective was the Concordat that by the end of the nineteenth century the construction program was nearing completion. Catholicism was reestablished in Haiti; its dignity had been repaired, and its work greatly increased in scope.

These reforms, however, had come too late. In spite of the fact that in the country's first sixty years as an independent nation the Haitian government, except during Soulouque's administration, had attempted to suppress Vodou, Haitian culture was imbued with Vodou practices. It had disseminated everywhere and anchored itself tacitly in Haitian religious life; it had also cast itself throughout the countryside within a Roman Catholic mold, adjusting itself to the pressures that attempted to suppress it. The government officials, the elite, fearing the rebuke of the state that had attempted to suppress Vodou, adhered to the religion only clandestinely. In contrast, the peasants interpreted the saints in terms of an already established Vodou pantheon of lwas. As is the case in contemporary Haiti, Roman Catholicism and Vodou formed two religious hierarchies, two parallel systems, which became juxtaposed. Each had its own divine power, and in the eyes of the worshipers the belief in one was not the denial of the other. That which permitted the shift from one system to the other was the process of reinterpretation by which the content of Catholic theology translated itself into Vodou beliefs.

While the new priests worked at their task with utmost devotion, they met no open belligerence from Vodou priests, nor did their adherents. Rather, they faced a folk religion that, during more than fifty years, had rooted itself in the Haitian's religious life—a folk religion which was tolerant in that it had worked out a system of reinterpretations by which its content absorbed most of Catholic theology, and rejected nothing of the spiritual aspect of life.

....

RELIGION IN HAITIAN LIFE: 1860–PRESENT

For the general purpose of this discussion I need not describe all the political events in the history of Haiti since 1860, but one of the most significant considerations has been the contact between the church and Vodou. The development of both religions can be examined in the light of many historical events. From 1860 to the present, Haitian politics has been troubled by a series of civil disorders. There have been no fewer than thirty-five presidents during that time, only five of whom completed their terms. One died while serving; one was killed when his palace was blown up; one was poisoned;

one was seized by a mob that dismembered his body; two resigned; and the others were ousted or threatened by political insurrections.

This political unrest is precisely what precipitated the American Occupation from 1915 to 1934. The instability from 1860 to 1915 had drained Haiti's economy. The relative absence of law and order during that period was caused by a number of factors, one of which was economic. Endeavoring to stimulate Haiti's economy, the government had encouraged foreign investors to settle in the country. Their numbers increased significantly,[13] and so did their financial control of many commercial enterprises, including the Banque Nationale de la République d'Haïti. Crowds of Haitians took to the streets from time to time to destroy these enterprises, and to protest what they perceived as the resurgence of whites' socioeconomic hegemony against which their ancestors had fought so valiantly.

In addition, the political instability between 1860 and 1915 necessitated the maintenance of a ready army, which was costly to the country. Haiti was forced to borrow money abroad.[14] These sums were to be paid back within an allotted period; otherwise, a foreign warship would appear in the Port-au-Prince harbor to collect the debt. Incidents involving the intimidating presence of foreign warships in the harbor were many during that period. English, French, German, and Spanish navy frigates that sailed the Caribbean stopped in Haiti not only to collect national debts due to their governments, but in some instances to impose on the Haitian government steep payments to be made to many of their influential and wealthy nationals settled in Haiti, who allegedly suffered financial losses at the hands of unruly peasants whom the Haitian government could not control.[15]

Following the public disorders in which President Guillaume Sam's body was dismembered by a mob in the courtyard of his palace, German ships anchored in the Port-au-Prince harbor to collect Haitian debts to Germany. To prevent a possible takeover of Haiti and Germany's military expansion in the Caribbean, and acting under the dictates of the Monroe Doctrine, the United States intervened to protect her economic interests, totaling about four million dollars (Ferguson 1989, 24) in the Banque Nationale and the Haitian-American Sugar Company (HASCO). On December 17, 1914, officials of the National City Bank of New York (whose investments in Haiti included among other holdings large tracts of land), accompanied by U.S. Marines, arrived in Haiti on board the navy destroyer *Machias*. With the blessing of the Haitian government (or perhaps due to unrelenting pressure from Washington), they entered the Banque Nationale in Port-au-Prince and transferred large sums of money in gold already earmarked to be deposited in U.S. banks to the City Bank of New York, sums that are currently in sundry accounts in that bank (Delbeau 1990, 38). The U.S. Marines landed subsequently in Haiti on July 28, 1915.

The American Occupation of Haiti achieved great strides toward progress. Roads were built, artesian wells for public water were drilled, in many important cities and towns water-distribution as well as drainage systems were installed, the first automatic telephone in the world was introduced in Port-au-Prince as an experiment before its U.S. installation, schools and government buildings were erected, and mail service and agricultural methods improved. For the elite, the occupation provided freer access to higher learning and the professions. The Université d'Haïti (later renamed the Université d'Etat d'Haïti) was reorganized with efficient schools of law, medicine, and agronomy. Industry flourished; productive sugar cane fields that had been turned into small gardens were cultivated again; and the Haitian bourgeoisie enjoyed the wealth of a flourishing market. A small mercantile class also emerged, which enjoyed an economic prosperity that Haiti had not known since the early days of Pétion.

In spite of these positive developments, however, the occupation by foreign troops also engendered profound resentment among the Haitian people. The large-scale public projects undertaken by the U.S. government required the marshaling of a large labor force, which urban dwellers alone could not provide. Thousands of poor peasants were compelled to abandon their soil, to join konbits (organized work groups), and to commit themselves to forced labor. The old corvée (forced labor laws) under Dessalines and Christophe returned. Dissatisfaction was so widespread that nearly five thousand armed guerilla peasants, or Cacos, inspired by the notable rage of the Petro lwas, revolted against the occupation—and the country was again in political upheaval. The suppression of these guerilla revolts required several years and was costly in terms of both lives and money.

In the midst of national disaster, economic instability, and the vagrant destruction of property by the Cacos, the violence of the urban streets did not go unnoticed by the elite. The sudden poverty of the peasants due to heavy taxation, coupled with the formation of urban ghettos occupied by former peasants who worked on public works, revived the antiquated assumption of the colonial days among the elite about the superiority of whites and the inferiority of blacks. Many of the mulatto elite came to feel that blacks could not govern themselves, that they could never build a civilization, or that they were unable to plan their own national destiny (Leyburn 1972, 107).

While the American Occupation revived many of the strong prejudices in the Haitian elite, it had little effect on their social structure, other than that it helped to strengthen their economic and political control. But it had a profound effect on the social structure of the peasantry. First, it weakened the organization of the rural *lakou* (an African-derived communal compound in which members of extended families lived) by bringing thousands of peasants into the dilapidated sections of cities. Second, many ill-nourished peasants had no contact with the outside world but were forgotten, deeply buried in the remote areas of the countryside. With no outside standard for comparison, they were indifferent to philosophical reflections about human rights or democracy, but merely wanted to continue to till their tiny plots peacefully.

Throughout the occupation, Catholicism enlarged the scope of its work in Haiti. Toward the end of the period, Haiti was divided into dioceses, each bearing the name of its principal city. The numbers of Catholics increased considerably from 1930 to 1972, as indicated by the following statistics:

	1930	1972
Archdiocese of Port-au-Prince	42,700	1,300,000
Diocese of Cap-Haïtien	453,000	650,000
Diocese of Les Cayes	628,000	800,000
Diocese of Gonaïves	475,000	700,000
Diocese of Port-de-Paix	153,590	290,000
Total	1,752,290	3,740,000

Source: 1930 statistics from Leyburn 1972, 128; 1972 statistics were obtained from the Roman Catholic Archevêché of Port-au-Prince during the summer of the same year.

The report of the Forbes Commission stated that in 1930 there were 205 priests, only 8 of whom were Haitians; 105 brothers; and 366 sisters. In a country of 10,000 square miles or so, there were 567 parishes and chapels (ABFI 1930, 16–17).

If the church made great strides after the signing of the Concordat, it was through the untiring efforts of young priests who worked diligently for its progress. Throughout the nineteenth century, Haiti had few relationships with other nations except for those that bought sugar, cotton, and coffee. Education remained almost nonexistent; the rate of illiteracy was high, and the profound ignorance that the slave master had encouraged persisted during the first hundred years of the republic's existence. Technology too was slow to reach Haiti. The rudimentary machete and hoe used during the colonial period are still being employed today. The draft plow and animals used in the colonial period are useless on small garden patches on steep hills, and even if they could be used, the poverty of the peasants would hardly permit them the luxury of feeding those animals adequately. Through many divisions caused by numerous inheritances the garden patches have diminished in size significantly, and they are no longer large enough to feed the growing number of large families that squat on them. Moreover, the planting of the same traditional crops each year for more than a century without applying adequate fertilizer has depleted the soil of its essential nutrients. The cutting of trees for use in cooking and for heating water, the systematic deforestation to reveal the hideouts of resistance fighters during the American Occupation (1915–34) and Papa Doc's administration (1957–71), and the endless erosion of the sun-baked soil have further diminished the crop production to a level below subsistence requirements. In addition, the lack of contact with the outside world has facilitated the preservation of old traditions from Africa; for example, in the domain of the arts, techniques used in weaving and wood carving show strong African influences (Weinstein and Segal 1984). In short, as regards the material aspect of culture, Haiti has not changed very much from what she was more than a century ago.

As a result of her cultural and political isolation, one of Haiti's few contacts with the outside world has been Roman Catholicism. The church has worked assiduously toward the education of her young people. In 1843, seventeen years before the signing of the Concordat, there were only 15 elementary schools and 1 secondary school, serving a total population of 2,000,000; all of these schools were non-Catholic (Bird 1869, 140). By 1875, fifteen years after the signing of the Concordat, a census reported the following:

Schools	Students
4 lycées	543
6 girls' elementary schools	563
5 girls' secondary schools	350
165 primary schools	11,784
200 rural schools	5,939
1 medical school	25
1 school of music	46
Total	19,250

Source: St. John, 1884, 293.

While the lycées and the medical school were under state control, 90 percent of the elementary, secondary, and primary schools were owned by the church. Statistics for 1919 show 29 Catholic girls' schools, 8 boys' schools, and 105 presbyterial schools with approximately 25,000 pupils. In 1972, out of 70 schools in the Port-au-Prince area alone 30 were Catholic, with a combined enrollment of more than 10,000 pupils (ABFI).

In the domains of technology and health, the church has been effective in the establishment of a practical curriculum that treats a variety of technical skills and agriculture. Until the end of the American Occupation, the church was also an active agent in the improvement of public health. Hospitals, both public and private, have traditionally been staffed heavily by Catholic sisters.

Yet in spite of the church's concentrated efforts among the Haitians, it has not been able to offer a satisfactory substitute for older religious traditions. The result has been that, as in the colonial days, most of those who proclaim adherence to the Catholic faith also adhere to Vodou; while there has been a Catholic influence, Vodou is more important in Haitian life. Since Haiti has never had an accurate census, it is difficult to say how many Haitians are Vodouisants. The impacts of the Code Noir, the harsh suppressions of Dessalines, Christophe, and Pétion, and the abuses and indiscriminate killings during the presidencies of François (Papa Doc) Duvalier and his son Jean-Claude (Baby Doc) by their secret military police or *tontons macoutes* (bogeymen), still persist in Haiti today—so that Haitians are often suspicious of census takers who probe into their personal affairs. Consequently, they do not usually admit their allegiance to Vodou. The Catholic church lists all non-Protestants in a diocese as Catholics, but it is clear that most Haitian Catholics still subscribe to Catholicism only nominally. The majority of peasants and elite alike frequent ounfòs, and spend large sums of money to buy ritual paraphernalia for Vodou ceremonies.

Generally, the church has been tolerant and open-minded about its Vodouisant adherents, but at times it has put strong pressures upon the government to outlaw and disband Vodou. It was in this spirit that in 1896, 1913, and again in 1941 the church conducted its Antisuperstitious Campaigns, burning and destroying hundreds of ounfòs and ritual paraphernalia throughout the country. In 1941 Opération Nettoyage (Operation Cleanup), instigated by Msgr. Paul Robert of Port-au-Prince, Father Joseph Foisset of Le Petit Séminaire Collège St. Martial, and three Haitian priests, Fathers Jean-Marie Salgado, Carl Peters, and André Solasge, attempted to "sweep all ancestral traditions" from the country (Hurbon 1972, 21). At the outset, Operation Cleanup was only the work of a few clerics, but within a year's time it had gained momentum. By the end of 1941, the church was given police support from the state. Around that period, a *Catéchisme* was also printed in the form of a pamphlet which circulated widely among Haitians and was taught in the churches, and in the public as well as the Catholic schools. Written in the traditional question-and-answer format of many such documents throughout the world, it encouraged all Catholics to "renounce their superstitious" practices, to promise "to renew their baptismal vows," to be fruitful members of the church, to abandon the practice of "feeding" and coercing ancestral spirits, and to raise their children according to the strict teachings of the Catholic church and no other (Hurbon 1972, 21ff.; Solasge 1967; Salgado 1963; Peters 1960).

More often than not, suppression destroys what is benevolent and gentle, while inspiring violent reactions on the part of those whose religious practices are endangered. As in the days of the revolution, Vodou's reaction to the Antisuperstitious Campaigns resulted in the reaffirmation of the Petro lwas. The violence of the peasants' resistance against the Campaign of 1941 was such that the country's national security was at stake once more. By 1942, the mulatto president Elie Lescot thought that it would be politically wise to abandon the Campaign and ordered it stopped.

Since 1942, the Haitian church has changed considerably, both among its clergy and in its attitudes toward Vodou. These changes have been caused by a series of events, the most notable of which were Papa Doc's efforts to creolize or indigenize the church. In 1957, the year of Papa Doc's rise to power, the Haitian writer Frank Durant published a contentious book in which he stated that for nearly a century after the signing of the 1860 Concordat, the Vatican did not abide by its articles. Taken in their entirety, these articles would have given more autonomy to the Haitian church. Article 4 in particular made provision for the president, in consultation with the Vatican, to name archbishops, bishops, and priests of local congregations. According to Durant, the church had not only failed to fulfill these obligations, but had not trained sufficient numbers of Haitian clerics to govern the church.

The publication of Durant's book led Papa Doc to creolize the church, replacing foreign priests with Haitian clerics to administer the affairs of the archdiocese. In 1960 he ordered the expulsion of French archbishop François Poirier from Haiti, appointing the Haitian priest François Wolf Ligondé in his place. Poirier was expelled under the pretext that he had reached "retirement age," and that he could no longer manage the affairs of his see. Rome did not take such developments lightly; in a letter addressed to the president in 1961, the Vatican reminded Papa Doc that canonic law made no mention of age as a consideration occasioning the removal of an archbishop from his post (Duvalier 1969, 147–288). But Poirier's expulsion was followed by other incidents. Between 1961 and 1964 the Society of Jesus, accused of conspiring in political insurrections, was expelled from Haiti; the Grand Séminaire Théologique was closed; three of the four white European-born bishops in the four Haitian dioceses, as well as many foreign curates and teachers, were exiled from the country. Papa Doc's actions merely increased Pope Paul VI's ire and caused a new, five-year schism between Haiti and the Vatican (1960–65). After years of deliberations, a new Concordat was signed, and in March 1966 a special Vatican delegation, headed by papal nuncios Msgr. Antonio Samoré and his assistant Msgr. Dante Pasquanelli, arrived in Port-au-Prince. During a special Mass at the national Cathédrale Notre-Dame, Ligondé was installed as the first Haitian archbishop. In the same year, the Grand Séminaire was reopened, staffed mostly by Haitian priests, and the previous appointments made by Papa Doc of Haitian bishops, pastors, and teachers were approved by the Vatican (Duvalier 1969, 241–48).

Papa Doc's measures had several effects on the church. The number of foreign priests decreased significantly between 1970 and 1980:

	1970	1980
Haitian priests	123	114
Foreign priests	118	78
Haitian brothers	45	45
Foreign brothers	113	113
Haitian sisters	425	525
Foreign sisters	425	472
Other Haitian functionaries	65	70
Foreign functionaries	187	191
Total	1,501	1,608

Source: Department of Cults, Port-au-Prince, Haiti, 1970 and 1980. Statistics for 1990 were unavailable during that year.

These figures show that while the number of foreign sisters increased by about 11.1 percent, Haitian sisters increased by 23.5 percent. And while the number of foreign priests in charge of the archdiocese and local churches dropped by some 33.9 percent, the number of Haitian priests decreased by only 7.3 percent.

This decrease in foreign priests meant that the Haitian clergy, freer from foreign control, could now be more tolerant of Vodou. Since 1970 the government has acknowledged its practice and has promised immunity to its adherents, a policy that was continued after Papa Doc's death in 1971 by his successor, his son Jean-Claude (Baby Doc) Duvalier (1971–86).[16] Hence, since 1972 Vodou ceremonies have been held openly in Haiti, and the age-old persecution by the government, together with the suspicion surrounding those who might have denounced local practitioners to religious and government officials, have now passed. Oungans and mambos admit their adherence to Vodou openly; and drummers are no longer required to obtain special permits to beat their drums.

From these developments, it would be difficult to make any firm predictions about the future relations between Vodou and Catholicism. It does seem, however, that if Haitian society remains stable and free of the political revolutions that have plagued it since Baby Doc Duvalier's departure in 1986, Catholicism in Haiti may well become more creolized, gradually "de-Europeanizing" itself by growing more flexible both in its ritual observances and in its theology, and appropriating indigenous folk traditions into that theology. (I will speculate further about this in Chapter 6.)

The simultaneous practice of Vodou and Roman Catholicism was generated by the historical circumstances in Haiti. As already noted, in the days of slavery, the church found it difficult to convert all blacks to Catholicism. Through intense programs of evangelization, religious acculturation took place, and some Catholic concepts took root and appealed to the slaves. But behind the veil of an apparent Catholicism, religious concepts from different regions of Africa became dominant and remained so throughout Haitian history. On the one hand, the maroon republics' isolation from European influence, as well as their residents' struggle in the revolution, engendered the crystallization of African ethnic beliefs and religious practices in Haiti. On the other, the missionaries' efforts to evangelize the slaves resulted in the incorporation of Catholic traditions into the slaves' beliefs and practices. Soon after independence, when Haitian customs and social institutions were being formed, the fifty-six-year breach with Rome altered the nature of Roman Catholicism in the country: Catholic priests who were not concerned with weaning the people away from their folk beliefs permitted Vodou to root itself solidly within Haitian life. The few Spanish priests who came to the country during the thirty years before 1860 spoke little French or Creole, and did little evangelizing to kindle Christian piety among Haitians. By the time the schism had been resolved, it was too late for Haitians to accept the catechizing efforts of the new priests; they could not be single-minded Catholics, at least not at the exclusion of what they had believed for more than a century. Haiti's long period of isolation in the nineteenth century (1804–60), during which other nations refused to recognize her as an independent nation, allowed her to maintain many more African cultural and religious traditions than most of the other nations in the Caribbean basin, whose colonial status lasted well into the twentieth century and whose continued contacts with European cultures tended gradually to abrade the African influences. Moreover, the cultural and religious frustrations generated in Haiti by the contact between European and African cultures resulted in Vodou's subdued millenarian tendency, which has surfaced from time to time in Haitian history—as in the recent insurrections and reprisals against former civil servants that ousted President Jean-Claude Duvalier from office on February 7, 1986.

The fall of Jean-Claude Duvalier from power in 1986 revealed the lack of religious single-mindedness among Haitians, for both Catholicism and Vodou contributed to his departure from office. In 1983, Pope John Paul II bowed and kissed the ground as he stepped onto Haitian soil from the papal plane as part of his tour of Latin America. On the platform especially erected for the occasion of his visit at the Port-au-Prince International Airport, and before thousands including the president, his wife, and their immediate entourage, he uttered the words that were to determine Haiti's destiny. Referring to the appalling socioeconomic conditions of the country, the intolerable social injustices caused by the government's abuses of power, the blatant embezzlement of funds by government officials, and the flagrant violations of human rights by Jean-Claude Duvalier's administration, he announced in the Creole language that "things must change in this country." In the ensuing three years the pope's announcement continued to ring in the ears of sympathetic listeners, and particularly the clergy who, influenced in part by liberation theology movements throughout Latin America, had grown weary of the Duvaliers' thirty-year regime. Sensitized by special broadcasts from the Catholic radio station, and by the impetuous Sunday morning homilies of disgruntled Haitian parish priests and other clerics, the most notable of whom was the Salesian priest Jean-Bertrand Aristide, thousands of young people in peasant or base communities throughout the countryside were joined by the urban masses who took to the streets demanding an end to social oppression. By February 1, 1986, the country had become paralyzed by comprehensive strikes in which the business community and government personnel participated. Under the pretext of celebrating the annual Mardi Gras, the people organized *raras* bands which paraded in the streets of various towns and cities throughout the country, demanding Baby Doc's resignation.[17] The rage of the Petro lwas, which had once inspired the slaves and the Cacos against their oppressors, returned once more, and the vividness as well as the success of the millenarian dreams for liberation that had inspired these rebellions reappeared in the imagination of many. These bands moved through the streets of Port-au-Prince, killing many of Duvalier's known partisans and publicly setting ablaze both the bodies and the extravagant homes of many notorious tontons macoutes. Under pressure from Washington to leave office,[18] and with no promise of military assistance from the Reagan administration to reestablish order in the country, Baby Doc summoned the French and American ambassadors to his palace on February 6, 1986, and made arrangements for his exile in France (Chiara 1988, 400). On February 7 Baby Doc, his family, and a number of close associates left Haiti clandestinely around three in the morning; they were flown to southern France in a U.S. Air Force C-141 transport plane stationed at Guantanamo Base at nearby Cuba. The country was left in the hands of a junta appointed by Duvalier.

Since 1986, Haiti has experienced much political turmoil. An unstable junta and at least five presidents have assumed power, most of whom have been ousted by military coups. Save for the election of December 1990, which nominated Father Jean-Bertrand (Titid) Aristide president by an overwhelming majority, Haiti has never had a democratically elected government; national elections have been fraught historically with blatant irregularities, including the intimidation and indiscriminate slaughter of many innocent voters at the polls. Hence, Aristide's election represented a momentous victory for democracy in Haiti; the voting, which proceeded without serious anomalies, could not have occurred without the presence of more than three hundred foreign observers who guarded the polls jealously throughout the country. Since 1986 the church, which was so active in causing Baby Doc's departure from office, has remained more passive in Haitian politics. Perhaps one of the most significant changes in the church recently has been its unofficial recognition of Vodou as a significant element in Haitian culture. But the efforts of many members of the clergy to indigenize the church have not caused more Haitians to become single-minded Catholics.

Any assessment of the importance of religion in the lives of Haitians can present some real difficulties, for in no other nation are outward appearances more deceptive. The beliefs of the Vodouisants are perhaps more easily examined than those of the elite, who either are professing Catholics or are not religious at all. Many attend church with unshakable faith and religious devotion. Others pay their weekly respect to the social and religious activities of the church and also pay frequent visits to their favorite oungans. Members of the elite must see their peers, and the Sunday morning Mass in an urban setting provides that opportunity for social contact. Social intercourse after Mass usually involves long discussions in which news of a general nature is exchanged. The city church also provides a place for the practicing of cultural refinement, and the formal rules of etiquette are observed with an almost religious devotion.

In contrast to the approximately 40 percent of the country's six million inhabitants who are urban dwellers, the majority of Vodouisants live rural lives. Their language is Creole, and when they speak it they do not strive for eloquence, nor intellectual brilliance, nor are they concerned about engaging in high-flown intellectual exercises of theology. Many remain relatively unaffected by contemporary urban developments, urban mores, and modern fashions. In the face of hard labor done with the relatively inefficient tools at their disposal for fighting the endless erosion of the soil that they cultivate, their principal concerns are reduced to making sure that they have the means of protecting and feeding themselves and their children. They dress modestly; they wear no English wool in sweltering summer temperatures, and their clothes are not as handsomely cut as those of the elite. But their life-style, as Leyburn notes, is by no means idyllic; nor can it be said by any stretch of the imagination that they are lazy (1972, 9). Their work is difficult, and the pressures of poverty and misfortune often cause them to see their economic position as catastrophic.

Proverbs in Haitian culture reflect the frustrated aspirations of Haitians. They reveal a world marked by the eternal triumph of those who are strong, and the defeat of those who are unfortunate and often forgotten. But they also reveal the wisdom of the destitute, the suffering of the poor, and the miraculous survival of the weak. Consider for example, the following Creole proverbs:

You step on my foot and you ask my pardon. What will the pardon do for me? (No amount of apologizing by the strong can change the lot of the poor.) [19]

The ant never dies under the weight of a sack of sugar. (The weak may suffer but do not die under the oppressive conditions imposed by the strong.) [20]

The stone in the water will never know the suffering of the stone under the sun. (The sufferings of the unfortunate can never be understood by the strong.) [21]

In short, Vodouisants are too rooted in their culture to have any room for such proverbs as "All things come to him who waits." They must stoically endure the trials and tribulations of life, tenaciously holding on to the reins of their daily existence, trying to avoid what they perceive frequently as their inescapable defeat, and trying to resolve their problems with the simplest possible means at their disposal, which seldom yield positive results. In the face of insurmountable economic disaster and unrelieved day-to-day strain, their last resort is to affirm in exasperation, "Bondye bon!" (The Good Lord is good!). This cry is a most emphatic assertion of what to them is a self-evident and integral part of their worldview: that the cosmos manifests, without a reasonable doubt, the existence of an inscrutable God whose wondrous and mysterious "face" reveals neither revenge nor goodness—a God with whom they must individually come to terms.

THE FACES

....

OF MYTH:

....

SYMBIOSIS

....

AND THE

....

CHANGING

....

SELF

3

The myths of any religious system are its source of power. This power resides in myths' ability to describe the lives of legendary cultural figures, powerful divinities, invisible spirits of the dead who mirror the depths of human character and its many existential predicaments. Myths, as Joseph Campbell noted, exhibit in imagination the "hidden processes of the *enigma homo sapiens*. . . . The entire spectacle is before us. We have only to read it, study its constant patterns, analyze its variations, and therewith come to the understanding of the deep forces that have shaped man's destiny and must continue to determine our private and our public lives" (J. Campbell 1972, 255–56). That these forces shape human destiny can be seen in the ways in which myths often transform the lives of those who recount them, hear them, or act them out in their rituals. By and large, myths are stories revealing great truths which cannot be put into scientific language.

When the storytellers of Haiti begin their recitations, they captivate the minds of children and adults alike. The unfolding drama of the beloved stories of Bouki and Ti Malice, Jan Lespri and Jan Sòt embellish the already rich oral tradition of the Haitian people, and radiate the special literary nature of Haitian folklore[1]—a nature in which the plot always assumes a simple form, and its significance rests in the realism and the picturesque images of the characters:

> "Cric," says the teller.
> "Crac," answer the listeners.
> "Time, time."
> "Bwa chèch."
> "Combyen li donnen?" (How many will he give?)
> "De" (Two).

And the storyteller is called upon to contribute two stories.[2]

The power of myths resides in a community's understanding that they authenticate life's crises and serve as authoritative and pervasive models for that community. Some myths call us to mend our ways and to raise ourselves above the corruption of the immorality of the community, while others reveal truths to which we should aspire. Mythological truths find expression in many forms: stories, riddles, and proverbs, which by their literary style or cleverness of phrase reveal their implicit wisdom.

To understand the function of religious myths in a society, one must recognize that they are more than literary techniques, for they possess a paradoxical capacity to express complex truths in everyday language, to use common words and familiar objects to reveal what is most sacred in life. Sacred wisdom resolves the existential struggles, the frustrations, the limitations, and the alienations of life. While changes occur in the daily lives of human beings, the sacred wisdom conveyed through mythology remains eternal, offering to replace the hardships of life with a more serene order of existence (J. Campbell 1972, 256). That order rests upon certain sacred truths that emerge out of the words of the storyteller. Myths are therefore powerful vehicles which can transcend the limitations of profane existence. They metamorphose a chaotic world into an orderly one where the tragedies of life are remedied. For example, Haitian Vodou sees the malice of human beings as recast by the cleverness of Legba, the trickster; the crushing power of the strong, by the invincible might of Ogou, the lwa of war. Poverty becomes a means of salvation; illness, a source of divine power; and death is suddenly transformed into life itself.

Thus, mythology often sees death as the cessation of the old being, but also as the birth of a new being—a life lived in the sacred abyss of the dead, constituting a return *ab origine* to the divine conditions of human selfhood before it assumed secular form. In Maya Deren's words, the paradox of death for religious persons is that it propounds two major themes of life: the lament and pain experienced in the death of a loved one, and the joy felt for the birth of a new being (1972, 23). Death, therefore, is not the cessation of being but the beginning of being: "As the land and sea define each other at the shore, so life and death define each other by exclusion. These which are the immediate neighbor in the realm of matter are separated by a difference which is as a vast distance in the realm of meaning. Myth is the voyage of exploration in this metaphysical space. The point of departure is the first meeting between the quick and the dead" (Deren 1972, 24).

Because of the conceptual nature of myths, and because the wisdom that they reveal is so often subjectively appropriated, the truths that they contain transcend the realm of empirical investigations. They are subject to neither the rules of logic nor the techniques of scientific investigation. The "unconscious" wisdom of myths is not superseded by new scientific discoveries, even though myths can be examined scientifically by those who study them.

Eric Dardel says that myths contain the "impassioned tonality" that vibrates certain verities within religious persons, "and remain serene and indifferent to contradiction" (1954, 42). These verities are "what we see in ourselves, the secret spring of our vision of the world, of our devotions, of our dearest notions" (1954, 50). Myths are beyond truth and falsity (Bidney 1958, 12); they claim an immunity to critical analysis not granted by empirical knowledge; their function and dramatic effectiveness lie in the fact that they hold the power to charge us with emotion, to affect our behavior, to commit us to action. Ernst Cassirer once noted that there will always be a chasm between our religious beliefs and our scientific certainties. History has demonstrated this, for Cassirer also notes that we have more often been willing to die for our religious beliefs than for our scientific convictions (Cassirer 1960, 12).

Myths have a positive value that rests in the fact that they are cultural, universal phenomena originating in the multiplicity of motives and involving all of our mental faculties. Engendered and nurtured in people's creative minds, myths are effective because they permeate the unconscious minds of those living in the myth-making culture. For example, Vodouisants' belief in the influence of the souls of their ancestors forms the basis of their family as well their communal organizations. Although myths differ in kind from one another, the development of the plot in the simple language of the storyteller points out the persistence and the importance of oral tradition. To the audience, young and old, to listen to a myth is to travel at "the edge of the cosmos" (Deren 1972, 24); it is to look upon the world through the eyes of humble sages, to transcend death, and to probe into the very primordial events that gave life its form. To Deren, "It is to enter in one's mind, the room which is both the womb and the tomb, to become innocent to everything except the motivation for myth, the natural passion of the mind for meaning. It is to meditate upon the common human effort to comprehend the human condition" (1972, 24).

Like all religious peoples of the world, Vodouisants have developed for themselves a body of myths reflecting the conditions of human life. These myths, many of which are yet to be recorded, are part of the rich oral tradition of Haiti. The purpose of this chapter and those that follow is to delineate some of the significant myths in the Vodou community.

Before proceeding, however, a word of caution is needed. Because Vodou has no clearinghouse, no seminary, no established orthodoxy, it is difficult to present a complete documentation of its myths. The task becomes more complex when one considers the multiplicity of mythological details, which vary widely from one ounfò to another as well as from region to region— but it is nonetheless possible to discover the internally consistent religious system that exists for each individual ounfò. What follows, then, is intended to portray, not universal beliefs and practices held by all Vodouisants, but those most commonly held by them.

The most commonly held Vodou beliefs can be summarized in the following creed:[3]

I believe in Bondye, the Almighty Father of the sky, who manifests his spiritual nature in me; in a large number of spirits; and in all things visible and invisible.

I believe in the lwas, the gods of Africa, and all the saints of the Catholic Church. Masters of the universe, they are manifestations of Bondye, who see all things and direct the course of all things; that some have made themselves known to us through our ancestors in Africa, and that others we have come to know, emulate, and serve in our new home in Haiti; that these lwas are potent enough to mount us, their children, in spirit possession; and that through their mounting, they can inspire us as to the needs of our community; that our moral duty is to faithfully serve them; that the lwas are capable, like us, of gentleness and mercy, but also of anger and revenge.

I believe in the power of ancestors who watch over us and serve us before the lwas; that they must be remembered and served faithfully.

I believe in the right granted to us by the lwas to interfere through magic in the normal flow of events as established by Bondye's will; in the efficacy of the medicines derived from the local fauna endowed to us by the lwas. I believe in the Holy Roman Catholic Church, in the communion of saints, and in life everlasting.

....

PARTICIPATION: THE COMMUNAL SELF

If one examines the details of the Vodou concepts of humankind, one finds resemblances to those in West Africa. Humankind was created by Bondye in his own image, and he has infused his divine energy into the physical body that serves as its vessel. Bondye also fashioned the physical body, which is constituted of clay and water. Hence, humankind is made of the same elements that constitute the world around it. As the trees, the waters of the rivers, and the materials from which we build our houses spring from the earth, so are we extracted from the sacred womb of Mother Earth. The body is then consumed by death which returns it to the earth, its original source. We are therefore not foreigners to the surrounding environment, nor are we pitted against a hostile world, but we and the cosmos are old acquaintances sharing the same elements.

In West African traditional religions, the physical and divine elements are closely related to each other, the divine being the centripetal force that draws to itself other selves in the community "in which subject and object are often no longer distinguishable" (Taylor 1963, 50). Instead of "I think, therefore I am," Africans might say, "I participate, therefore I am" (Taylor 1963, 50). As O. J. Oldham writes of this spirit in the case of Africa, the isolated self in Africa is an abstraction: "We become persons in and through our relations with other persons. The individual self has no independent existence which gives it the power to enter into relationship with other selves. Only through living intercourse with other selves can it become a self at all" (quoted in Taylor 1963, 65). The self is thus conceived as a member of an extended family, which not only contains the living of whom Oldham writes, but extends itself to include the invisible spirits of one's ancestors (Taylor 1963, 66).

Oldham's observations about this sense of community apply to Haiti and can be seen particularly in the lakou. Like the African compound, a lakou is an area in which are gathered approximately five to six conjugal families. They live in separate dwellings, sometimes with one hut that serves as the temple (Davis 1988, 39–40). The members of the lakou share the same courtyard around the hut of a patriarch (*chèf lakou*) who is often the oldest member of the group.[4] The patriarch's responsibilities vary from the settlement of domestic quarrels to social and political matters affecting the survival of each member of the group. His decisions are respected and dutifully obeyed by all. He counsels those who need economic and social advice, and his honorific title has earned him the right to participate actively in all of the lakou's festivities and religious ceremonies. Perhaps the most important function of the patriarch is that of calling the spirits of the ancestors from their abode, and he is often possessed by the lwa rasin (root lwa) recognized as the ancestral divine protector of the lakou's members. In a sense, the patriarch may be considered as the symbolic axis mundi of the lakou because he stands at the crossroads of the social and religious life of the community. He is the social focus and likewise the religious fulcrum on which the sacred and the profane worlds rest in equilibrium, in that he is a "family tree" whose "roots" are anchored in the world of the "living" as well as that of the lwas. He not only is a physical symbol of the ancestors and lwas before the people, but also stands before the sacred world as the organic representation of the entire community.

Despite the fact that the lakou has almost disappeared in Haiti recently, the spirit of community in Haitian life has persevered in the face of drastic socioeconomic changes currently occurring in the country. The prospect of employment in the cities has driven many young people from the countryside where lakous were most prominent; few have returned, except for occasional visits. But the spirit of the lakou has not been erased from the Haitian mind, where it continues to survive in ideology rather than in reality. The persistence of that spirit is evident in the lakou's reappearance in immigrant communities in the diaspora, especially in urban areas in the United States, such as New York, where "house systems" are prevalent. A house is analogous to the lakou. It consists of an entire building in which several conjugal families live in individual apartments, but share and exchange their domestic and financial resources. They gather around a oungan or mambo whose apartment combines living quarters and ounfò; there, ceremonies are held regularly. The religious specialist replaces the patriarch in the lakou. He or she is the symbol of communication between the sacred world of the lwas and ancestors and the profane world of humans.[5]

Both in the Haitian lakou and in the house system in the United States, Vodouisants conceive of each individual life as a connecting link in a continuous chain of humanity. A son's life is the continuation of the dead father's, the grandfather's, and so on, extending in retrogression through his entire lineage to the lwa rasin. Thus, as in African traditional religions, the individual is conceived as a "single-branching organism whose existence extends beyond the visible aggregation of other organisms and enlarges its circle out of sight to include limbs beyond this life" (Taylor 1963, 98–99). The result of this communal participation among Vodouisants, as with Africans, is an unconditional desire to share whatever one possesses. It is a complete surrender of one's individuality for the sake of the community, and the understanding of selfhood through one's dependence upon the visible and the invisible human family.

To say that a person participates in the visible and the invisible communities is not to equate the two and to give them equal importance. That which distinguishes the two worlds is death, which confers upon an individual a sacred character not to be attained in this life. The moment of death constitutes a separation from the community of the living and a transferral into the sacred abyss, the world of the ancestral spirits (Ginen), where the individual takes on the divine, original, and essential bodiless form that it possessed before the creation of the world. Thus, the immortal spirit enters Ginen and becomes an archetype; its ethereal nature transcends the struggles and limitations of profane existence.

As already noted, Vodouisants believe that the human body is a manifestation of Bondye. This body contains a spirit (espri) that derives from the divinity, but is constituted of two compartments, characterized by their separate psychic functions within the body. In some ways, the Vodou notion of the compartmentalized self is analogous to Freud's description of the theoretical divisions of the human psyche. Deren provides ample descriptions of the Vodou teachings regarding the compartments of the self (1972, 24), and they need not be discussed here in detail; I will merely summarize the characteristics of each of these compartments that relate to symbiosis as described above in Chapter 1. The first compartment of the soul is the immortal, cosmic spirit of Bondye, which is manifested in the body; it is known as the gwo-bon-anj (literally, "big-good-angel"). It is a life-force, an internal dynamism planted within the body that serves as its shell. It derives its subsistence from, and is an offshoot particle of, Bondye; it is sustained and molded by the same "stuff" from which creation flows. In the physical world, Bondye is conceived, like the Godhead in most African traditional religions, as an impersonal deity who is identified with eternal motion in the world, a dynamic cosmological Principle that ensures the flow of the rivers and the rotation of days and nights (Idowu 1973, 169–201). Bondye's force is manifested in the majesty of the mountains of Haiti, and in the thunderous clashing of the ocean's waves on the rocks of the island's shoreline; and his gentleness, in the stillness of the night, in the warmth of the tropical morning sun, and in the refreshing coolness of the early evening rain.

Like Bondye, the gwo-bon-anj is conceived as motion: the sinuous motion in the succession of human generations, and the invisible driving force that generates action in a person's body. It is thought of as the root of being, consciousness, the source of physical motion, the inherent principle within the body that ensures life; it is identified with the flow of the blood through the body, and the movements of inhalation and exhalation of the thoracic cavity. Breathing and the throbbing of the heart are vital signs of life, but the gwo-bon-anj is not breath or palpitation itself; rather, it is believed to be the life-source from which these motions originate.

The gwo-bon-anj is also associated with varying degrees of intelligence, creativity, and overall disposition. It is identified with the blood within the body, and like blood's, its motion may increase or decrease according to the body's social and physical contexts. In Haitian folklore and the Creole language, a person with *movesan* (bad blood) is one whose deportment or speech manifests vexation, hostility, or resentment, and symbolizes a decrease in the gwo-bon-anj. In contrast, a person who displays creativity and intelligence—that is, an unusual ability for rational discrimination—is said to have *lespri* or much spirit (Deren 1972, 25). In short, the gwo-bon-anj is not some "vague, mystical evanescence" but is "a point of reference to the energy of action of the mind which as a state of consciousness and as a repository of material and moral knowledge and experience, is the source and the act of judgment, decision, desire of all the motivation, and the will projected in man's visible action" (Deren 1972, 25).

Just as Bondye transcends the cosmos but manifests himself within it, so too the gwo-bon-anj is an immortal and divine spirit that manifests itself in human life. Vodouisants believe that the other compartment of the soul is the ti-bon-anj (literally, "little-good-angel"). It is personality, conscience, the moral side of one's character, which reveals itself through one's general deportment; it is that element in a person which is the physical manifestation of his or her gwo-bon-anj. It mirrors the gwo-bon-anj in that it constitutes moral behavior, that psychic element in the self that makes it possible to detach oneself from the pressures of the world in order to make morally upright and responsible decisions. The ti-bon-anj is the conscience that distinguishes between "good" and "bad" behavior, between actions motivated by love and by hate. Through the ti-bon-anj, the individual feels happiness or satisfaction, elation or guilt, joy or regret resulting from that individual's behavior toward others.

Apart from its moral function, the ti-bon-anj is the ego-soul. It represents the unique qualities that characterize an individual's personality. It is also that which manifests visibly the gwo-bon-anj's disposition—be it happiness and laughter on festive occasions, or tears on the occasion of the tragic loss of a loved one. The ti-bon-anj is thus the essence of personality; its power is expressed when one person captivates another, holds another spellbound.

Vodouisants believe that throughout life a harmony must be maintained between these two "compartments" of a person's spirit. While the gwo-bon-anj and the ti-bon-anj have their separate functions, one is the visible manifestation of the other. Vodouisants do not understand their spirit as a dualism—that is, as two irreconcilable entities, one of which negates the other; rather, the two parts constitute an organic process, a dynamism which comprises divinity, authority, influence, morality, and wisdom (Deren 1972, 27). The two aspects of the self mirror one another—the first manifesting itself in the second, and the second bound to the first in the life of the individual.

....

RITES OF PASSAGE: THE TRANSFIGURED SELF

Death: The Fractured Self

At death, the harmonious relationship between the twin compartments of the self is fractured and each follows its separate destiny. The expiration of the last breath is the expulsion of the ti-bon-anj from the body. Liberated, the ti-bon-anj is believed to enter into heaven. It is hard to say precisely what Vodouisants mean by "heaven." There are many local variations, but it seems to be generally thought to exist in a place higher than the sky where the liberated ti-bon-anj exists as an anonymous and depersonalized entity of no further use to the living. The Vodou conception of the ti-bon-anj in heaven seems to correspond to the Roman Catholic doctrine of the soul, for Vodouisants believe that it "appears" before Bondye to stand before the heavenly tribunal where it is arraigned for its misdeeds, and must suffer the appropriate penalties.

In its new state, the ti-bon-anj is believed to have no independent power and no further relation to the living. It can neither intercede with Bondye or the lwas in the living's stead for personal favors, nor mount the living in spirit possession. Moreover, it cannot be used in magic or divination. Because of its incapacity for spiritual manipulation, it plays a minor role in the death rituals.

In contrast, the gwo-bon-anj is of much concern to Vodouisants in their death rites. Because the ti-bon-anj has transpired and the body is no longer animated, all intelligence and conscious experiences are believed to fuse with the gwo-bon-anj. The death rituals performed by oungans or mambos and the entire community send the gwo-bon-anj to Ginen to join the community of ancestral spirits, the living-dead in Ginen.

Much as in the case of heaven, there is no agreement among Vodouisants as to the exact location of Ginen. One commonly held opinion is that it is under the sea, or under the bed of a local river (Herskovits 1972). But some believe that it is located in the bowels of the earth; still others hold that it is above the sky. Whatever its location, it is the domicile of the gwo-bon-anj, whose residence there initiates the process of its deification. How this happens is not clear, but when the appropriate ritual sequences are performed by the community, the gwo-bon-anj can be reclaimed from Ginen and become an important influence in the lives of the members of the community.

The Vodou death rituals move a community toward the future; they celebrate the birth of the gwo-bon-anj into a new dimension of life. The death rituals restore the gwo-bon-anj to its primordial state before it assumed form—a condition of freedom from the limitations and struggles of human existence. At the moment of death, the body loses its role in the visible dimension, and the gwo-bon-anj is returned to its original, invisible form. Because a new life must be given to the gwo-bon-anj after death, the desounen (literally, "uprooting of the sound"; hence, removal of life from a person's body) rite of passage is performed. It is said to "desacralize" the body, extricating from it all divine manifestations, and at the same time freeing the gwo-bon-anj to be initiated among the community of the dead.

Desounen, which separates the soul from the body, is a religious observance that can only be performed by a priest. It is analogous to the Fon death ritual in Benin. The Fon dokpwégâ (priest) comes to the house of the deceased with a large quantity of cloth, two goats, and one rooster. He goes to the center of the room in which the body is laid; as he sacrifices the animals to the gods and the ancestors, he orders the soul and the protector deity residing in the head of the deceased to leave the body and to enter their respective abodes: the deity to the sky, the soul to the world of ancestors (Herskovits 1963, 1:368–89).

In Haiti, desounen is designed to dispossess the body of its gwo-bon-anj and its mèt tèt (master of the head, or guardian angel), the third part of the soul, the guardian lwa, which throughout the person's life has protected him or her from harm, has been the subject of constant service and spirit possession at regular intervals. Desounen sends the three compartments of the self into their respective dwelling places: the ti-bon-anj to heaven, the gwo-bon-anj and mèt tèt to Ginen, and the perished body to the navel of the earth, where it will disintegrate and await its refashioning by Bondye and the lwas (Deren 1972, 45). The ritual in all of its details has been described amply by Alfred Métraux and others. What I will do here is to recall those aspects of my field observations of desounen that relate to cultural symbiosis.

In the central portion of Haiti, an eminent member of a small community not far from the town of Ville-Bonheur had passed away. The surviving members of the family called the oungan to the house of the deceased shortly after death. He came with a bottle of kleren (crude rum). After drinking from the bottle, he did not swallow the kleren but spewed it out in the shape of a cross to the four cardinal points, to recognize Bondye and the lwas at the four corners of the universe. He also sprayed the corpse in a similar fashion to cleanse it from any defilement that might hamper the effectiveness of the ritual. While shaking his *ason* (rattle),[6] he lit a candle in the middle of the room, then called the names of the deceased and the mèt tèt, occasionally whispering their names in the dead person's ear, ordering them to leave their lifeless shell. At the moment when the gwo-bon-anj and the mèt tèt were believed to be extracted from the body, the oungan became spirit-possessed by the man's mèt tèt and stepped outside the house into the adjoining courtyard. The dead man temporarily forgotten, the community encircled the oungan to hear the lwa's pronouncements to the community. As the lwa left the body of the oungan and he came out of his profound trance, he was born anew. The lwa had used his body as an intermediary before returning to Ginen; but empowered by the lwa, the oungan was reborn, a symbolic and organic rebirth of the community in microcosmic form. This part of the ritual symbolized that the deceased man's death had occasioned his mèt tèt's solemn pronouncements, which will remain as a living legacy to the community. Henceforth, members of the family will observe the same service and obligations that the deceased had contracted with the lwa. The lwa demanded that his "liturgical" color be worn on the day attributed to him; he asked absolute devotion, sacrifices, and the unlimited right to invade the body of members of the family with his sacred will. The divine essence of the life of the deceased became a prolonged, functioning force in the household of his family.

As for the gwo-bon-anj, it was now released from the body that had appropriated and imprisoned it; desounen had dispatched it to Ginen to be incorporated among the community of the living-dead. There it will stay for one year and a day, after which period it will be absorbed into the family of Gede (Ginen's guardian and chief of the ancestral spirits); then it may influence the human community through Gede's manifestations in his devotees' bodies by spirit possession. The period of one year and a day may be a religious interval adopted by Vodou from Roman Catholicism, for the Haitian church has traditionally asked of its adherents that, at the end of the first year following death, a special Mass be sung to free the soul from purgatory. Unlike Roman Catholicism, however, Vodou does not teach the physical resurrection of the body. Deren notes that the Haitian is "too close to the constant limitations of the flesh, its vulnerability to disease, its insatiable and harassing need for food, and its too frequent mortality for that" (Deren 1972, 42); Vodou myths could not reflect what to Vodouisants seemed unreasonable. But since many Christians who do believe in the resurrection of the body have experienced hardships similar to those of many Haitians, perhaps there is a more historically valid explanation: deriving their views from the African concepts of life and the experience of death, the Vodouisants do not see the logic of the resurrection of the body.

The body now exists as an abandoned tomb, dissociated from Bondye, its life-force, its source of animation and vitality; it will disintegrate as nature reclaims it as one of her own, and will never be fashioned and animated again in the same form. This is the reason why the burial of the man near the town of Ville-Bonheur involved a number of ruses to circumvent any possible bodily resurrection. As part of desounen, the oungan cut tufts of the dead man's hair and pieces of his fingernails which he put in a jar to be placed later in the coffin and buried with him—a precaution that served as an impediment to local sorcerers, who might want to raise the body and prevent the gwo-bon-anj from ever entering Ginen. In Haiti, as in many parts of the world, sorcerers are believed to acquire tufts of hair and nail clippings of persons whom they seek to harm. If it were discovered in this case that the nails had been clipped from fingers other than those designated by the oungan, then it would be a telltale sign that a sorcerer had tampered with the body. A few branches of hoholi (the sesame plant, sesamum indicum) were also included in the coffin; each branch contained a very large number of seeds which any sorcerer coming to raise the body would have to count—a feat that could never be accomplished before sunrise.[7] The nostrils and ears of the deceased man were stuffed with cotton so as to prevent him from ever breathing again, or from ever being awakened by the clatter of the living. The man was also buried in his socks to prevent the sound of his feet from disturbing the living if he should decide to return to this world. His knees and big toes were tied together to prevent him from ever walking again. His mouth was tied shut by a cloth placed under his chin and securely fastened on top of his head, to prevent his speaking and interfering in the affairs of the living. The pockets of his garments were turned inside out to prevent him from transporting objects to Ginen that might give him control over surviving members of his family, or from carrying the souls of the living with him to the abyss. Care was taken in the disposal of his personal objects, such as tools, toothbrushes, soaps, and combs; they were included in the coffin in order to avoid his returning to seek them. In short, every precaution was taken to hinder the return of the man among the living. As for the body, it was entirely needless, doomed to its inevitable dissolution—a return to its primordial condition of clay and water before being given form by Bondye again. As in Fon mythology, dead bodies return to the navel of the earth to wait for the Godhead and the gods to refashion them from earth and water into new bodies, to reanimate them, to give them life again.

As for the gwo-bon-anj, the time it spends in the waters of the abyss is not conceived of as a period of purgation. The coldness and wetness of Ginen, notes Deren, strikes the imagination of Vodouisants as one of extreme discomfort because they have hardly enough with which to protect themselves against the torrential rainfalls of the tropical Caribbean. Stripped of its fleshy substance, the gwo-bon-anj remains in Ginen and awaits its reactivation as a quasi-divinity in its own right (Deren 1972, 45).

Desounen is performed for the preservation of the Vodouisants' divine heritage. It is said that if the family neglects to call the oungan to perform desounen, the mèt tèt and the gwo-bon-anj can use the body to "bully rage" against the surviving members of the family by inflicting disease and death upon them. Moreover, not to perform desounen would prevent the gwo-bon-anj's passage into Ginen, and would leave it wandering on the face of the earth forever. It could not emerge as a quasi-god, nor could it manifest itself to the community of the living in the future; because it had no permanent abode, it could never join the ancestral community from which it could be recalled to reincarnate itself in a descendant's new body, or to assist the living in times of need. The ancestral line too would be broken, for Bondye's life-giving Principle as contained in the gwo-bon-anj could never be inherited by the deceased person's progeny.

Burial: The Transitory Self

After desounen, the family of the deceased sends for the bather (benyè)—usually a person of the same sex as the dead. The bathing of the corpse is a highly complex ritual that involves placing the body in a trench dug on the dirt floor of the house to allow the collection of spilled, defiled water that might otherwise flow out of the house to pollute the community of the living. Cold water is mixed with ethyl alcohol and infusions of green oranges, lemon, mint, and korosòl (soursap) leaves. Soap is also used to wash the corpse. During ritual washing, the benyè often speaks to the corpse and explains that it must be thoroughly cleansed in order to make it acceptable to all the ancestral spirits. Métraux notes that benyès are often charged with the responsibility of conveying to the deceased messages from members of the community, in the hope that they will transmit these messages to dead relatives in Ginen (1958, 219). The back of the corpse is washed first, to allow mucous to flow from its mouth. Collected in a bowl, the mucous, like the spilled water, is discarded at night in a secret place as a precaution against the machinations of sorcerers. The bathing of a corpse is often accompanied by wailing, which begins as soon as the person approaches death. In a tropical region where temperatures often soar to thirty-eight degrees Celsius, a cadaver kept for more than one day decomposes quickly, creating a health hazard for the community.

Among the many social activities and religious rituals performed on the day of the death is the wake (veye) during which family and friends come to visit the immediate family of the deceased. The members of the family provide visitors with a meal and with nonalcoholic beverages. A significant characteristic of the wake is the inclusion of Catholic elements: a table is customarily placed in the room near the deceased with lithographs of the Catholic saints, a crucifix, vases of flowers, a scapulary, a kerosene lamp, and sometimes a plate containing food for the gwo-bon-anj of the deceased.

According to Haitian custom the funeral rites usually follow the traditions of the church, but they may vary considerably in their elaborateness. For instance, the financial resources of the family determine the duration of the tolling of the church bells, the number of acolytes assisting the Catholic priest, the number of lighted candles on the altar, and the duration of the church ceremony. Vodouisants at all levels of society believe that a dead body must be accompanied to its final resting place. Placed in a wooden coffin, it is carried out of the house followed by a cortège on its way to the church and then to the cemetery. The prèt savann often leads the cortège to the cemetery. In an effort to prevent the body from being animated by the gwo-bon-anj or from retracing the steps of the cortège, the pallbearers ordinarily take certain precautions: they may turn the coffin counterclockwise, or they may follow a zigzag path to the church and to the burial grounds.

Although the prèt savann performs no active function in the church ceremony, he assumes a significant role at the cemetery. There, he reads a few Catholic prayers. In the midst of the uncontrolled wailing of the family and friends gathered around the grave, the pallbearers turn the coffin counterclockwise as a last precaution and lower it into the trench. The participants remain until the gravediggers (còk mò) fill the trench completely. Then everyone returns home.

The day of the funeral, the *case kanari* (breaking of the clay pot) ritual is held at the ounfò. The kanari is a large oval clay jar about two and a half feet high and one and a half feet in diameter. The case kanari, as the name indicates, is a ritual in which this pot is solemnly broken to commemorate the close of the funeral ceremonies; it can only be performed by the oungan or mambo. At the appointed time, the members of the family of the deceased and friends watch the oungan rub the jar with kleren and numerous concoctions made with oranges and lemon leaves. Placing the kanari in a trench dug in the dirt floor of the peristil, the oungan strikes the pot with a steel pipe several times until it has been reduced to dust. He then pours a libation of kleren to the lwas on the tiny pieces of the clay vessel that lie at the bottom of the trench. After drawing the *vèvè* (the geometric symbol of the appropriate lwa), he fills the trench with its dirt, which had been carefully piled around it.

In Vodou, case kanari recaptures the entire funeral rites in one religious ritual. First, the washing of the jar symbolizes the ritual washing of the body; second, the clay jar itself is a symbol of life, or in this case the deceased person's head containing his or her gwo-bon-anj and mèt tèt; third, the violent beating of the jar represents death's brutal separation of the person from the community, and the escape of the gwo-bon-anj and the mèt tèt from the head; fourth, the trench on the floor of the peristil is the grave; and fifth, the burial of the pieces of clay replays the burial rites at the cemetery.

The religious rituals performed after death include not only the religious services at the ounfò, but also a number of Catholic observances at the home of the deceased. On the night following the funeral, the prèt savann is invited to the home of the family of the deceased to officiate at a *novena* which ends with the final prayers (*dènyè priyè*). On that occasion, family and friends gather around a table decorated as it was at the wake. After reciting Catholic prayers, the prèt savann collects his fees and leaves.

In piecing together the details of these death rituals, one is struck by the interplay of Catholic rituals and Vodou ceremonies. It is this interplay that has caused Haitian and foreign scholars to refer to Vodou as syncretistic. In their forms, the rituals do appear to reflect syncretism; but (recalling my observations in Chapter 1) desounen and the funeral rites also illustrate the phenomenon of religious symbiosis, in the following manner:

1. There is no agreement among Vodouisants as to what they mean by *heaven*. Although this observation applies to Ginen as well, the concept of Ginen is much more definite than that of heaven. Moreover, Vodouisants are also unsure of the status of the ti-bon-anj after it has ascended into heaven. Indeed, the entire cycle of rituals that follows desounen deals with the gwo-bon-anj: much concern is given to its "travel" to Ginen, and to the numerous precautions during and after the funeral to prevent it from ever returning among the living.

2. Although many Vodouisants believe, similar to Catholic belief about the soul, that the ti-bon-anj in Vodou is judged by Bondye, this belief is not held everywhere in Haiti. It exists primarily in the cities where the proximity of Catholic churches has influenced Vodou's theology. In the remote mountains, where the practice of Vodou is most prominent, many Vodouisants believe that after nine days, both the body and the ti-bon-anj are dissolved into the navel of the earth.

3. Symbiosis can also be seen in the efficacy of the Vodou ceremonies as compared to the Catholic rituals. From the point of view of the family of the deceased and those who attended the cycle of religious observances, the Vodou rituals described above occupied a prominent place because they dealt with the lwa mèt tèt and the status of the gwo-bon-anj in Ginen. On the one hand, desounen expelled the gwo-bon-anj from the house of the deceased, and protected the living by preventing their harassment if the gwo-bon-anj were angered. On the other hand, the prayers addressed to the lwa also served to protect the living against danger by establishing an intimate relationship between the family of the deceased and the lwa.

In contrast, the Catholic rites had no effect on the lwa or the gwo-bon-anj. In their observance at the home of the deceased, no mention was made of the lwa (Gede) or the gwo-bon-anj. They were not intended to expel the gwo-bon-anj from the house of the deceased. Even the prayers of the prèt savann on the way to the cemetery had no effect in barring the gwo-bon-anj from reanimating the body and returning it to its home. Indeed, the turns and the zigzag movements were no more able to summon the lwas or the gwo-bon-anj than was the Catholic priest or the prèt savann to exercise power over them.

Moreover, the Catholic rituals did not even have any purpose in ensuring the ti-bon-anj's victory before the court of Bondye. As already noted, most Vodouisants believe that Bondye is good, meaning that in his goodness, he can never prevent the ti-bon-anj from residing in heaven.

4. Symbiosis can be observed in the function of the prèt savann as opposed to that of the oungan. First, it may be pointed out that no Catholic ritual was performed at the ounfò. After desounen, the oungan remained silent until case kanari. He attended neither the wake, the novena, nor the church funeral services. His role in the ritual cycle limited itself to the Vodou rites performed to assure the status of the gwo-bon-anj in Ginen. The rituals of the church were not performed simultaneously with the Vodou, and the rites led by the Catholic priest or the prèt savann did not require the cognizance of the oungan.

These observations show once more that the Catholic rituals performed at the church and at the home of the deceased are in mosaic juxtaposition to the Vodou rites. This "symbiosis by ecology" can be seen in the spatial juxtaposition of the locations at which the Catholic and the Vodou rituals were performed, and in the spatial juxtaposition of sacred objects from the church and from the ounfò placed at the makeshift altar at the home of the deceased, both on the night of the wake and at the novena.

5. As concerns the funeral and post-funeral rites, Vodouisants insist not only that the corpse must be brought to the church for funeral services, but that, in accordance with the teachings of the church, a special Mass for the dead must be said a year after the death. The church in Haiti teaches that on the first anniversary of a death, a requiem must be performed to free the soul from purgatory, and to secure its entrance into heaven. In the mountains of Haiti, however, the requiem often is not performed at all, or it may be postponed for at least a year. Urban Vodouisants interpret the requiem as the specific gesture of placation to the power of Bondye (as opposed to the propitiation of any other spirit) in the reclamation of the gwo-bon-anj. But if a family's means are not sufficient for both the requiem and the Vodou rite of reclamation, the church ritual is either omitted altogether or postponed indefinitely. In contrast, the Vodou rite of reclamation is never postponed. In addition, the actual reclamation of the gwo-bon-anj, as will be seen later, is

not achieved by a Catholic priest in the church but by a oungan in the ounfò. This statement finds support in the comment made to me by a oungan outside the city of Gonaïves: he noted that "no Catholic priest could reclaim the gwo-bon-anj from Ginen," and that "neither Vodou nor the gwo-bon-anj could ever be the business of the Catholic priest."

From Vodouisants' attitudes toward the Catholic rites, one might infer that they do not believe in the religious efficacy of Catholic death rituals, but demand that they be performed because social custom dictates them. As already noted, Haitians have been forced by historical and social circumstances to practice Catholicism and have learned to see in it analogues to their African religious values. The police ruling of 1758 prohibited the slaves from congregating under the pretext of celebrating weddings or grieving over the body of a departed friend because they often met to perform what authorities referred to as superstitious ceremonies. The ruling stated that these meetings "covered the assemblies with a veil of obscurity and that of the Catholic religion," and that in cases of death, slaves could congregate in the church only for the burial rites led by a Catholic priest (Gisler 1965, 79). Today, Vodouisants still live under the shadow of this and other rulings of the colonial period, and they see the Catholic death rites as having no other function than to provide a veil under which African (in this case the Fon) religious practices can be carried out. The practice of Catholicism and Vodou can be considered as a symbiosis—symbolic acts that derive from historical circumstances and whose functions are social rather than religious.

Reclamation: The Incorporated Self

In Benin, reclamation ceremonies serve, among other things, as opportunities for members of a clan to construct a memorial shrine in honor of their ancestors. My field research in Benin revealed not only the elaborateness of the Fon ceremonies of reclamation, but many parallels with similar rites of reclamation in Haiti.

In Benin, the construction of the memorial shrine (dexóxô) by clan relatives of the deceased is done in honor of the clan's ancestors, and provides a place where ritual ceremonies to these ancestors can be carried out in a compound. When the head of a clan decides that it is time deify his ancestors, he tells members of his clan to contact the priest and relate his intentions. The priest asks the names of members of the family who have died and the length of time since their death. If the required period of three years has elapsed, he asks the head of the clan to furnish him with the paraphernalia needed for the ceremony. Fowl of various kinds, small pots, cloths, cowry shells, and numerous mats must be provided by the family of the deceased, the number of mats corresponding to the number of ancestors to be deified. The priest then calls together the local work group (dokpwê) of the compound and designates an area to be cleared where the ceremony is to take place. Once the area has been prepared, the priest places the mats on the ground, folding them so that each forms a "small house." In each one he places a cowry shell for the ancestor whose soul is about to be reclaimed. At the side of this aggregate of folded mats, he makes a large house for the souls of ancestors from other clans. Two large bamboo structures of different sizes are also constructed. In the smaller house, the descendants of the persons to be deified sleep for four nights, the period consumed by the entire ceremony; in the larger house the dokpwê and the priest, together with their sacred rattles and drums, lodge for the same period (Herskovits 1963, 1:194–208).

At the beginning of the ceremonies, the members of the clan leave their house, bringing with them pots, clothes, many young chicks, and a moderate quantity of palm oil, and go to a crossroads where the priest has already prepared leaves and several pots containing certain sacred objects. While the clan members remain at a distance, he traces numerous circles in the sand in which he stands the pots, placing in them the maize, the palm oil, and the young chickens brought by the members of the family. He whispers certain secret words whose esoteric meaning is imparted only to priests during the period of training. This ritual is important, for the Fon believe that if it were omitted, the souls of the dead would not be able to find their way to the world of the living when they are summoned, but would wander endlessly, eternally lost to that clan—a consequence that would prevent the reincarnation of the soul, and would bring about the eventual dissolution of the clan (Herskovits 1963, 1:194–208).

After this ceremony, the entire clan goes to the sacred ceremonial spot where the mat dwellings have been erected. There, the priest calls the head of the clan and asks him to utter the names of the ancestors to be deified. As the reply is given, the priest whispers each name sixteen times; for each name he holds outstretched in his hands a clay pot in which he places a young chicken that acts as a substitute for that ancestor. The head of the clan stands nearby with many of the cloths he has brought with him. When the priest has covered the opening of a pot containing a chicken with his hand, he presents the pot to the head of the family group who swathes it at once with a cloth. At the end of the ceremony, the priest no longer speaks. He groups the pots according to the sex of the ancestors, and later places the pots inside the mat houses. In front of each mat dwelling a lighted lamp is placed, whose flame must burn day and night during the four days of the ceremony.

The remaining three days are filled with complex ceremonies in which rams, chickens, and other food offerings are brought to the mats. During that period the priest remains silent, while under his direction, the remaining portions of the ceremonies are carried out by the members of the clan, each of whom takes a turn in tendering personal offerings to his or her reclaimed ancestors. Drums are played and dances are performed to welcome the new deities among the living; meals are prepared in honor of these deities; offerings (to Legba or Fa, the god of the crossroads of destiny) are deposited in the clearing of a sacred forest, where they are immolated; and finally, guests who have traveled long distances to attend the ceremonies present farewell gifts to the members of the clan and depart. After the four days the members of the clan return to their compound where they will build a dexóxô or "house of the deities." But nothing will be placed inside the shrine for a period of about three months, after which it will be consecrated; then the clay pots will be brought from the mat houses to the permanent dwelling of the deities (Herskovits 1963, 1:194–208).

The importance of the deification ceremony in Benin is that the reclaimed ancestors become quasi-deities who can be summoned to guard the living against disease and suffering. They will "buy back" the wandering souls of those who have not been interred and deified properly by including them in the compound's family of ancestors (Herskovits 1963, vol. 1). In time, those ancestors whose individual names cannot be remembered will emerge as members of a family of ancestors (tohwíyo). These ethereal beings are the earliest ancestors, the founders of the clan, who lived so long ago that even the clan's origin myth does not tell of them. As a group, they are respected, and their influence in the community is significant because they intercede for the members of the clan with the deities. They accord the members certain personal favors and help them in their difficult moments of life. As souls who are to be reborn in the future, they are in the preeminent position to deal with matters related to life in general.

From their permanent abode in the compound, the ancestors insure the virility of young men after they undergo circumcision without injury. In return for placative offerings suggested by the priest, the ancestors protect their clan members from disease, war, drought, and natural cataclysm. Their power is summoned to protect members from the machinations of sorcerers by shielding them from the malevolent spirits and forces that may cause them harm. From the mouths of the vessels that act as their substitute bodies, they will come forth to possess their heirs, using the bodies and mouths of the latter as media through which to utter advice and warnings to the community. Like humans, these mythological creatures are believed to love ceremonial display and to resent being forgotten in the daily round of life. They are angered if they are not called upon to participate in the religious rituals of the community and to "consummate" the ceremonies in which the deeds they performed while on the earth are reenacted by those possessed by them (Herskovits 1963, vol. 1).

In short, the reverence given by the Fon to their ancestors is of paramount importance. Ancestors stand between them and the deities who personify the forces of the universe. Their respect for their ancestors may be thought of as a unifying force that gives meaning and logic to life.

The Fon rite of reclamation has its parallel in Haitian Vodou. As already noted, one year and a day after death, a person's gwo-bon-anj is reclaimed from the water of the abyss and placed in a clay jar or a bottle (*govi*) where it receives new form. Here, the disembodied spirit provides Vodouisants with the wisdom drawn from the experiences of a person who has completed the cycle of life and death. This spirit, which has accumulated a person's intelligence, past experiences, and creativity, is reborn in a substitute body, and the vessel that contains the spirit becomes a valuable legacy preserved for the future prosperity of his or her progeny.

Ouete mò nan ba dlo (extracting the dead from the waters of the abyss) is a ritual that separates the gwo-bon-anj from the community of the living-dead and reincorporates it into the community of the living. Among the Fon, the rite of reclamation is considered the birth of a person, and so is Vodou's ouete mò nan ba dlo. Both religions teach that a person is formed out of clay and water. The human shape, which is slowly molded in the mother's womb, captures the soul or the gwo-bon-anj. After that shape is expelled from the mother at birth, it matures. The second birth occurs when the gwo-bon-anj is separated from the body to join the family of ancestors. In its newest birth, the disembodied spirit is separated from the community of ancestors, and brought back among the living in the substitute body of the govi. From the mouth of this vessel will flow sacred wisdom and counsel about matters related to magic, divination, and the dilemmas of life in general. In it all of life's experiences are preserved as an active divine force for an ancestor's descendants.

Living in the vessel, the gwo-bon-anj becomes a grandfather or a great-grandmother. Soon, those who knew these spirits in their physical lives die, and with them the memories of their faults and weaknesses. Then, as among the Fon, the gwo-bon-anj emerges as a quasi-lwa in its own right. What was once physical returns again, but in a new form and in another dimension of life. Those who seek counsel with that spirit through the oungan become empowered to solve the riddles of life. What was once a resident of Ginen is now at the center of communal life; what was a being "out there" has been transmuted to a driving force in the community of the living (Richman 1991, 16); what was once an objective physical entity has now become a spiritual force to be appropriated by the living, inspiring them to actions of reverence and propitiation.

The sacred status that a gwo-bon-anj achieves in a vessel gives it power over all humans. What the Fon and Vodouisants insist is that no living person has the right to possess another, for possession means the mounting and the controlling of a person's will (Deren 1972). It means that the possessed person's gwo-bon-anj is temporarily displaced by the influence of a foreign element whose incommensurable power accords that person the capacity to perform feats that are humanly impossible under ordinary circumstances. The possessed lose their memory, intelligence, and responsibility for their actions, and no living person can impose such a will on the living.

Although the possessed gain no immediate personal reward from their experience, the ancestral gwo-bon-anj (now the lwa) that rides them fulfills a cohesive function within the community. For the most part, possession is a public occurrence that takes place in the peristil where the community is gathered. The manifestation of the lwa's personality, vocabulary, and mannerisms through the body of a medium provides a spiritual force with which the entire community can identify. In general, the lwas are considered wise, and they use the bodies and voices of the possessed as conduits through which they impart their wisdom to the community. In return, they expect to be recognized and called by their names by those whom they visit, to be greeted by all members of the community, to be treated respectfully, and to be given the devotion and piety due to them. In short, when the lwas visit the peristil, they become the nucleus of the community.

In order for the dead to participate within the living community, the rite ouete mò nan ba dlo is necessary. And the family's failure to have it performed can result in illness, misfortune, and death. The failure to reclaim the spirit of the living-dead is a betrayal of responsibility, not only to the ancestral spirit but to the entire community as well. To examine the details of this ritual, and to enable its comparison with the Fon rite of reclamation, it will be useful to relate one such experience from my field research.

A year and one day after the death of the same man, I returned to the Artibonite Valley, in the central portion of Haiti, to witness one of these rituals. A small community had gathered in the peristil of a ounfò to reclaim the man's gwo-bon-anj. The dim glow of an electric bulb hanging by a wire from the ceiling barely dissipated the darkness of the peristil, and one could barely see the oungan emerge through the door followed by his *laplas* (assistant). In the corner of the room, a tentlike structure made of *nates* (mats) of dried banana leaves had been erected. Although this had been carefully closed, with its sides hanging to the floor, it was possible to see through the cracks a large wooden vessel containing food offerings of various kinds. The wooden vessel was covered by a board on which a candle was placed. The oungan later explained that the structure and its contents were for the deceased man's gwo-bon-anj—the food to allay his hunger, and the covered sides for his privacy.

The ceremony began around eleven at night. As the oungan crossed the peristil, he greeted the members of the dead man's family and the other guests. The three drummers sounded the rhythm appropriate to the ritual and the gathered devotees began to dance, first to Legba and later to Gede. Soon the oungan's assistant entered the room carrying a number of nates; he placed these on the dirt floor of the peristil and then covered them with white sheets, putting pillows at one end. From the northern door of the peristil emerged a procession of female devotees (*ounzis*) in white dresses, carrying a vessel. As they approached the structure, they walked on the sheet-covered nates, which were quickly picked up behind them and placed in front of them again so that their feet never touched the dirt floor of the peristil. When they reached the tent, after placing the vessel on a small table covered with a white tablecloth, they lay down on the nates with their heads on the pillows, their bodies entirely covered by the sheets upon which they had walked during the procession. The drums had now fallen silent. The oungan stood near the western wall of the peristil and began to shake his sacred rattle (*ason*) around the tent vigorously, then put his head in the tent, calling Gede, the master of Ginen, to release the gwo-bon-anj of the deceased person. After some time, a member of the community became possessed by Gede, an indication that the lwa had responded to the oungan's plea.

The oungan then asked a member of the family of the deceased to call out the dead man's name, and he also entered the tent to call out the name. He emerged from the tent possessed by the spirit of the man being reclaimed. At the appropriate moment during possession, the oungan took the vessel, removed its lid as if to inspect its contents, quickly sealed it, and then handed it to one of the surviving members of the deceased man's family. Symbolically, the reclaimed gwo-bon-anj of the dead man entered the vessel to be kept there indefinitely. The oungan then ordered the ounzis to rise from the mats and to carry them, as well as the tent, outside the peristil.

In this ritual the community re-created the death ritual in its entirety. The bodies of the ounzis lying on the nates and covered with white sheets recalled the body of the deceased in the coffin; the tentlike structure represented not only the grave in which the deceased body was deposited but Ginen as well, for both Gede and the gwo-bon-anj were believed to emerge from it. This ritual was also a reenactment of desounen, for the gwo-bon-anj's name was called by the oungan and by one of the surviving members of the family.

In short, ouete mò na ba dlo reminded the community that the body was to be dissolved after death and that the gwo-bon-anj was not to include the deceased body. The spirit had once been separated from the body; it was now being separated from Ginen. The indeterminate time of transit which the spirit took as it traveled to Ginen to live with the gwo-bon-anjs was now retraversed once more, the sojourn in the realm of the living-dead was ended. For several generations henceforth, the man's gwo-bon-anj would increase in the community of the living.

As time passes, the man's gwo-bon-anj will become to the living an abstraction deprived of any individuality; he will be slowly absorbed by the family of Gede, the deceased man's mèt tèt. His power and the reverence given to his spirit will increase as what was once a person becomes a *Papa* or lwa. The stories of his life will be preserved and will have a special place in the mythology of the local ounfò. From the lips of the future storytellers in the community will come powerful words of wisdom related to this man's life. He "will solicit the fidelity of his descendants to the legacy" that he will have left for members of the community (Richman 1991, 16). Moreover, surviving members of Papa's family will seek his counsel in matters related to their service to the lwas, and to the daily and practical round of life, such as marriage, childbirth, disease, or the planting of crops.

In many ounfòs throughout the country, ouete mò nan ba dlo includes another ritual known as *boule zen* (literally, "burning of the jar"). In this variation, the reclaimed gwo-bon-anj extracted from Ginen is placed in a vessel that is exposed on the ounfò's altar or placed in the branches of a tree in the countryside, until such time as it is burned by the sacred flames of the boule zen ritual (Métraux 1958, 219). The significance of this ritual is that, by its immolation, the gwo-bon-anj is returned to its divine source in the cosmos to join the company of the lwas.

In ouete mò nan ba dlo we can see certain parallels to the Fon rites of reclamation. In the structure of the rites themselves, the use of the folded mats to form the small tent, representing the world of the ancestors from which the spirits are to be reclaimed, the special portion at the beginning of the ceremony dedicated to Legba and Gede, the silenced drums during the ouete mò nan ba dlo ceremony, the extensive use of the ason by the oungan to call both the man's gwo-bon-anj and the deity, the secret words of the oungan to call the lwa and the ancestral spirit in the earthen vessel, are all parts of the Beninois rite of reclamation which, with some differences, have been re-created in Haiti.

The major departures of the Vodou rituals from those of Benin are creole phenomena, which can be summarized as follows: In Haiti the rites of reclamation are performed entirely in the ounfò, and the ceremony lasts, not four days as in Benin, but one night. Similarly, the Haitian ritual calls for a single mat house or tent, rather than the several used in Benin. The complex pageantry of the Fon ritual also has been simplified in Haitian Vodou by the elimination of the elaborate sacrifices and offerings. These differences can all be explained in light of the many Antisuperstitious Campaigns conducted in the nineteenth and twentieth centuries, and by the police rulings mentioned in the previous chapter. These attacks on Vodou prohibited Vodouisants from performing their ceremonies openly; instead, they were confined to restricted, secret places outdoors, or the ounfòs. The use of a single tent in the Vodou rites of reclamation can be accounted for by the lack of suitable space in these enclosures. By the same token, the unavailability to the slaves of materials used in ritual offerings caused the Vodou ritual offerings to be less elaborate. Similarly, the rigid work schedule of the slaves would not have allowed them four consecutive days to devote to the performance of the ritual; hence, in Haiti the length of the ritual would have been limited to one night.

In spite of these differences, however, in both the Fon and Vodou rites the deified ancestors have an important function in the life of the community and represent a religious affiliation within the community. As among the

Fon (and in other parts of West Africa, for that matter), altars in the homes of members of a Haitian community are dedicated to the deified ancestors, and the gathering of the family around this sacred area of the house reinforces the bonds between its members. Moreover, in the local temple as in the ounfò, the community frequently assembles to revere the deified ancestors with elaborate ritualistic offerings. In Haiti as in Benin, the revered ancestors stand between the community of the living and the lwas who personify the forces of the universe that threaten to destroy it. Communal appeals are made to them for their indulgence, particularly in matters related to marriage and childbirth. As already noted, since the deified ancestors are also spirits of those who are not yet born, they play a significant role in dealing with matters related to the future life of the community. In short, as an integral part of the family organization on the one hand, and of the religious and mythological expression of the individuals in the community on the other, the reverence of the ancestors can be seen as one of the great unifying forces that, for both the Fon and the Haitian, give meaning and logic to life.

Baptism: The Empowered Self

Just as the gwo-bon-anj in the earthen vessel is consecrated to the service of the community in the ounfò, so too persons and substances must also be initiated into the service of the lwas in the ounfò. After the ritual ceremonies connected with death, the rites of initiation are the most important religious observances in Vodou. They are meticulously performed.

In Haiti when a ounfò's sacred chamber (bagi), which contains the altar and the ritual objects, is constructed, the entire edifice and the objects within it are purified and dedicated to the service of the lwas. The importance of the initiation rites lies in their theological meaning. By their initiation, ritual substances are imbued with divine power and thus become the physical residences of the lwas. Henceforth, these substances will be the hallowed portals through which communication will be established between the community of the living and the world of the lwas. Just as the gwo-bon-anj in the vessel serves the community by interceding with the deities, so too consecrated substances provide a channel through which the living can enter into relationships with the ancestors and the lwas.

Like edifices and ritual objects, Vodouisants who have been initiated into the service of the lwas can be possessed by them. Through the medium of their voices and their bodies the lwas can reveal their will and power to the community of the living. The initiation of Vodouisants is an ordeal requiring the neophytes (*ounzi bosals*) to submit themselves to pecuniary obligations and physically painful ordeals lasting through a long training period. Devotees resilient enough to endure the painful stages of this adventure receive certain degrees as members of a local ounfò, whereby they achieve a closer relationship, not only with the lwas, but with the living community as well.

The degrees in the Vodou rites of initiation remind the observer of West African religions. As do the West Africans, Vodouisants give to the initiated new names at the moment of their consecration (Mugambi 1989, 184). In all cases—whether the initiated be a person, a ritual object, or an edifice—the name is that of the deity to whom they are sanctified. Names are of such vital importance to these rites that no ceremony can take place until a name has been ascribed to each substance. The importance of the name lies in its very denotation. Because the power of the lwas is believed to reside in their names, affixing the name of a lwa to persons or substances has the function of infusing into them the power of that lwa. In this sense, the name is not merely a word but becomes part of the personal property of the bearer, property that must be protected and whose use is exclusively and jealously preserved by the bearer. The name functions as a proxy for its bearer; hence, to pronounce it is to call into being not only the person, but his or her very self, the divine essence with which he or she is undissolvably linked.

The assigning of a sacred name is what makes a person an individual; it marks a metamorphosis in that person's state of being. In Benin and other parts of West Africa, the mythology conceives of a person not as something fixed and unchanging, but something in flux, whose being passes through phases—each phase being reflected by changes in his or her new self. At birth, a person receives a name. At puberty, that same person receives another name, because the initiation rites that accompany consecration mark a rebirth. The person ceases to be a child and becomes an adult. The taking of many names throughout life serves not only to mark the stages of development of a personality, but also to protect the individual against impending danger by taking different selves, whose forms make one unrecognizable. In a sense, the close connection of a new name to that of a deity reflects the source of power through which an individual can draw the divine substance necessary to such protection. The African and Haitian use of names for the purpose of protection against impending danger can be compared to Western manufacturers' practice of naming a new automobile after some wild animal, to appeal to the buyer's secret longings to identify with the power of such an untamed and uncivilized beast.

Not only in naming do the Vodou initiation rites reflect the re-creation of West African traditional religions, but in their use of water as well. In Haiti, water is used to purify persons or substances in preparing them to embody the lwas. Melville Herskovits observed that in Benin, water is the symbol of purification whereby neophytes, shrines, temples, and rituals are washed and cleansed of their impurities before they can be consecrated to a deity (1963, 1:234). The Ewe in Benin believe that their priests are "called" by God; before someone becomes a priest, he is first trained, and then undergoes the ritual ceremonies involving the pouring of a libation to God, after which his head is washed, cleansed, and consecrated (Mbiti 1969, 21–22). A similar initiation ceremony is performed during the Vodou initiation rites: a vital part of the ceremony, known as *lave tèt* (washing of the head), consecrates the novice to the service of the lwas in the ounfò.

Because these rites include the use of water, Vodouisants refer to them as baptisms (*batèms*). The term *baptism* itself is borrowed from Roman Catholicism, but Vodou interprets the rite differently. Although most Vodouisants would agree with Catholics that baptism is a rite of purification that introduces the initiates into the sacred community, there is a further meaning in the rite: for Vodouisants, it also implies the instilling of the power of the divinity within the person or substance being initiated so that it becomes a vessel in which a lwa resides.

An examination of Vodou baptisms is important to the study of symbiosis of Roman Catholicism and Vodou, for in no other ritual are the rites of the church so intermixed with elements that are both creole and African. Indeed, in no other ritual are outward appearances so deceptive. To the untrained eye, the Vodou rituals might seem a replay of the church's baptismal rite cast in a Vodou setting, and it is easy to perceive in them the syncretism, or fusion, of Catholicism and Vodou beliefs. What deceives casual observers is the presence and apparent officiation of the prèt savann. As already noted, he is a tangential member of the temple hierarchy who is expected to read the prayers and to chant the canticles of the church, as well as to sprinkle the persons or substances being baptized with holy water. However, a closer examination of the status of the prèt savann in the numerous baptismal ceremonies I attended during the course of my research reveals that his role in these rituals was actually perfunctory.

First, while the prèt savann recited the prayers of the church at the opening of the ritual, he remained silent during the ritual itself. It was the oungan, rather, who directed the actual initiation and was the sole religious functionary with the power to summon the lwas.

Second, whenever the lwas manifested themselves in the possessed bodies of devotees in the ounfò, they addressed special salutations to the oungan as to one whose sacred duties earned him that honor; they offered no such salutations to the prèt savann.

Third, although the prèt savann sprinkled holy water as if baptizing the person or substances, he did so only at the start of the ceremony; the actual baptizing or initiation was carried out by the oungan.

Fourth, in many of the ounfòs I visited throughout the country, particularly in the remote areas, the prèt savann was nonexistent; in these cases there was no recitation of prayers of the church, nor singing of canticles. In many cases, the only portion of the rituals that reflected some Catholic influence was the sprinkling of water on the persons or substances by the oungan, and this was a mere preliminary to the actual baptism. After witnessing these ceremonies, I questioned the oungans about the prèt savann. They were unaware of the significance of the term. Even after the role of the prèt savann was explained to them, they were uncertain as to how he would function in their rituals (although they also seemed to think they ought to have heard of him), and they appeared embarrassed by what they felt to be their ignorance. My many interviews and conversations with these oungans about the role of the prèt savann revealed that they had no need for his services, "since they had their own way of dealing with the lwas." Moreover, the Vodouisants in these regions felt no sense of deprivation because they had learned to establish an intimate relationship with the lwas and knew how to summon them whenever they needed them.

These observations support the definition of symbiosis stated earlier in this study by showing that the occurrence of prayers and canticles of the church in these baptismal rites was not only unimportant but actually unnecessary to the Vodou initiation rites. Rather, the presence of the Catholic elements in the initiation rites of some Vodouisants reflects the juxtaposition of the two religious rituals, one occurring next to the other with no effort on the part of practitioners to work out the relationship between the two. This judgment is based on the following arguments. First, if these baptismal rituals showed a fusion between the rites of the church and of Vodou, the prèt savann would be granted a significant portion of the ceremony where he would be allowed to perform the actual act of baptism separately from the oungan. Second, if the role of the prèt savann were necessary in these rituals, the lwas would accord him special recognition when they manifest themselves in the possessed body of the devotees or oungans during the ceremonies. Third, if he were essential to the baptismal rites themselves, his presence would be necessary in all such ceremonies throughout the country. Finally, if the prèt savann's role were of consequence, his service as an officiant would require the acknowledgment of his participation in these rites by the oungans. Since these conditions are not fulfilled, the occurrence of the Catholic rituals in these ceremonies can be described as symbiotic rather than syncretistic.

Here, the juxtaposition of the two rituals is made clear by the presence of the prèt savann. In the urban areas where the churches are numerous, and where their influence on the organization of the ounfò's hierarchy is extensive, the function of the prèt savann is separate from that of the oungan. Because the church does not approve of Vodou and has attempted so often in the past to control it, Vodouisants feel the need for some symbol of the church's sanction of their religious activities in order to create an overt similarity between the two religious systems. They therefore have attempted to provide, within the structure of their rituals, what they consider as desirable to Catholicism. On the one hand, for the historical reasons that have caused the persistence of African religion in Haiti, Vodouisants still value that heritage—a value symbolized by the role of the oungan in the community. On the other hand, the magnificence of the church as reflected in its liturgy and its sacerdotal vestments has taught them to admire Catholicism as well—an admiration symbolized by the role of the prèt savann in the community. The prèt savann is, therefore, a symbol of the church in the baptismal rites. His place in the urban ounfò is guaranteed in his ability to bring to the baptismal rites elements of a competing religious system, which the oungan or mambo operating under the framework of African traditions cannot provide, but which Vodouisants nevertheless feel are necessary.

In spite of this analogy, however, the prèt savann and the oungan or mambo are not homologous. The prèt savann's prestige among Vodouisants is not as great as the oungan's. His function as the unofficial representative of the church has placed him between the oungan and the Roman Catholic priest. Although Vodouisants accept him as an officiant in the baptismal rites in the ounfò, they have learned to distinguish between a baptism performed by a Catholic priest and one done by a prèt savann. One important distinction is that in Haiti a prèt savann is traditionally black, whereas (until recently, when the number of black Catholic priests in Haiti has increased) a Catholic priest in Haiti has traditionally been white. Until the late 1960s or so, the old tradition lingered in the minds of many Vodouisants that "Christian baptism by a black priest (Catholic or prèt savann) will not stick" (Leyburn 1972, 114), but that in the sacrament of baptism in the church, one needs the intercession of whites—just as the Vodou lwas need to be summoned by a native oungan.

In conclusion, by analyzing the details of Vodou baptisms, we can make several observations:

1. The theological concepts behind the Vodou baptismal rites derive essentially from West Africa. Although the term *baptism* has been borrowed from Catholicism, Vodouisants, like most West Africans, use it to denote a means whereby divine power is instilled in a person, an edifice, or an object.

2. In their form, Vodou baptisms resemble many West African initiation rites, in that they involve ritual washing whereby a baptized substance becomes the portal through which communication is established between the sacred and profane worlds. The utterance of the substance's sacred name frees the lwa within it from its residence in that substance.

3. Unlike Roman Catholicism, whose ceremonial objects retain their sacredness unless it is removed by special ceremonies of "degradation," the sacredness of Vodou objects is limited to the rituals that accompany their use. Once these rituals cease, the divine powers that have occupied these objects depart to return to their sacred abode. Hence, the power of a divinity comes and goes according to the circumstances in which an object is handled. Deren is therefore right in stating that Vodou has a "quality which can be described as a constant 'disappearingness,'" for when the sacred function of an object is fulfilled, it ceases to be sacred; she notes that the peristil, which during a ceremony vibrates with the power of the lwas, becomes the next morning a place where chickens and dogs may wander about and where men and women sit to gossip, giving no attention to the presence of the lwa to whom the entire ounfò and its contents are dedicated (1972, 187).

4. The role of the prèt savann during the baptismal ceremonies is perfunctory. Not only do the lwas in the body of the possessed oungan accord the prèt savann no special attention such as might be due to an officer of a local ounfò, but the actual washing that infuses the power of the lwas into the substance or the persons being baptized is performed solely by the oungan. Moreover, the prèt savann is part of the ounfò's hierarchy primarily in areas where the Catholic church is present and where it influences the life of the members of the community.

In such areas, symbiosis between Roman Catholicism and Vodou takes two forms. First, the presence of the ounfò near a Catholic church accomplishes the spatial juxtaposition of Catholicism and Vodou. Second, the elements of the Catholic rites, such as the sprinkling of water and the prayers and canticles chanted by the prèt savann, effect the temporal juxtaposition of the two religions.

THE FACES

....

OF THE

....

COSMIC

....

GODS

4

As ritual objects and persons baptized in the service of the lwas harbor spirits and thus become the portals to divine perception, so too the entire cosmos is filled with the dynamic power of the lwas to become a conduit through which these lwas can show their "faces" and be apprehended. Like many other traditional religions of the world, Vodou teaches that the universe is peopled by thousands of invisible spirits who are inherent in all persons and things, and who direct the physical operation of the universe. Hence, the repetitive patterns of change in substances in the universe—the rise and decay of things, the rotation of days and of astral bodies, the cycle of seasons, and the succession of human generations—are all parts of a grand cosmic scheme which are perceived as the manifest faces or personae of the lwas. The lwas are therefore identified not only with the substances in which they are infused, but also with the manifest changes in these substances.

But the identity of the lwas with physical substances should not lead us to conclude that Vodou is animistic. Initially coined by British anthropologist E. B. Tylor ([1871] 1970), this term was used to classify traditional thought and refers to the belief that a spirit or *anima* is an "invisible double," a shadowy "vapor" that resides in a substance, manifests itself through that substance, and is indistinguishable from the very thing that harbors it (Bergounioux and Goetz 1958, 84). In these terms, Vodou might seem to be an animistic religion, and indeed many writers have defined it as such (Salgado 1963; Métraux 1958; Price-Mars 1928). Upon closer examination, however, it becomes clear that Vodou is far from animistic, for although Vodouisants believe that the lwas reside in all matter in the cosmos, substances serve merely as vessels or conduits through which the lwas can show their faces, or manifest themselves. The relationship of a lwa to an object that harbors it is analogous to the relationship of a spirit to the body of a possessed devotee, or the relationship of the reclaimed gwo-bon-anj to the jar that lodges it. The changes in personality and deportment of a possessed Vodouisant, or the changes in physical appearance of a jar (such as its discoloration because of its age), are attributed to the spirits that are believed to reside within these substances. But these spirits are said to transcend the substances that shelter them, for they exercise their autonomy by leaving these substances and entering others as they travel from place to place either at their own will, or when they are commanded to do so by oungans or sorcerers. In short, Vodouisants perceive the faces of the lwas when these manifest themselves in matter or in the possessed body of a devotee. They address the substances initiated in the service of the lwas by their divine names, because the lwas within them provide palpable demonstrations of abstract principles. But they perceive two modes of reality in the world by making a succinct distinction between the lwas themselves, and the substances that harbor them.

Moreover, if Vodouisants can identify the lwas with the principles that govern the universe, it is because these lwas manifest themselves not only in the material world but also in the lives of the devotees as well. Because Vodou imparts to its devotees a set of moral convictions upon which the life of the community depends, it does not ask that they understand its teachings abstractly. As already noted in Chapter 1, Vodou is a religion that does not lend itself easily to high-flown theological exercises. Instead, it makes use of every possible visible technique to involve the devotees in its rituals. Vodouisants come to know the lwas by dancing, drumming, and singing, and by reenacting or mimicking the envisaged personalities of the lwas. In Robert Marrett's sense, Vodou, like many other traditional religions, is a religion that is "danced out" rather than conceived intellectually—that is, it is imitative rather than meditative (Marrett 1920). It does not separate the mind from the body, but claims the entire person. The devotees become acquainted personally with the moral and metaphysical principles of their religion by embodying the lwas in spirit possession, by being transformed by them in mind and body, and by appropriating their envisaged personalities.

Hence, Vodou's teachings about the lwas are based upon the premises that they manifest themselves in nature, and that devotees gain knowledge of them through ritual observances in the community. It is upon these premises that the pantheons of lwas will be discussed in this chapter and the next. The order in which the lwas are to be described reveals not only the devotees' worldview, but also the manner in which the lwas are thought to participate in the devotees' daily round of life. The description of the mythological details in the personae of the lwas reveals the subtle emphases and nuances by which each lwa, each universal principle, is distinguished from all the others.

The description of the Vodou nanchons is here divided into two parts. This chapter deals with the lwas who manifest themselves most often in nature, and the following chapter describes the lwas who are most clearly related to the devotees' public and communal life. Both chapters will attempt to elucidate the three main principles mentioned in Chapter 1: first, the relationship between the African gods and the lwas; second, the nature of the transfiguration of these lwas in terms of Roman Catholicism in Haiti (to determine if the relationship between these two religions is indeed symbiotic); and third, the nature of the creole elements associated with them that are phenomena indigenous to the island. Before proceeding, however, we need to note that the existence of lwas closely related to public life does not mean that offerings, sacrifices, and other public rites are not tendered to the cosmic lwas. The reader is reminded that the present classification of the lwas as cosmic versus public is merely for the purpose of facilitating the discussion of the faces of the lwas and their relationship to Catholic saints.

....

THE NANCHONS: THE CLASSIFICATIONS OF THE LWAS

When Vodouisants speak of the lwas, they group them in families, pantheons, or nations, called *nanchons*. Each of these pantheons has its own characteristic ethos, which demands of its devotees corresponding attitudes. There are generally held to be seventeen nanchons of lwas, but most Haitians know only a few of these by name. They include the Wangol, Rada, Petro, Ginen, Kongo, Nago, and Ibo. Of these, the Wangol and Nago (or Anago) are the least known in Haiti; they have generally been absorbed into the Rada nanchon. The Kongo and Ibo nanchons, on the other hand, are well known, and many of their lwas have been absorbed into the Petro. The lwas of the Ginen (from Guinea) nanchon have also been absorbed into the Rada, and are the central objects of ancestral reverence of the ounfò. Although most Vodouisants recognize the Wangol nanchon (which originated in Angola), in my field research I found that no one, including oungans and mambos, could cite their names.

The Rada, Petro, and Kongo (and in some provinces, Ibo) nanchons are by far the best known in present-day Haiti. *Rada* derives from *Arada*, the name of a prominent kingdom in Dahomey during Haiti's colonial period. Similarly, the Kongo lwas originated in the Bakongo region of West Africa, which provided thousands of slaves to Haiti during the colonial period. In Vodou these words no longer designate geographical locations; rather, they characterize "categories" of lwas who are known in Haiti particularly for their cosmic functions as sustainers of the universe. *Petro* reportedly derives from a mythological character, Dom Pedro, a leader of the maroon rebellion during the latter half of the eighteenth century.

Many of the Rada lwas have Petro, Ibo, and Kongo counterparts. As if their images were reflected in a mirror, the personalities of these Rada lwas become inverted in the Petro pantheon or nanchon. In designating the Petro lwas, Vodouisants use the Rada name for each lwa and add epithets, such as *Flangbo* (Afire), *Je-Rouge* (Red-Eye), or *Zarenyen* (Spider), to designate their Petro or Kongo affiliations. For instance, Gede in his Rada persona does not usually inflict illness upon a devotee, but in his Petro persona as Gede-Zarenyen who, as the name indicates, crawls and stings like a spider, he does. Likewise, Rada's Ezili, the beneficent lwa of love, becomes Ezili Je-Rouge in her Petro affiliation, a dangerous and offensive spirit who can cause harm to recalcitrant devotees.

From early in Haitian history, the impression has persisted among scholars that the main distinction between the Rada and Petro nanchons is that between good and evil. Nothing could be more erroneous than this attempt to fit the Vodou nanchons into such rigid theological and ethical categories. It is true that in the past, the Petro lwas were most often connected with malevolent magic, while the Rada lwas were connected with benevolence (Métraux 1958, 76–78). Consequently, the Petro lwas have earned the reputation of being destructive, aggressive, and violent, whereas their Rada counterparts are said to be the gentle guardian powers of the universe. But these distinctions are not absolute. The Petro lwas can still protect a person from danger. Similarly, while the Rada lwas are usually beneficent, they can also inflict diseases on devotees who fail to fulfill their religious obligations toward them. For instance, Rada's Legba, the beneficent lwa who directs the course of human destiny, can be, in his Petro persona Kafou Legba, not only the maleficent trickster-lwa who causes accidents to alter that destiny, but also the malicious agent whose power the sorcerers propitiate in sorcery. Yet in spite of his maleficence, Kafou Legba can also protect a devotee from sorcery. The protective charms that a devotee wears to guard against misfortune are initiated in Kafou Legba's service.

Hence, the characteristic differences between the various Vodou nanchons' representations of the personalities and functions of the lwas cannot be understood exclusively in moral terms. This statement does not imply, however, that Vodouisants are morally obtuse, or that they are incapable of differentiating between good and evil. On the contrary, they have a clearly established set of ethical standards which they feel correspond to a natural cosmological order. From the point of view of empirical science, Vodouisants would say that the entire cosmos, including all of the principles inherent in its mechanical, biological, and stellar functions, can be reduced to one higher Principle, Bondye, who is the ensurer of universal order and the source of all human actions. The highest wisdom consists not only in recognizing the wholeness of the universal order as contained in Bondye, but also in affirming that same wholeness in the human community. All of life belongs to Bondye. He summons it into being and preserves it.

The strengthening and the preservation of life are Bondye's gifts to the lwas and to humankind. The divine will is a vital principle of life which expresses itself through a hierarchy of forces existing in the universe. But Vodouisants differentiate among these forces by distinguishing between "higher" and "lower" ones, all of which descend from Bondye to the lwas, to humans, to animals, and finally to physical objects in the world. World order is maintained by Bondye who controls the interaction between these forces, but each of these forces occupies a position in the order of the world and each derives from the same source.

Vodouisants' concepts of good and evil correspond to their idea of the forces that operate within the universe. They distinguish between good as a higher force and evil as a lower one, and correlate both with the natural order of forces in the world. A good act is of a higher order because it increases Bondye's power in the world, while a bad act is of a lower order because it decreases that power. Hence, every act, every detail of human behavior that militates against Bondye's vital force or against the increase of his power in the maintenance of order in the universe, is bad. For instance, Vodouisants consider murder wrong because, by a person's death, Bondye's divine influence is decreased in the human community. Sorcery is not wrong, because it increases the power of Bondye, as the sorcerers "tap" it from one of the lwas. The willful eradication of life is thought to be a sacrilege since it is not only a departure from Bondye's will for orderliness in the world, but an actual destruction of that order as Bondye established it.

The idea of Bondye as the ultimate source of power can also be seen in Vodouisants' concepts of the personalities and functions of the lwas as they present themselves in the Rada and the Petro nanchons. As already noted, the lwas have dual personalities and functions, each being the inverse of the other. In spite of the notable differences in these personalities and functions, Vodouisants do not understand them to represent two distinct divine entities, the one symbolizing beneficence and creativity and the other maleficence and destruction. Rather, they believe that both personalities and functions are attributes of the same being. This corresponds to Mircea Eliade's notion of *coincidentia oppositorum* (Eliade 1959, 174–78). On the one hand, a lwa expresses the diametric opposition of two divine personae sprung from the same Principle; and on the other, it is the nature of these personae, in the bodies of possessed devotees, to present themselves by turns, or even sometimes simultaneously, as beneficent or terrible, as creative and destructive. Although a lwa's personae appear to oppose one another, they are nevertheless reconciled (or rather transcended) by Bondye's vital force, which not only permeates the universe but fosters the forces of good and evil.

As already noted, the Petro lwas represent a *tertium quid*, New World creations whose personalities bear the marks of neither Africa nor Europe. This can be seen particularly in the *bizango* secret society, which exists in Haiti today and whose origins probably date back to the colonial period. The bizango is a Petro secret society of sorcerers whose art includes among others the phenomenon of zombification amply described by Wade Davis (1988) and others (Craan 1988; L. Douyon 1980). As we have seen, not only does the emergence of the Petro nanchon reflect the slaves' rage against the cruelty of their masters, but the distinctions between the personae and functions of its lwas in each corresponding nanchon also reflect the theological diversity of Vodou, both during the colonial period and today. Hence, although the Petro nanchon is an extension of the Rada, it clearly reflects the socioeconomic conditions in Haiti, both past and present.

In short, the word *nanchon* in Vodou does not primarily designate the historical origin of the lwas, nor does it indicate an exclusive distinction between beneficent and maleficent forces in the universe. Rather, it presents the ethos of the lwas as well as the characteristic attitudes with which the devotees approach them. In both their Rada and Petro characterizations, or at least in the way in which these characterizations are manifested through the lwas' possessed devotees in religious ceremonies, the lwas appear as beneficent and maleficent, and possessed devotees act out these personae as the community envisages them in their local mythology. In the bodies of their devotees, the lwas are often decorative and whimsical; their notable accoutrements, which are kept in the ounfòs as part of the ritual paraphernalia, and which they wear or use when their devotees are spirit-possessed during ceremonies, lend concrete physical form to their mythological personalities. Through their devotees' mannerisms, their carriage, and their dress, the lwas manifest their personalities as these correspond to the nanchons with which they are identified. By such manifestations, the community is able to recognize not only which lwa has come to "visit" it in the peristil, but also which nanchon is represented. In a sense the living depiction of the lwas in the bodies of their devotees replaces the literary and artistic vehicles upon which mythologies of other cultures often rely for the portrayal of their deities; one comes to know the lwas only by observing them, or by "becoming" them.

Vodouisants admit that there are more than one thousand lwas, who manifest themselves in all phenomena. Some are known to humans, but most are not. The Vodouisants can learn, however, to differentiate the personalities of many of them, and thus come to know intimately the powers that control the various events of their lives. By learning the variety of the lwas, they discover the nature of Bondye, the sacred life-force who controls the universe and who manifests himself through the multitude of the lwas. By his characterizations, each lwa reveals the varying cosmic principles inherent in the universe. Some express life and fecundity, while others are related to death and sterility; some do good, while others are maleficent. But whatever their characterizations, each reveals a different facet of that ultimate Principle. Each is, in musical terms, a variation on a theme, depicting a different cosmic Principle. Each embodies what Vodouisants deem most important to life: a life-force, which ensures fertility in the animal and vegetable kingdoms, and which establishes a power as represented in the visible community of men and women; a dynamic Principle whose beneficent and maleficent powers can be tapped and channeled through magic or sorcery. In short, the lwas are different aspects of one cosmic Principle, whose faces manifest different personae of Bondye, and whose outward appearances vary according to the context in which it operates in physical substances and in devotees' lives.

....

VODOU COSMOLOGY

Beginning with the one universal Principle, the world of the lwas is rich, vast, and largely unexplored. By and large, Vodouisants say that the permanent residence of the lwas is in Dahomey in Africa, which is a mythological island below the sea, or more specifically in Ginen's mythological city of Vilokan. The events that occur there are no living person's business, though everyone has conjectures about them. It is said that few living persons have been allowed to enter Vilokan, those privileged few having been taken there accidentally by the lwas.

Although few Vodouisants have ever visited Vilokan, most believe in its existence because they have established contact with it through the medium of the oungan in the ounfò. The oungan makes this contact at the outset of a religious ceremony by invoking Legba, the keeper of the gates to Vilokan. In Haiti, as in Benin or Nigeria, the gods are said not to speak the same language as the devotees who serve them. Legba is then the divine medium through whom human requests can be channeled to the respective lwas invoked. He is the interlocutor, the interpreter, the principle of crossing and communication with the divine world. Legba is the Hermes of the Vodou Olympus, the polyglot who translates the supplications of the devotees to the respective lwas for whom they are intended.

Legba is the one who opens the gates that separate the profane world of the living from the sacred world of the lwas. Therefore at the beginning of each religious ceremony the devotees sing to him:

Atibo Legba, open the gates for me
Papa Legba, open the gates for me
Open the gates that I might enter
When I will return (from Vilokan), I will salute the lwas.
Vodou Legba, open the gates for me
When I will return, I will thank the lwas.
     Ayibobo![1]

This invocation to Legba is an important part of the Vodou ceremony. As the community dances and sings it, the oungan solemnly traces Legba's symbolic, geometric figure (vèvè), an act which is said to open the gates to Vilokan to permit passage of the devotees' supplication to the divine world.

The focal image of this vèvè is Legba's symbol, the cross. In its form this cross resembles the Christian cross, but its significance is entirely African.

The symbol of the cross is central to Vodou ceremonies. Indeed, Vodouisants revere it wherever they encounter it, not only when it is traced on the floor of the peristil, but in their daily lives as well. For instance, in what might be called a territorial rite of passage, Vodouisants who pass a sacred edifice (a Catholic church, a school, or a hospital) may cross themselves reverently; to them, the Christian cross that dominates the building symbolizes Legba, the medium through which contact can be established with the world of the lwas.

Because Vodouisants usually appear to revere the Catholic cross and because the cross image has such a symbolic significance in Vodou meetings, many scholars who have written about the religion have argued that Vodou crosses are borrowings from Roman Catholicism. However, while it is true that Catholic crosses in Haiti may well have been invested with Vodou meaning, the cross symbol in Vodou did not originate in Catholicism but in African mythology. In the Fon traditional mythology in Benin, for example, the universe, as described by Paul Mercier (1968, 219–21), is conceived as a sphere transected by two mutually perpendicular and intersecting planes which, perceived in a cross-section of the sphere, represent the arms of a cross (see figure 1); these crossed planes provide the framework and supporting axes of the sphere. In the myths, this cross resulted from the movements of Mawu Lisa, the Godhead, to the four cardinal points of the universe when she created the world.[2] The Fon creation myth compares the universe to two halves of a gourd that are welded to each other and whose edges match perfectly;[3] the plane along which the two halves are joined constitutes the plane of the horizon. Fon mythology also conceives of two different crosses in relation to the plane of the horizon: first, it conceives of the four cardinal points of an earth that stretches flat along the plane of the horizon; second, the vertical plane intersecting the mid-point of the horizontal plane forms a cross with the horizontal plane, and the ends of these planes which penetrate the gourd represent the four cardinal points of the universe (Mercier 1968, 220–21).

Fon traditional mythology also conceives of the gourd that constitutes the cosmic sphere as surrounded by a larger gourd welded in the same manner as the small one. Beyond the larger gourd is the abode of the gods. Since the small gourd is mobile, it is said that the "little calabash floats in the larger one" (Mercier 1968, 220). The small gourd contains the visible world with its four elements: earth, water, fire, and air. In traditional societies of both

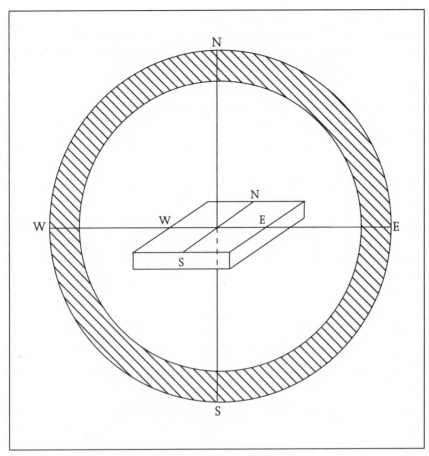

Figure 1. The Fon traditional worldview

Benin and Haiti, the earth is conceived to be a flat disk within the smaller cosmic sphere, surrounded by and floating on water. This is why Fon and Vodou traditional beliefs teach that one finds water when digging deeply into the earth (Mercier 1968, 220–21).

According to the Fon, when Mawu arranged the universe from preexisting materials, she did so in four days, the traditional Fon week. She traveled throughout the universe, stopping at the four "quarters of space," which correspond to the four cardinal points of the cosmos. At each halt, she gathered materials with which she formed the halves of the gourd, solidifying the dirt from which the earth is composed and determining the location of the waters.[4] The path of Mawu's primordial movements formed a cross: from west to east, and then from north to south.

The Africanness of this symbol is made clear by the fact that the cross is sig-

nificant not only in the Fon traditional worldview but in those of other parts
of Africa as well. Germaine Dieterlen (1951, 2–33) noted that the figure of the
cross is an important symbol in the Bambara traditional worldview. Bambara cosmology is founded upon two cosmological principles: the eternal
vibrations of matter, and the movement of the universe as a whole. According to the myth, the original germ of the world came out of emptiness or
nothingness (glã or fu), which is enveloped by a sheath (Zuesse 1979, 153–
54). Glã is also the profound silence that lies at the core of cosmic space. The
first act of creation occurred when glã emitted a primal sound, which not
only produced its twin (or an echo), but set in motion a series of vibrations
or oscillations of "energy principles" that moved up, down, and sideways
to trace the lines of a cross. From this primordial pair flowed all organic
and inorganic substances in the cosmos—substances which Faro, the Godhead, later arranged at the four corners of space (Zuesse 1979, 154). The
vibrations still exist in the universe today, and are responsible for the recurring dynamic flux of all world phenomena: the emergence of things, their
existential changes, and their eventual destruction.[5]

Hence, the Bambara base their worldview on three active principles: a
profound silence, which is an unmanifested yet most sacred primordial
energy-force; the phenomenon of twinness (or the principle of efficient
cause in matter and of biological reproduction in the deities and humans)
deriving from that primordial energy-force; and the symbol of the cross
(connecting the four cardinal points of the universe), which establishes cosmic order. The cross is the metaphysical axis around which the universe is
constructed. On the one hand, it holds the entire universe in equilibrium;
on the other, it provides the path for the infinite extension of the universe
by the continual progression of matter. Dieterlen adds that the symbol of
the cross appears in many sacred ritual objects and on many of the cooking
utensils (1951, 2–3). It is also drawn on the ground at religious ceremonies
and serves to frame a game of a quasi-ritualistic nature called sumangolo, a
game to which Bambara of "all ages and both sexes abandon themselves" in
order to contribute to what Dieterlen refers to as the ever-increasing "marche
du monde" (1951, 2, nn. 1–5).[6]

An examination of the cross symbol in Vodou will make it clear that both
its ritual and its theological significance derive from African mythology and
not from Roman Catholicism. Like the Fon, Vodouisants see in it a cosmographic image that symbolizes their worldview. It is used in religious
ceremonies that establish contact between the profane and sacred worlds.
The cross represents the fact of communication between the two worlds,

and the nature of the difference between their modes of reality. In the first of these symbolisms, the horizontal line of the cross represents the profane world of the living, and the vertical line the medium of communication with the sacred abyss (Deren 1972, 35). In the second symbolism, the vertical line represents the other world itself, its verticality indicating that the reality there is the inverse of the reality in the profane world of the living. This latter symbolism becomes clear when one realizes that in the Vodou worldview, the metaphysical world of the lwas is not vague and mystical, but a cosmic mirror which, like the personae of the lwas, reflects the images of the profane world of the living and in so doing inverts them. The lwas are often referred to as mirror images reflecting the deportment and personalities of the living (Deren 1972). For example, when the oungans or mambos address or call upon the lwas, they do so in terms that describe them as reflectors of humans: Loco-Miwa (Loco in the Mirror), or Agasou-Do-Miwa (Agasou in the back of the Mirror).

Moreover, during Vodou ceremonies the mirrored image of the world of the living is symbolized by a number of ritual observances. When the oungan greets his assistant (laplas), the two face each other while holding hands, bow to each other (reflecting the inverse motion of the other), and then perform a number of turns—first clockwise, then counterclockwise—to represent the sights of the profane world of the living as reflected in the sacred, cosmic mirror of the lwas. The double handshake, with both the right and left hands superimposed, not only traces the configuration of the cross (or the four cardinal points of the universe), but symbolizes the profane world and its mirrored inversion. Further, as Maya Deren notes (1972, 34), a mother who customarily carries her baby on her right arm will hold it on her left arm when she presents it to the lwas in the ounfò. And the ritual dance in the peristil revolves in a counterclockwise motion around a central pole (potomitan), which serves as an axis mundi.

Not only is the physical world inverted in the cosmic mirror of the sacred world, but so too is time. The oungan who is about to begin a ceremony often enters the peristil by emerging through the door of the holy of holies (bagi) backwards; this reverse motion symbolizes the retrogression through time to primordial times when the world was being created. The opening of the Vodou ceremony represents the sudden halt of profane time. The entire ceremony in which a large number of lwas "mount" their devotees is the archetypal reconstruction of the cosmos ab origine, and as the deities appear in succession, the devotees participate in the symbolic re-creation of the world. At the start of the ceremony, cosmogony is reactualized; the devo-

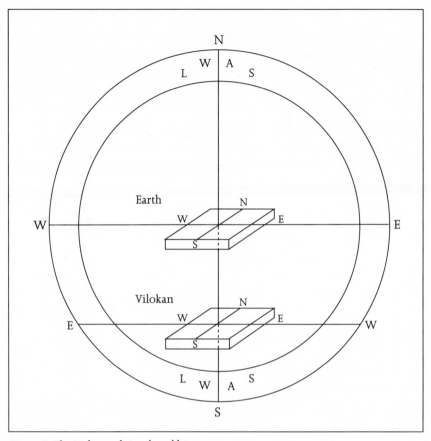

Figure 2. *The Vodou traditional worldview*

tee's possession is the re-creation of the Vodou nanchons; the world of the living is refashioned, and the individual, as well as the community, is born anew (Eliade 1959, 41). The repetition of the archetype is the temporary suspension of profane time.

The principle of inversion and retrogression is fundamental to Vodou theology as well as to its rituals. Hence, in Vodou the relationship between the cosmic mirror and the profane reality that it represents takes the cosmographic form of the cross. In the cross, Vodouisants see not only the earth's surface as comprehended by the four cardinal points of the universe, but also the intersection of the two worlds, the profane world as symbolized by the horizontal line, and Vilokan as represented by the vertical line (see figure 2). The foot of this vertical line "plunges into the waters of the abyss" to the cosmic mirror where the lwas reside; there, in this sacred subtelluric city, is Africa (or Vilokan), the mythical home of Vodouisants, the place of the lwas' origin, and Ginen, the abode of the living-dead (Deren 1972, 36). The point at which the two lines intersect is the pivotal "zero-point" in the crossing of the two worlds. It is a point of contact at which profane existence, including time, stops, and sacred beings from Vilokan invade the peristil through the body of their possessed devotees.

The cross symbol, as Deren observes, is therefore one of the most important ritualistic symbols in Vodou, appearing wherever communication or traffic between the two worlds occurs (1972, 35). The following examples will give some idea of its pervasiveness in Haiti.

Perhaps the most prominent example is the structure of the peristil itself. It is a microcosmic representation of the universe. The four poles sustaining the structure symbolize mythologically the four cardinal points of the universe, covered by an overarching roof that represents the cosmic vault above the earth. Like the horizontal lines of the cross, the floor of the peristil symbolizes the profane world, while the vertical pole (potomitan) in the center of the peristil represents the axis mundi, the avenue of communication between the two worlds. Although the downward reach of the potomitan appears to be limited by the peristil's floor, mythologically its foot is conceived to plunge into Vilokan, the cosmic mirror. The point at which the potomitan enters the peristil's floor symbolizes the zero-point. During the ceremonies, the potomitan becomes charged with or "polluted" by the power of the lwas. Hence, before tracing the geometrical symbols of the lwas (the vèvès), the oungan or mambo may touch the pole, a ritual act that empowers him or her to summon the lwas into the peristil. Thereafter, like the potomitan, the oungan's (or mambo's) body becomes in itself the source of power, a repetition of the microcosmic symbol, a moving embodiment of the vertical axis around which the universe revolves.

The cross structure of the peristil is repeated in the drawing of the vèvès, which are central to the rituals,[7] and the disposition of the vèvès on the peristil's floor also reflects the concept of inverted symmetry. Since each lwa has his or her own vèvè, the area where it is drawn is consecrated to him or her. In drawing each vèvè, the oungan or mambo often traces the cross (or kwasiyen) first; cornmeal is held between the thumb and forefinger of the right hand, and is sifted onto the floor in the configuration appropriate to each lwa. The complex representation of the deity's personality appears to hang on the two intersecting lines of the cross, and the opposing personae of each lwa are often drawn opposite each other, as if mirroring each other, on either side of the horizontal or vertical line of the cross. Once finished, they appear to the worshipers as both static and dynamic. As the principal posts

Figure 3. The vèvès drawn at a Vodou ceremony

of a building support the beams, so the lines of the cross provide a structure on which these images, like the cosmos, hang in equilibrium (see figure 3). Once drawn, notes Deren, the cross is like a revolving door; it seems to spin as if to throw off these images to the outer limits of the earth's surface (1972, 36). Both of these analogies are appropriate, for Vodouisants see the horizontal line of the vèvès as representing the secular world, while the vertical line reaches the cosmic realm of the lwas, and plunges into Vilokan.

Like the myths that they represent, vèvès can be elaborate and complex symbols, or they can be simple lines that cross each other. But their meanings are profound, for at the center of these diagrams is the zero-point of contact, where the horizontal and vertical lines intersect each other; it is the location at which all human dialogue, all the supplications of devotees that accompany the tracing of the vèvès cease to travel horizontally as they are forced downwards to Vilokan (Deren 1972). Spirit possession accompanied by glossolalia is common among devotees during the tracing of the vèvès. Possession represents a nonmaterial achievement—a profound willingness on the part of a lwa to intervene in the profane activities of humankind. That is why devotees wish to have it conferred upon them often. The possessed devotee, like the oungan, becomes the ambulant axis mundi, the point of contact between the sacred and profane worlds, and is polluted by the power of the lwa. A possessed devotee becomes a medium whose feet are planted in the sacred mirror and whose body is the vertical line whereby the revitalizing forces of the universe flow to the community.

From this examination of the use of the cross symbol in Vodou, several conclusions can be drawn. First, as among the Bambara, the tracing of the vèvès at Vodou ceremonies can be interpreted as the symbolic re-creation of the universe. In this sense, by the intricate tracery of the vèvès, and by the intervention of the lwas, Vodouisants relive the cosmological archetype not only in their retrogression through time, as represented by the movements of the oungan and his assistant as they enter the peristil, but by being possessed as well; in possession, they participate in the re-creation of the world as their bodies, now ambulant potomitans, support the world in a microcosmic way. Hence, "creation" for Vodouisants, as for the Bambara, is not a static event but a dynamic process, an ever-recurring *marche du monde*. Second, the Vodouisants' worldview corresponds to that of the Fon. In a macrocosmic dimension, Vodouisants conceive of space in the universe as limited by four cardinal points; these points are connected by intersecting lines that take the form of a cross, a metaphysical axis supporting the entire universe. In a microcosmic dimension, the peristil is the symbol of the universe. The space within it is limited by the four posts that support the structure, and the metaphysical lines that join these posts cross the floor of the peristil to form a horizontal cross which is also limited by the area of the peristil. Moreover, the vertical potomitan, around which the devotees dance in a counterclockwise direction, intersects the floor of the structure, which mythologically supports the entire structure of the universe. As the cosmic reflection of the profane world, Vilokan is conceived by Vodouisants to be structured much like the peristil, for the potomitan that traverses the floor of the peristil also traverses the sacred world of the lwas. As already noted, during the ceremonies the vèvès and the bodies of possessed devotees become a further microcosmic reduction of the potomitan.

Hence, the cross in Vodou cannot be seen as representing a syncretistic relationship between Roman Catholicism and Vodou; rather, it is the direct product of African mythology on Haitian soil. It may be true that the African symbol of the cross among the slaves would have disappeared (as did many aspects of African religion) if it had not been reinforced by the parallel symbol in Roman Catholicism on the island during the colonial period. Yet in response to the early missionaries' catechizing efforts, the slaves learned to interpret the Catholic cross in the light of their own African traditions; if the Vodou interpretation of the cross during the colonial period was similar to that found in Vodou today, it may be conjectured that it was this interpretation that provided the slaves, as well as Vodouisants today, with the necessary means by which they could adapt themselves to a foreign religious system. Moreover, it may also be conjectured that the presence of the cross in Vodou may act to disguise actual religious practices, among Haitians today as among the slaves, under an appearance of conventional piety.

....

THE COSMIC LWAS

Legba: Keeper of the Gates

According to Vodou mythology, one of Bondye's first creations when he fashioned the world was the sun. Without its existence, the lwas, human beings, and all the multiplicity of things could not exist. All derive from this primordial light. Among the Fon, this light, which is the fire of life, is identified with the creative power of Legba (Herskovits 1963, 2:220–30), a characterization that explains why in Haiti fires are often lit for Legba during Vodou ceremonies. Moreover, in the ritual invocations addressed to him, one finds such words as *clèronde*, meaning circle of brightness, and *kataroulo*, meaning the four wheels of the sun's chariot as they roll on their daily path across the sky (Deren 1972, 299). In Vodou, the sun with which Legba is identified is a regenerative life-force whose rays cause the vegetation to grow and ensure the maturation and sustenance of human life.

In Vodou, as in Fon traditional beliefs, Legba is the patron of the universe, the link between the Godhead and the universe, the umbilical cord that connects the universe to its origin. Bondye fashioned the universe; Legba has nurtured it, has fostered its growth, and has sustained it. Legba is also said to be androgynous; hence, his vèvè contains the symbol of his sexual completeness, and he is invoked in matters related to sex.[8] Both the Fon and Vodouisants (as well as the Yoruba in Nigeria) know him chiefly as the cosmic phallus, and the imagery for him also expresses his androgynous nature: the potomitan of the peristil symbolizes his phallus, and the open space around it in the entire ounfò is his womb (Laguerre 1980b, 45).

Both as phallus and as umbilical cord, Legba is the guarantor of the continuity of human generations. Vodou drawings on peristil walls show him as an old man smoking a pipe; a small sack in which he carries morsels of food dangles by his side from a strap that passes over his shoulder. He totters slowly, leaning on a cane known as baton Legba (Legba's cane). This cane represents his phallus, the source of human life, the symbol of man's virility, and the virtual link between human generations. As cosmological symbol, Legba's cane also corresponds to the potomitan in the peristil, the "odd pole," which is the source of his power—the vertical shaft that establishes contact between the sacred and profane worlds. Like the potomitan, his power reaches the depth of Vilokan and rises to the upper regions of the universe, a cosmographic image that symbolizes his virtual access to both sides of the cosmic mirror. In short, Legba's symbol is the cross; he is a mediating principle in Vodou between the sacred world (as represented by the vertical potomitan in the peristil) and the secular (the horizontal intersecting line as symbolized by the floor of the peristil), between the center of the universe (again represented by the potomitan) and the outer edges of the cosmos (represented by the four poles that uphold the structure at the four corners), between humankind and the lwas, and between one human generation and another. Likewise, his androgyny makes him the mediating principle between the sexes, for he is identified with the entire ounfò, a space symbolizing a sacred cosmic womb "impregnated" by its central potomitan, from which emerge the regenerative divine forces that invigorate the community of the living.

Because Legba's symbol is the potomitan, he is conceived as the keeper of the gates to Vilokan. He is also known as the lwa of the crossroads, or the lwa Gran Chemin (Master of the Great Way to Vilokan) (Courlander 1960, 36). As noted in the previous section of this chapter, he is believed to hold the keys to the portals of the sacred world. He is often compared to a policeman who controls traffic at a busy intersection in a large city: just as the policeman directs the orderly passage of automobiles, Legba controls the order in which the lwas appear in the possessed bodies of his devotees when they summon him to the peristil.

Vodouisants say that Legba has two personae, each corresponding to one of the aspects of his total personality. Rada's Legba is the sun, the regenerative force, the lwa of the crossroads, the mediating principle between opposites. His reflection, known as Mèt Kafou Legba (Master Legba of Intersections), is his inverted image in the Petro nanchon. Legba commands the traffic of the Rada nanchon through the potomitan, while Kafou Legba directs that of the Petro nanchon. Legba is the source and sustainer of life, whereas Kafou is a destroyer of life; his symbol is the moon (Deren 1972, 101). The persona in which Legba manifests himself varies according to the circumstances: as a Rada lwa, he is the guardian of destiny, the one who holds the keys to that destiny and makes certain that a person's life follows the preordained plan sealed by Bondye at creation; as a Petro lwa, he is the trickster who arranges unexpected accidents to cause human lives to deviate from the Almighty's plan.

In his function as the guardian of universal and individual destiny, Legba is of Yoruba origin and is known to the Fon as "Fa." The name of Fa is not known to the Haitians, but his persona is familiar to them. He holds the keys to the secrets of life, and assists Bondye in sealing the destiny of the world. As phallus, he shapes one's destiny at conception, and as umbilical cord, he sustains that destiny by maintaining one's relationship with Bondye and with the lwas. Vodouisants also imagine him to be the celestial arc, the path traveled by the sun during the day. As such, he has many lives, each corresponding to a different part of the day. In the early morning, he is as frail as a new-born child; at noon he is as fertile as a young man in the prime of life; and in the late afternoon he is a venerable and poor ancient, whose humility is like that of the revered sages of India. In this latter characterization, he is one whose age has given him a wisdom attained by no other creature, including the lwas (Deren 1972, 98).

As one who has lived through all the phases of human life, Legba knows the past and the future of the world. In Haitian folklore he is often depicted as carrying a sack that contains the world's destiny, which he dispenses at the four corners of the universe as he traverses the sky each day. He is the witness or the advocate of the destiny of humankind and the lot of the lwas: he is conceived not only as one who has access to both sides of the cosmic mirror, but also as one who has knowledge of the future as well. Because he holds such positions Vodouisants seek his advice in moments of crisis by consulting a diviner. In divination, offerings are made to him in an effort to appeal to his benevolence, and devotees "sound the cosmic mirror" to reveal what the future will bring to them. Like the Fon and the Yoruba, Haitians believe that the place that a devotee occupies in the world is established at birth. Legba determines that destiny by making a series of pronouncements, most of which may be revealed through a diviner, promising prosperity, wealth, and security to his poor devotees. He guides them through the successes and misfortunes of life.

From this idea of destiny, one might conclude that Haitians believe in an absolute determinism that enslaves each person; but like the Yoruba and Fon, they do not believe that fate binds a person inescapably. Humans have some freedom of choice, for when Legba assumes his Petro persona as Mèt Kafou Legba, he is a trickster who invents stratagems that upset the ordinary course of that destiny. Vodouisants dread this persona because he holds the power of life and death over them. They picture Kafou as a malicious mischief-maker quite capable of causing confusion, subtle enough to complicate simple situations, and cunning enough to stimulate malice among humans.

Vodouisants believe that if there were no gates to the Petro nanchon, the worlds of both lwas and humans would be more just and less full of malice. Legba would then be free to execute the destiny of the world as Bondye and his lwas planned it. Since Kafou is an inversion of Legba, so too is his effect upon the human community's destiny an inversion of that protected by Legba. For if Legba functions to support life, Kafou attempts to undermine it. If Legba is the lwa of the four cardinal points of the universe, Kafou is the "lwa of the points in between" (Deren 1972, 19). If Legba is life as symbolized by the light of the sun which radiates during the day, Kafou is death as symbolized by the moon, the "rising sun of the night," whose mysterious nature perplexes every Vodouisant (Deren 1972, 101).

The lwas of the day are of the Rada nanchon. They are just and bring misfortune only if they are angered by the negligence of their devotees in regard to rituals, sacrifices, and offerings. At times these lwas are forced to strike hard at their devotees, but then they withdraw. Such punishments are just, because they have the purpose of disciplining recalcitrant devotees. Kafou, who releases his demons during the night, knows no mercy. The sufferings that he inflicts upon devotees do not stem from human negligence, but from the malevolent nature of Kafou and his demons. If Vodouisants believe that Kafou can inflict disease or even death on them despite their supplications to Legba, it is because they feel that ill-chance is sometimes an inescapable part of human life. As the Haitian proverb notes, "When the day of suffering arrives, even curd milk can break your head."

Because Kafou is identified with the night, Vodouisants say that he is instrumental in the nocturnal machinations of bòkòs (sorcerers).[9] They avoid contact with the mapou (silk-cotton tree)[10] at night, the reputed sacred rendez-

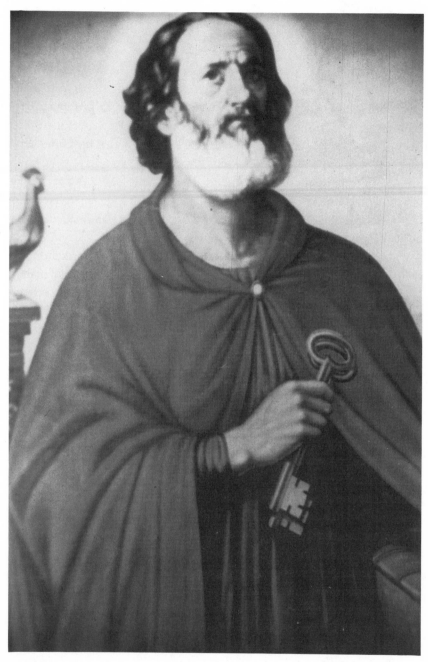

Saint Peter or Legba

vous in which Kafou and his demons meet to plan their blood-curdling activities. In his Petro characterization as Legba Pie Case (Legba with the Broken Leg) Kafou commands demonic legions that are believed to live in families, the most famous of which are the bakas, envisaged as small, red-eyed, fleshless mythological creatures with black-and-red skin stretched over their bones. Under the direction of bòkòs who summon them, Kafou changes his bakas into animals or lougawous, believed to be messengers of bad fortune. They roam throughout the countryside during the night to "eat people" (Métraux 1958, 89)—that is, to injure or kill them.

If All Saints' Day is reserved to commemorate Legba, it is because Legba and Kafou Legba are referred to in Christian terms. Because Legba is the keeper of the keys, many Vodouisants have identified him with Saint Peter.[11] This identification derives from lithographs of Saint Peter, popular among Catholics and Vodouisants in Haiti, which depict him holding the keys of the church (see illustration 2)—an iconographic image that derives from his official position as the keeper of the keys to the kingdom of heaven (Matthew 16:10–20). In Vodou, this image has been construed to be that of Legba who holds the keys to human destiny. The same lithographs also depict Saint Peter with a rooster, an image that derives from the New Testament's account of Peter's denial of Jesus. Vodouisants believe that the rooster is not only a symbol of Legba, but also his faithful companion; this perhaps explains why they always tender a rooster as an offering to him.

Although these symbols may suggest a syncretism of Vodou and Catholicism the connection is merely superficial, for Vodouisants have construed the symbols of the lithographs in African terms, as their interpretation of the details clearly shows. First, unlike Haitian Catholicism, which sees Peter as a purely benevolent saint, Vodou, as already noted, assigns two functions to Legba, corresponding to his two personae, and one of these is malevolent. Second, although the symbol of the keys in the lithographs is the principal point of contact between the saint and the lwa, Vodouisants interpret them in African terms. Nowhere else in Vodou do the keys appear—not in drawings on the walls of the ounfòs baptized in his service, in the vèvè that symbolizes him, or in the ceremonies performed in his honor. Rather, Haitians, like the Fon, identify him with the symbol of the cross. Nor is the rooster a Christian borrowing, for Melville Herskovits notes that the rooster is associated with Legba in Fon religious traditions. Two or three times a year the Fon, like Vodouisants, sacrifice several roosters (or chickens) to Legba. These ceremonies involve the pouring of the blood of the animal or the placing of cooked chicken as food for Legba (*manje lwa*) at crossroads in the countryside—religious practices similarly observed in Haiti.

Thus, symbiosis can be seen in the use of Catholic lithographs, some of whose details are interpreted in the light of African religion. Furthermore, symbiosis by ecology can also be seen in the calendrical connection between All Saints' Day and the function of Legba as the master of traffic of the lwas. Among the Fon, Herskovits notes that special religious ceremonies to Fa and Legba are observed at the beginning of each traditional new year. The first day of the year falls sometime during the harvest period. Since the slaves in Saint-Domingue were forced to adopt the Roman calendar,[12] they made the logical association between All Saints' Day and Legba by virtue of his function as master of the gates to Vilokan. All Saints' Day (November 1) falls during the period of harvest in Haiti, for, like Benin, Haiti has two rainy seasons: the first begins in March and ends in late June; the second begins about the middle of August and ends by late October or early November. Haitians, like the Fon, plant their crops shortly before the rainy season and harvest them after that season ends; the months of July and October, and the early part of November, are therefore periods of harvest. Hence, it is logical to assume that the slaves made a connection between All Saints' Day and the Fon ceremonies to Fa or Legba.

In short, symbiosis can be seen from two points of view. First, the Catholic symbols associated with Saint Peter gave Vodouisants a basis to establish the connection between Legba and the saint. Second, such a connection meant that the Catholic symbols in the Christian calendar were adopted to the African feast day in honor of Legba at the beginning of the traditional year. Here too, Vodouisants have fitted the Catholic holy day into the African harvest ceremonies held for Legba.

Gede: Master of Ginen

Just as Legba initiates time, so Gede ends time, for he is the master of Ginen who rules over death. Just as Legba, the lord of the sun, plunges into the sea at sunset to await his rekindling at sunrise, so too the gwo-bon-anj of the dead must remain lifeless and await its reclamation from Gede's abyss. In a sense, Gede is Legba's opponent, for whereas Legba as the sun is omnipresent during the day, Gede is lord of the night and is symbolized by the moon. Whatever Legba constructs, Gede tears down; whatever Legba sets in motion, Gede arrests; whatever Legba conceives, Gede aborts; and whatever Legba sustains, Gede destroys, for he is the lord of death, the master of destruction of things.

Although these two divine forces appear to have opposite functions, and indeed are inversions of each other, they nevertheless are similar in many ways, for both participate in the creative forces at opposite ends of the spectrum of life. Both control traffic between the profane and sacred worlds, Legba at Vilokan's gate and Gede at the portals of Ginen. Just as Legba facilitates the lwa's rebirth in the body of a possessed devotee, so too Gede ensures the reclaimed gwo-bon-anj's rebirth in the jar (govi) that serves as its vessel. To Vodouisants, Ginen is analogous to Vilokan, for both represent temporary cosmic birthplaces and cosmic graveyards from which spirits emerge and to which they return.

In a sense, therefore, Legba and Gede are divine relatives governing two distinct worlds, each of which is, for Maya Deren, the tomb and the womb of the world.[13] Gede, the master of Ginen, is lord not merely of death but of life as well. This is why Haitians often identify him with his regenerative rather than with his destructive powers. Even in his official capacity as lord of death, Vodouisants use such appellations for him as the "Giver of Life" and the "Rising Sun." These similarities explain why both lwas are represented by the symbol of the cross (Deren 1972, 102).

Because Gede is identified with life, he is also seen, like Legba, as a phallic deity. Indeed, he symbolizes the inevitable sexual element in humankind. Pictures of him drawn on peristil walls show a man with enlarged nostrils indicating breathing, a symbol of life, but with petrified arms and feet. His large thoracic cavity is depicted as that of a skeleton, a symbol of death. In contrast, his erect phallus is large, to symbolize life; for Vodouisants say that when he walks, the movements of his body (gouyad) recall the sexual act (Laguerre 1980b, 95).

Vodouisants reserve these graphic motifs of life and death not only for their artistic expressions of Gede, but for objects and buildings initiated in his name. In the sacred chamber dedicated to his service stands Petro's Baron la Koa, represented by a black wooden cross similar to those erected on tombstones and cenotaphs at cemeteries. The tools of the gravedigger, such as pickaxes and shovels, also decorate the peristil's walls. Piles of stones, dried leaves, and skulls lie on the floor of the ounfò's sacred chamber. Amidst the macabre decor of what could be a dark and damp cosmic graveyard is the symbol of life, for dominating this grotesque arrangement is a large wooden phallus, a combination symbolizing the unity of life and death.

In the body of a possessed devotee, Gede speaks with a nasal resonance—

the sound that, Vodouisants say, would be produced by a corpse if it were allowed to speak. Usually this sound incites nervous laughter on the part of those attending the ceremonies, because it reminds them of their eventual lot. The lwa is particularly noted for his rich repertoire of stories, narrated in a nasal tone and in a vocabulary that, under other circumstances, any Haitian would consider obscene. Gede always tries to provoke his devotees with his ribaldry. His stories and his songs describe the secret love affairs of the members of the community, omitting none of the lewd details. If members of the community consider sex sinful, or appear uncomfortable and embarrassed by his wantonness, he enjoys the opportunity to taunt them, displaying before them the most unrestrained and immoral mannerisms. Adept in his voluptuous art, Gede is neither ashamed of his reputation nor bothered by those who are publicly contemptuous of his sensuousness; he knows that they cannot evade their eventual confrontation with him (Deren 1972, 103).

Although Gede's devotees see him as a witty clown (Métraux 1958, 100), he nevertheless symbolizes their destiny. With a keen memory, he remembers their past lives, shrewdly watches them in their present communal life, and makes of their existential dilemmas objects of mockery and laughter. But his jocularity can never mask his omniscient and unlimited power over his devotees' destiny—a power which he does not have to manifest in the body of his devotees because they need no reminder of such a universal fact as death. Perhaps this explains why his demeanor often takes the form of mockery and defiance. When he comes to possess his devotees, he adopts the role of a young and cheerful clown, as Petro's Entretoute, or that of a frail beggar, burdened by illness, old age, and poverty. These paradoxical manifestations are reminders of the somber moment of death as an inevitable and inescapable reality from which, ironically, mirth becomes the only temporary avenue of escape.

While Gede enjoys his role as a clown, his devotees consider him wise. As lord of life, he is instrumental in giving advice to them regarding which crops they should plant, or which woman or man they should marry, or which children will be more promising. His wisdom is discernible even in his lighter moods; he is most generous in carefully advising those who seriously ask for his assistance.

Gede is probably the most complex character in Haitian folklore, for he reveals more than thirty personae,[14] each of which is associated with a different function. As Petro's Baron Sanmdi, whose fearless wife is Manman Brijit, the guardian of the past, he is the preserver of the community's religious heritage, and the protector of the history of the human race. As Baron

Cimetiè, he is the "guardian of old bones" and sits at the gates of graveyards as represented by his black cross; this symbol appears at the entrance of every Vodou burial ground, to remind visitors that they are about to enter a territory where Ginen and the profane world are said to intersect each other. A graveyard is thus like the potomitan in the ounfò, the zero-point of contact between the sacred and profane worlds. He is depicted in the Vodouisants' imagination as wearing a frock coat and striped trousers, formal apparel once worn by government officials at funerals. Amusingly enough, he has no shoes, smokes an old pipe, and wears a threadbare coat and a frayed black straw hat (Métraux 1958, 101), the stereotypical accoutrements of the Haitian undertaker. At times these accoutrements are completed by smoked glasses, which are necessary, Vodouisants say, to protect his eyes from the bright tropical sunlight, for he spends much of his time in Ginen's darkness. All the Gedes also cover their faces with thick coats of white powder, their nostrils and ears blocked with white cotton to simulate the dead. Appareled thusly, Baron holds in his hand a pickax (or hoe) and a shovel. Those who address special prayers to him may also address him as Kongo's Gede Nibo— that is, the one who lives in the shadow of the black cross. Devotees "feed" him often by bringing calabashes of food, which they place at the base of the cross. In exchange for their gifts, he counsels them on domestic matters that impinge upon the life of the community.

Baron's power, like Legba's, can be channeled through the bòkò's malevolent machinations. He can set in motion invisible forces that can harm his devotees. Whether as Baron Sanmdi, Cimetiè, Capitèn Gede, or any other characterization, his malevolent power is said to range from assisting the bòkò in animating zombis to releasing his bakas to harm those whom the sorcerer curses.

Since death consumes the world, Gede is also known for his gluttony. When his plate is set before him at a ceremony, he eats rapaciously, stuffing his mouth with both hands. In the body of a possessed devotee, he does not hesitate to snatch morsels of food from other devotees' plates, and then rushes to a corner of the peristil to eat the food privately, or runs outside to bury it. He is said to return at night, several days later, to eat it after it has decomposed (Métraux 1958, 102). In the personae of Toapel, Fatra, or Pete [15] he appears even more malevolent, as his hunger turns him not only against devotees but against other lwas as well. Angry at his devotees' occasional neglect, he invades their bodies unexpectedly, even at ceremonies not performed in his honor, to participate as an uninvited guest at sacrifices and to eat at ritual meals offered in honor of other lwas. His effrontery is per-

Representation of Gede painted on a peristil wall

haps most evident in the ceremonies for his younger brother, Kouzen Zaka (or Azaka).

In some ways the Vodou characterizations of Zaka resemble those of Gede, but for the most part he is differentiated from Gede by characteristics that are strictly his own. These perhaps reflect the way in which Haitian mythology conceives of him as well as the position he occupies in Haitian society. Pictures of Zaka painted on the walls of peristils (and ritual clothes worn by those possessed by him) show him dressed as Haitian peasants once did: he wears a straw hat, a blue denim shirt, trousers with one leg rolled to his knee, and a machete attached to a strap placed about his waist. With his straw sack, hung on one side of his body by a strap over his shoulder, he is believed to roam the countryside to inspect the tilled fields. Although Zaka's cosmic domain may not be as eccentric and glamorous as that of his brother, he is nevertheless the farmer's hero, for he is lord of agriculture. In this function, reminiscent of the early period of the country's history shortly after independence, he becomes an inspector of agriculture—a role that often gives him a pompous posture of authoritarianism.

Zaka is characterized as a crude and ignorant lwa. As younger brothers often do, he slavishly attempts to emulate Gede's mannerisms and character but consistently fails in his efforts. Like Gede, Zaka is said to have a ravenous appetite, but unlike Gede, Zaka's speech is neither eloquent nor his gestures clever enough to incite laughter. Gede speaks defiantly with bold vulgarity, whereas Zaka is inarticulate, his speech being the mere bleating of a goat. Gede is most often boisterous whereas Zaka is passive and quiet. In short, this unsophisticated and gauche "peasant Pan" (Deren 1972, 110) is the sort of character whom Gede would ridicule. Moreover, Zaka is docile, gentle, and kind. The Haitian peasant sees in Zaka's affection and admiration for his brother a welcome change from the fears and anxieties that Gede, as Baron, often generates in him. For although Gede produces laughter by clowning, his presence creates a sinister atmosphere which no laughter can obscure.

Little is known about Gede's origin. Because there are no exact accounts of him in Fon mythology, it is difficult to establish a connection between Benin and Haiti, but speculations can be made on historical as well as ritualistic bases. It seems that Gede may have originated from the exploits of the Ghédévi clan in ancient Dahomey whose mythological ancestor and founder bore the name "Ghédé." In the latter part of the eighteenth century, Abomey in Dahomey became a very wealthy and powerful kingdom, having profited from the sale of slaves to the Portuguese and the French. According to Fon oral tradition,[16] Andanzan, king of Abomey, was an aged monarch whose only ambition was to enrich the state treasury by whatever means possible. He warred incessantly with neighboring peoples and plundered many of their villages, carrying away whatever wealth they possessed; he captured men, women, and children whom he kept in slave camps for a time and later sold to European slave traders. It seems that Andanzan's mother (whose name is not mentioned in the story) became displeased with her son's behavior and attempted to replace him with his younger brother Ghezo.

In order to deprive Ghezo of the counsel of his mother in the usurpation of his throne, Andanzan enslaved her as well as sixty-three of her retainers, members of the Ghédévi clan who had sided with her. Andanzan later sold them to the Portuguese and French slave traders. They were transported to Brazil and to Haiti, where they found many Dahomeans. When the descendants of Ghédé arrived in "Ame'ika," they founded the "cult of the Dahomean city." When Ghezo took his rightful place as king of Abomey, he dispatched a Portuguese friend, Da Sousa, to the New World to find his mother. After an extensive search, Da Sousa found her in Brazil, and later returned her and six other Dahomeans to Abomey. There, she is said to have ruled by the monarch's side for eighteen years until his death in 1840.

If this story is true, it would account for the connection between Dahomey and the New World, and would explain the presence of Gede in the Vodou pantheons in Haiti and in Candomblé in Brazil.[17] It would also explain why he would have been an object of ancestral reverence. As the head of a clan, and similar to the founding ancestors of other clans in Abomey, Ghédé would have been regarded as one of the focal points of social and political organizations; an altar would have been erected in his name, and clan priests who bore his name would devote their lives to him. Moreover, Ghédé would have a significant influence on the behavior of his descendants. They would have sought his counsel in matters related to marriage, and to breaches of faith between his descendants and the members of other clans. He would have been the giver of children by participating in Dã, the life-giving element of fecundity that provides continuity in perpetuating the clan, allowing the passage of ancestral souls from the underworld to be instilled in the refashioned bodies of newborns within the Ghédévi clan.

The connection between the Haitian Gede and Dahomean Ghédé can also be seen in the similarity between the Vodou rituals performed in Gede's honor and those performed by the Fon in honor of their ancestors. First, both in Dahomey (or Benin) and in Haiti, these ceremonies involve the sacrifice of chickens and goats. Second, the sacrificing of animals includes collecting their blood into calabashes, and pouring it onto the altar, or Baron Sanmdi's black cross. Third, the ceremonies in both countries take place around a tomblike structure behind which is a table serving as a shrine to the ancestors. Fourth, both in Haiti and in Benin the participants kiss the ground before they present offerings of cooked and uncooked food. Fifth, the Fon rituals, like those in Haiti, are not only an act of reverence, but are also often used for therapeutic purposes, to cure a devotee of a disease.

Because the Haitian Gede is associated with the welfare of his descendants, Vodouisants have identified him with Saint Gérard. According to Catholic hagiology, Saint Gérard was born to a wealthy family in Venice in the eleventh century. He renounced his family's wealth for the monastic life and spent much of his time healing the sick, whom he is said to have treated with uncommon tenderness. His reputation as a healer has survived in Haiti. Lithographs of the saint (which circulate widely throughout the country) depict him as dressed in a black robe, holding a bishop's crosier in his right hand. Vodouisants recognize that lithograph to be Gede not only because of the saint's reputation as a healer but because of the color of his robe: black has traditionally been the symbolic color of the saint, as well as that of Gede. Among all the lithographs of the saints in Haiti, Saint Gérard is the only one dressed in black.

Since Gede is Zaka's brother, Vodouisants say that Saint Gérard is the brother of Saint John the Baptist, with whom Zaka is identified. It is difficult to establish Zaka's origin in Vodou mythology and folklore; most scholars provide few details about him. It is plausible that the name "Zaka," or "Azaka," is a relic of Haiti's prehistory. A brief etymological description of *zaka* shows that it probably derives from the Taino Indian word *zada*, meaning corn, or from the related *azada* or *azadon*, Taino words referring to the agricultural activities of hoeing and digging. In the northern part of Haiti, Zaka is also known as "Mazaka," a derivation from another Taino word for corn, *maza*, from which comes the English word *maize*. If this is right, Zaka, Azaka, or Mazaka in Vodou has an agrarian significance dating back to Haiti's pre-Columbian Amerindian culture (Deren 1972, 280). The inclusion of the word in Vodou mythology may have been the result of the maroons' contact with Indian culture in the interior of the island during the colonial period.

Despite these linguistic connections to the Taino, the Vodou characterizations of Zaka and the Vodou rituals related to him correspond to those for the Fon deity of agriculture, Yalóde. According to Herskovits, the rituals to Yalóde in Benin vary according to the types of crops being harvested and also according to the time of the year. As already noted, in Benin as well as in Haiti there is a well-recognized agricultural calendar based on the variations in seasonal rainfall during the year. In both countries the peasants plant, among other vegetables, corn, yams, carrots, beets, and plantains. Zaka, like Yalóde, is particularly identified with yams rather than corn. The yam harvest occurs twice during the year: during February and March, and during July and August. These are the periods of religious ceremonies in honor of Zaka and Yalóde. In both Benin and Haiti, these ceremonies involve offerings of numerous yams and of at least one chicken and one goat. In both countries, the meat from the sacrificial animals as well as the vegetable offerings are cooked and eaten at the site of the ceremony.

If Zaka is identified with John the Baptist it is not because of the saint's life or ministry, but because of his depiction in the lithograph that is said to represent him. In reality, the lithograph that Vodouisants identify as John the Baptist is that of Saint Isidore, the patron saint of farmers and food-growers in Catholic hagiology—but Vodouisants are unaware of Saint Isidore's name,

Saint Isidore, believed to be Saint John the Baptist or Zaka

and even less aware of his persona and the symbols associated with it in Catholic iconology. In the lithograph representing Saint John (or Saint Isidore), he is depicted as a poor man wearing a blue robe, carrying a large sack hanging from a strap that passes over his shoulder and crosses his chest and back. Vodouisants identify Saint John with Zaka because his clothing and his sack resemble those of many Haitian peasants when they work in their fields. His blue robe is interpreted as the blue denim shirt and trousers that Haitian peasants have traditionally worn; likewise, Zaka's sack becomes the sack in which peasants put their personal belongings and the vegetables that they harvest as they till their fields.

By piecing together these details concerning Zaka and Gede, several conclusions can be drawn. First, unlike Zaka, Gede is entirely Fon (Herskovits 1972, 247).[18] His persona and function derive from an ancient Dahomean clan, and the Vodou rituals performed in his honor may well have originated in ceremonies performed for the royal ancestor of the Ghédévi clan in Dahomey. Second, the identification of Saint Gérard with Gede is based upon Christian hagiology and the traditional role of ancestral figures in Dahomey. As Roger Bastide suggested in the case of Brazil, the early missionaries to Brazil, as in Haiti, may have recounted stories about Saint Gérard's life to the slaves; these accounts were then interpreted in terms of African tradition (1978). Since both Gede and Saint Gérard concerned themselves with healing the sick, it seems reasonable that Vodouisants would have made the logical connection between the African persona of Gede and the saint. Moreover, the saint's symbolic color and that of Gede were the same, so that Vodouisants would have identified them with each other.

Vodouisants' penchant for identifying a lwa with a Catholic saint on the basis of his accoutrements is made particularly clear in the case of Zaka. The Vodouisants' identification of Zaka with Saint John the Baptist rests entirely upon the similarity of the saint's accoutrements, as depicted in the lithograph that they mistakenly think represents him, to those of Haitian peasants.

Hence symbiosis can be seen in two ways. First, in the contact situation between Catholicism and African religion on the island, the African mythological personae were revived in the personae of both Gede and Zaka. Although Zaka's name is a creole phenomenon that probably derived from the contact between the Indians and the maroons during Haiti's colonial period, both the function and the persona of Zaka are essentially Fon. Second, symbiosis in the identification of these lwas with the saints is not based upon Catholic symbolism, but upon the accoutrements of the saints in popular lithographs. Moreover, these depictions have been transfigured in African terms. Third, the rituals performed in honor of these lwas recall those of Africa rather than the Catholic tradition.

Damballah: The Gentle Snake of the Primal Seas

In Fon mythology (Mercier 1968, 220–21) the story is told that at the beginning of the world Mawu Lisa traveled to the four corners of the universe in order to arrange it. She was carried in the mouth of her benevolent snake-servant Dã Aida Hwedo. Wherever Mawu directed him to take her, mountains appeared, composed of Dã's excrement.[19]

When Mawu had completed her task, she noticed that the earth would not remain buoyant upon the primordial waters, for the mountains rendered it too heavy. Like a ship weighed down by a heavy cargo, the earth was slowly sinking into the primordial waters below it. Mawu asked Dã to coil himself below the earth and form "carrying pads" to hold the earth in place. To support the earth, Dã also constructed four pillars of iron, one at each of the cardinal points of the universe, and implanted them into the cosmic waters below. The tops of these pillars were elongated to support the sky, while holding the flat and thick earth buoyant and stationary in the middle. Dã is said to have then twisted himself around these pillars in order to reinforce them and to hold them in their original position.

The Fon agree that Dã is not stationary. It is said that he also revolves around the earth by extending himself under it and across the vault of the sky, providing the circular trajectory for the sun during both day and night. Because of Dã's revolution around the earth, he is identified with eternal motion in the universe. This motion is characterized by the passage of all physical phenomena from birth to decay. According to the Fon, whatever assumes form is subject to destruction, and each world phenomenon is a link in the chain of progression of existent things. Hence, the passage from formation to destruction is seen as part of an inherent, eternal cosmic motion. This motion stems from Dã's divine energy-force, a divine essence in all world phenomena which produces the physical displacement of objects in space and in time and which manifests itself in the incessant motion of the waves of the ocean, the waters of springs and rivers in which Dã is said to reside in the form of a snake. Dã animates the wind, ensures the alternation of day and night, and impels the cyclical motion of the astral bodies. In short,

Dã is a living quality expressed in all dynamic motion in the cosmos, in all things that are flexible, sinuous, and moist, in all things that fold and unfold, coil and recoil.

In humans, this energy-force is the giver of children. It is identified not only with the eternal motion of human bodies but also with motion as seen in the cycle of life and death and in the passing of human generations. The Fon, like the Haitians, give much consideration to the importance of children in the ancestral line of continuity. Children must be born not only so that the physical line can continue, but also so that the parents may be kept in a state of immortality by their children's remembrances.

Many of these characterizations of Dã have been retained in Vodou mythology and folklore in the personae of Damballah. Although few of the Fon tales about Dã have survived among Haitians, their mythological details have persisted. Like the Fon, Vodouisants say that Damballah is an aged, noble father who assisted Bondye when he created the universe. Indeed, it is said that Damballah is so ancient that in a sense, he is the father of the universe (Herskovits 1963, 2:250). As in Fon mythology, Damballah is the snake lwa, the one who twines himself around the four pillars that support the universe, and analogously around the four poles in the peristil. In some ounfòs, as in temples in Whydah in contemporary Benin, he is symbolized by a snake that lives either in an enclosed area of the temple, or in a pool of water specially constructed for him.

In the body of his devotees, Damballah crawls on the ground and speaks with an incoherent hissing. One can never communicate precisely with him, notes Maya Deren, for in his cosmic grandeur and venerable wisdom he refuses to be bothered with the petty precision of human speech (1972, 115). Yet, in spite of his aloofness, Damballah comforts Vodouisants by his willingness to possess them. As if unaffected by the events of human history, the cold, static snake-lwa's presence in the peristil brings to the devotees the assurance of a stable world whose future is secure. By each of his manifestations in the body of a devotee, Damballah promises that motion will continue to be the essence of life: time will flow, and with it physical objects will form and deteriorate, and children will be born and die, their bodies returning to the navel of the earth to await their reshaping by Bondye and his lwas.

As in the Fon solar myth, Vodouisants identify Damballah with the daily path of the sun as it travels over and under the earth, as the following song sung after sunset in Vodou ceremonies would seem to indicate:

Oh the one in the mirror
Damballah, you are the venerable one.
Don't you see him leaving
Oh the one in the mirror
Damballah, you are the venerable one.
Don't you see him leaving.

And at dawn, as a ceremony that has lasted throughout the night reaches its close, the community will sing:

Snake, Snake oh!
Damballah Wèdo, Papa,
Oh, Damballah Wèdo
I am calling you snake oh!
The snake cannot wake up
Damballah, Papa, you are a snake oh!
Ayibobo!

To this song Damballah answers through the body of a possessed devotee, as he unwinds himself to prepare the sun's path across the sky:

When they need me, they call me: "Papa."
The day that they don't need me, they say that I am a snake, oh!
Damballah has a bad disposition, oh!
Papa, they greet everyone else,
Why don't they greet me?
Papa, they greet everyone else,
Why don't they greet me?
Papa, has a bad disposition
Let me navigate!
Ayibobo!

Damballah's "bad disposition" in the song refers to the devotees' rude awakening of their lwa as they summon him to rise from his deep nocturnal sleep in the waters of the abyss to visit the peristil. The mention of navigation conjures up the image that Damballah must swim in the primordial waters under the earth before he can pass across the sky to establish the sun's trajectory at sunrise.

Vodouisants believe that when Damballah is satisfied by his devotees' devotion to him he manifests himself, as in Fon mythology, in the form of a multicolored snake, which can be seen by all the lwas and their devotees in the form of a rainbow on the horizon. One half of the arc is Damballah, and the other half is his female consort Ayida Wèdo.[20] Such manifestations reflect Damballah's sexual completeness (Métraux 1958, 92). Since they are members of the Rada nanchon, both Damballah and Ayida are conceived to be benevolent. The oungan announces Damballah and his consort with the words,

> Calling Wèdo!
> Who is this lwa?
> They tell me it is you, "Dan e!"

As this song is intoned, the drums sound the rhythm of the *yanvalou*, an electrifying dance that thrusts the possessed devotees' bodies into serpentine motions from shoulder to ankle. The devotees' voices surge into a powerful unison that reflects personal fulfillment, devotion, and excitement.

As one who participates in the motion of the universe, Damballah is associated with other members of the sky pantheon: Badè or Badeci, the wind; and Sogbo[21] or Agasou Tonè, the thunder. In Vodou mythology and folklore Agasou and Sogbo are inseparable companions. They share their divine functions, as the following song indicates:

> Badè is blowing, blowing
> He blows, Badè
> Agasou roars, roars
> He makes the roaring thunder.
> Nadè [the wind] came from Ginen
> He blows, he roars.

As Rada lwas, Badè and Sogbo are benign natural forces. Badè appears as the gentle rainfall that disperses the scorching heat of the tropical sun; while Sogbo, the thunder, heralds Badè's coming: he mounts his chariot and drives across the sky, throwing lightning bolts in the clouds. Conversely, in their Petro manifestations, Badè's gentle wind becomes a hurricane that damages crops, while Sogbo becomes a thunderstorm so violent that it shakes the earth. These latter characterizations are evident in cases of spirit possession in ceremonies in which Badè and Sogbo "mount" their devotees simultaneously. Such possessions are often violent and potentially destructive to the devotee who harbors their forces. In their brutality, it is said that Badè and Sogbo can cause death to persons who harbor them. Those sturdy enough to be occupied by them produce sounds that resemble the whistling of the wind and the roaring thunder.

Because of the notable violence that Badè and Sogbo manifest in their devotees, possession by them occurs infrequently. Indeed, in some parts of the country they have been forgotten. According to Deren, Badè and Sogbo may well be vestigial remains of another period of Haitian history. In the regions of Haiti where they are known, they may be identified with the lakou's lwa rasin. As already noted, the disintegration of the lakou in Haiti in recent years may have reduced them to mere vestiges. Yet precisely because of their vestigial nature, they embody the historical development of the lakou. Ceremonies that invoke them resemble a kind of retrogression in the lakou's history, a return to certain past events around the figure of deities who no longer are central to religious practices. As Deren notes, to revere them is to "stretch one's hand" into history and to "gather up all history into a solid contemporary ground beneath one's feet" (1972, 116).

Since by his very nature as encircler of the universe Damballah is a positive force, his contrasting equivalents in the Petro nanchon are not believed to be malevolent. However, he also has several counterparts in another frame of reference, magic. In this context, he becomes Simbi, who shares functions and characteristics not only with Damballah but with the other major deities of the Rada and Kongo nanchons. It would be logical for Simbi to be part of the Kongo pantheon rather than the Rada, for his original does not derive from Benin but from Kongo, where he is identified with pools of water (Courlander 1960, 327).

As one who is said to straddle both nanchons, Simbi epitomizes the principle of religion. He is a lwa of the crossroads, between the Kongo and Rada nanchons. In a sense, he and Legba are divine relatives, not only because he provides a path for the sun, but also because he permits communication with the lwas of the Kongo nanchon. Indeed, his vèvè shows all the symbols of Legba surrounded on both sides by two intersecting snakes. Vodouisants also say that in his Kongo persona as Simbi-yan-dé-zo (Simbi-in-the-twin-waters), he straddles the waters of Ginen and the waters about the inner cosmic gourd of the world that separates humans from the lwas (Deren 1972, 117). In his function as a Rada lwa, Simbi is the master of springs and of ponds. Pools of water are often created in a ounfò's courtyard as a symbolic representation of his abode. Like Dã among the Fon, he is the vital force that ensures the eternal motion in the waters of the rivers. In Vodou art, he is often depicted as a powerful snake who inhabits the rivers, one who shows his strength by uprooting trees and rocks and carrying them downstream during tropical storms. In his function as a Kongo lwa, his body encircles its prey and chokes it to death. Because of these manifestations of power,

Saint Patrick or Damballah

Simbi is the patron lwa of magicians. In his Rada persona, he is most often summoned to assist the oungan in benevolent magic or the bòkò in his sorcery. This role is a natural one, since in his pivotal position as lord of all crossroads his power radiates to all four corners of the universe.

In both characterizations, Vodouisants believe that Simbi is a lazy lwa. He is reluctant to enter the ounfò; during meetings he is believed to coil himself outside the peristil, and, like a small child in the company of adults, he is bashful in exhibiting his knowledge. In this characterization, Simbi opposes Damballah, for while Damballah is a creative force out of which surges the energy-force that accounts for eternal motion in the universe, Simbi counteracts Damballah's creative momentum by always struggling to instill within the cosmos a lingering, static quality.

Because Damballah and Simbi are associated with snakes, Vodouisants identify them with Saint Patrick or with Moses; the first because of the well-known story about Saint Patrick driving the snakes out of Ireland, and the second because of Moses' miracle performed before the Egyptian Pharaoh when he threw down his staff on the ground and turned it into a serpent. In both cases, the personalities of Damballah and Simbi are identified with the same Catholic lithograph, which depicts Saint Patrick standing near the seashore. Wearing the liturgical accoutrements of a bishop of the church and holding a crosier in his left hand, Saint Patrick is surrounded by snakes at his feet, which he casts into the sea. Vodouisants interpret this action to mean that Damballah and Simbi possess magical power over the snakes, power that permits them to master them.

In analyzing the depiction of Damballah in the lithograph, two observations can be made regarding symbiosis. The first deals with the interpretation of the lithograph itself, and the second with the personification of Damballah. First, the stories by the early missionaries related to the life of Saint Patrick or Moses have not been retained in Haiti. When Vodouisants are presented with the lithograph representing the saint, they identify him immediately with Damballah or Simbi. Like the Fon, they see in Damballah the manifestations of a dynamic life-force in the universe. Second, by analyzing Vodouisants' concepts of Damballah's personality, one sees that the similarities between Saint Patrick and Damballah are only apparent; for although lithographs of Saint Patrick hang in every ounfò, Vodouisants never refer to these as Saint Patrick but as Damballah. Thus, in the case of Damballah, symbiosis consists in the adoption of a lithograph, symbolic of the saint's life as depicted in Catholic hagiology, to depict a Vodou lwa who remains essentially Dahomean in character.

THE FACES

....

OF THE

....

GODS AND

....

PUBLIC

....

LIFE

5

In analyzing, in this chapter, the lwas whose personae relate more directly to Vodouisants' public life, I will give special attention to the public rituals offered to these lwas. And in keeping with the thesis of this discussion, I will consider symbiosis as it occurs in the myths about these lwas as well as in the rituals. The chapter ends with a description of Bondye's envisaged personae because, although he does not enter directly into the lives of Haitians, the mythology that surrounds Bondye includes that of all the other lwas.

....

THE LWAS OF PUBLIC LIFE

Ezili: *The Luxurious Virgin Mother*

If motion is ensured by Damballah, and if, as generating principle, the phallus is symbolized by Legba and Gede, Ezili represents the cosmic womb in which divinity and humanity are conceived. She is the symbol of fecundity, the mother of the world who participates with the masculine forces in the creation and maintenance of the universe. As mother, Ezili cooperates with the sun lwa Legba, who ensures the florescence and nurture of all living things. When she cooperates with Gede, she symbolizes Ginen's cosmic womb from which the released ancestral gwo-bon-anjs are reclaimed. She is represented not only by the govi or clay jar in which the gwo-bon-anj is believed to reside, and whence it emerges to possess the living, but by the devotee's possessed body, which serves as her temporary vessel, and from which her personae emerge as she manifests them to the community. In combination with Damballah, Ezili guarantees the flow of human generations. Vodou mythology conceives her as the mother of the lwas and of humanity. She is believed to have given birth to the first human beings after Bondye created the world, and since that time her powers of provision have continued to grant children to the human community.

Because Vodouisants see her as sexually fertile, they invoke her in matters related to conception and childbearing. Indeed, without her patronage a woman would not be able to conceive. In the peristil, it is to her that women sing:

I said: "Ezili you are the venerable one, oh!"
Extend your hand, gives us children, oh!
I said: "Ezili, you are a venerable one, oh!"
Ezili, oh! you are the venerable one, oh!

As a symbol of fecundity, Ezili is not identified merely with sex. Like the Virgin Mary, to whom she corresponds, she is imagined as the symbol of womanhood, the image of exquisite beauty that fills every man's dreams. Maya Deren says that in Ezili, "Voodoo has given the woman an exclusive title to what distinguishes humans from all forms, their capacity to conceive beyond reality, to desire beyond adequacy, to create beyond need" (1972, 138).[1] Ezili is therefore the embodiment of human longing for an ideal in which human fantasy transcends the limitations of mundane reality and the exigencies of privation. She is the lwa of love, the Homeric Aphrodite[2] whose wealth and physical beauty are beyond all imagination; it is in these roles that she symbolizes not merely the mother of fantasy but the mother of mythopoeia as well, for around her persona Vodouisants have developed an oral literature: a large complex of poems, songs, and stories extolling her virtues.

In Haitian mythology and folklore, Ezili is depicted as an astonishingly wealthy upper-class mulatto woman of luxury whose exquisite taste is revealed in her choice of flamboyant dresses (Métraux 1958, 97). She possesses a large collection of pink as well as blue dresses made of satin and silk, of sheer, embroidered, and lace-trimmed fabric; she also owns necklaces with ornate pendants, earrings, numerous wedding bands, and rings carved and decorated with jewels. All these accoutrements are kept in the ounfò's sacred chamber, and worn by devotees (male or female) who are fortunate enough to be possessed by her.

As lwa of love, Ezili is believed to be preoccupied with establishing erotic liaisons with male lwas as well as humans (Laguerre 1980b, 71). Indeed, her life as depicted in Haitian mythology abounds with scandals which, by normal standards of morality, would be considered disgraceful conduct. Her partners in spiritual *plasay* (concubinage) include not only her male devotees, but many lwas as well. Among the latter are Legba, Damballah, Gede, and Ogou and Agoue (the lwas of war and the sea), to name a few. Human devotees celebrate their spiritual bonds with her in a special ceremony of "baptism" or initiation (also referred to as a wedding ceremony) in the ounfò, in which they become her "husbands," bearing her name or variations upon it. But such a distinguished relationship with Ezili is not without its price: twice weekly, she requires of her husbands sexual abstinence from their human partners, of whom she is notably jealous; and she demands special food offerings on the day of the week that is reserved for her.

When Ezili comes to a Vodou ceremony in the body of a possessed devotee (male or female) she requires gifts in the form of money which she appropriates freely from the oungan and distributes among her male "companions." In return, she expects to be treated generously by them; she awaits the finest gifts that her devotees can afford, including expensive jewelry, French perfume, lace-bordered kerchiefs, silk underwear, and imported liqueurs. A festive meal that includes some of the finest dishes is also part of the ritual in Ezili's honor. In short, her devotees ration nothing when she visits the peristil; in everything that is done, there is always more than enough. She gives of her love abundantly in return for her devotees' gifts and devotion. Deren notes that Ezili's expectations may appear to transcend her poor devotees' financial resources, but in another sense, she is very much like them; she shares their impatience with life's economies and with the causes of excessive thriftiness (1972, 138).

So abundant is Ezili's generosity that any devotee becomes captivated by the freedom with which she is said to give herself. It is in order to feel her love that her devotees respond to her desires, however demanding they may be. Her cherished perfumes and soaps, cosmetics, French wines and champagnes are kept in a separate chamber for her use. At times, when her devotees cannot meet her demands, she manifests her Petro rage in the body of a possessed devotee as Ezili Dantò. In this persona, she pronounces their punishments, inflicting upon the recalcitrant devotees grim promises of horrifyingly painful diseases.

At other times, she becomes Rada's Metrès Ezili. In this persona, she manifests herself as a dejected old woman, whose body is so bent forward that she must support herself with a cane; her body is twisted, deformed by arthritis, and trembles when she walks. When Metrès comes to the peristil, her devotees participate in her physical pain by singing the plaintive song:

The Ville-Bonheur Church

Ezili, I have no bones [to support me]
I have no bones
Ezili, oh! I have no bones in all my body
Ezili, oh! I have no bones.

To this song Metrès replies:

Metrès Ezili in back of the gate [to Ginen]
I speak, speak, and they refuse to listen to me,
I speak, speak, my children.
Ezili in back of the gate
I speak, speak, they refuse to listen to me.

Such vivid depictions of Ezili's personae have given rise to special rituals performed in her honor. So prominent is she in Vodou's ritual cycles that its liturgical calendar consecrates three days to her annually. The oungan encourages the devotees who have caused her to weep to reconcile themselves with her in order to avert her anger against the community. Aside from the numerous festivities given in her honor in the ounfò throughout the year, Vodouisants also make a pilgrimage to the sacred site outside the town of Ville-Bonheur where she is said to have once appeared.

Oral tradition has it that Ezili appeared to a crowd as the Blessed Virgin Mary, in the branches of a palm tree near the waterfalls outside the town of Ville-Bonheur (in the central portion of the country). Overwhelmed by this unexpected event, the people fell on their knees in reverence to the Virgin. They summoned the white Catholic vicar of the nearby Ville-Bonheur parish to come and witness the apparition and to pray with them, but when he arrived, he could not see the Virgin, although everyone else could. He then accused the people of blasphemy and ordered the area closed. In order to suppress what he considered mere "superstition," he called in the local police captain, who placed guards in the vicinity with orders to shoot the apparition, but the Virgin is said to have moved to another tree at every shot. The Catholic priest then asked that the tree be cut down. It is said that those who were present saw the anger of Ezili Dantò rise in the air above the area. Additional guards were then placed to prevent anyone from returning to the site. As the Catholic priest returned home, word came that the presbytery had burned down and nothing had been saved. He is reported to have died soon after from a sudden paralytic stroke. The captain's fate was not as disastrous as that of the priest, for he was merely afflicted with a temporary madness that caused him to wander aimlessly throughout Ville-Bonheur and its surrounding area. He was healed soon after this incident, and returned to the place of the apparition to ask the Virgin's pardon. Fire subsequently burned the Ville-Bonheur church, a fire said to have been caused by the powerful anger of Ezili Dantò. The area of the apparition remained closed for a while, but when the nation's chief of police in Port-au-Prince heard of the Virgin's anger and the fates of both the vicar and the captain, he ordered the area to be reopened.

Today, the place where the Virgin appeared has become a sacred place to Vodouisants. Two waterfalls adjacent to the palm tree are said to have been carved into the hillside by her; one is dedicated to Damballah, and the other to Ayida Wèdo. It is also said that those who bathe in these waters will first be possessed and later healed. For these reasons, many pilgrims come to the falls throughout the year. But the largest crowd gathers on the anniversary of the Virgin's appearance, July 15, the Catholic holy day dedicated to the Virgin in Haiti. In addition to the Catholic masses sung in honor of the Virgin on that day, numerous Vodou ceremonies are held near the falls on the eve and on the night of the anniversary. Pilgrims tie blue and pink cloth girdles around their waists, colors symbolic of Ezili and the Virgin, and remove them when they reach the falls, ritualistically fastening them around neighboring trees. This ritual is one of purification by which pilgrims seek her protection from whatever defilement might threaten their persons or communities, thus ridding themselves of disease and misfortune. The Vodou ceremonies at the falls and near the palm trees, as well as the Catholic masses in honor of the Virgin at the Ville-Bonheur parish, occupy an important place in the complex rites of the liturgical calendars of the Haitian church and of Vodou. The feast is known today as the Fête de Saut d'Eau.

From these examples, it is apparent that the worldview of the Haitians and the motivations that underlie Haitian religious life cannot be understood unless the contributions of both Roman Catholicism and Vodou are held in mind. The symbiosis that characterizes the relationship between the two religions can be seen in two ways: first, as symbiosis by ecology; and second, as the system of identification by which Catholic saints are identified with Vodou lwas.

Symbiosis by ecology can be seen both in the calendrical observances of the Fête and in the location at which the Vodou festivities are held. Since no written record has survived of the original event or the early forms of the Fête, it is not possible to tell exactly what occurred, if indeed any event of that magnitude occurred at all. Because such stories about the apparition of the Virgin were common in Catholic European folk tradition around the latter half of the nineteenth century and the beginning of the twentieth, it is highly possible that a similar story was told by Catholic missionaries to arouse their parishioners' piety and reverence for the Virgin. In any case, Vodouisants have appropriated both the story and the Fête and have fitted them within the framework of their own theology. They have most likely modified the original story, and they have adopted a Catholic holy day for the performance of their own rituals. Thus, the Fête that commemorates the apparition of the Virgin can be seen as an attempt on the part of Vodou to adapt the church's liturgical calendar to itself.

Symbiosis by ecology can be further seen in the fact that the Catholic masses take place in the village, whereas Vodou ceremonies are celebrated in the countryside at the falls. In my field research, I found a marked change in the religious attitudes of the devotees as they traveled from the Vodou site to the village, and vice versa: in the countryside, they "served" the lwas by loud singing and by violent possessions, while at the church they showed more subdued devotion by quietly praying before the statues of the saints. During the entire period of the Fête, there were no Vodou ceremonies in the village. The devotees attended the numerous masses during the day of the Fête, received communion, and lit their votive candles to the Virgin and to the other saints that adorn the church's sanctuary. Moreover, I found that

Cloth girdles tied around trees near the waterfalls at Saut d'Eau

at the Vodou site the lwas were not revered by their Catholic names; rather, both oungan and devotees referred to the Virgin as Ezili, and to Saint Patrick as Damballah. Conversely, although the Vodou rituals were not hidden from church authorities, no mention was made of the lwas during the Catholic rituals. This reflects the mosaic quality of Haitian religious observance; for though the rituals of the two religions share the same day (and hence are juxtaposed to one another), they are celebrated not only at different times but also quite separately.

Symbiosis can also be seen in the identification of Ezili with the Virgin. As already noted, Vodouisants see Ezili as the pure mother lwa whose beauty is celebrated in many songs and poems. Yet she is also said to have had many children with numerous lwas. Vodouisants see no contradiction between the purity, or virginity, of Ezili and her plasay (concubinage) with humans or with the lwas. For as Deren rightly observes, the interpretation of the virginity of Mary in Vodou differs from that of Catholic theology: it does not refer to her physical condition, but to her beauty and transcendence, as one who does not belong to the world of the living. For a devotee to call Ezili (or Mary) a "Virgin" is to say that "she is of another world, another reality," and that her life transcends her devotees' financial and existential problems (Deren 1972, 144). To assert Ezili's virginity, then, is to say that she is untouched by the corruptions of the living. Vodouisants do not see her promiscuity as a sign of corruption, for plasay is commonplace in Haitian society. The mythology that depicts Ezili's persona mirrors the realities of Haitian life. Thus, the identification of Ezili with Mary is not based upon Mary's virginity, but upon her physical beauty and her persona.

The faithfulness of her devotees can be seen in the pervasiveness of the service that Vodouisants render to her. Throughout the country, her devotees pay their veneration to her in a more or less uniform way, for the personae which she expresses through their bodies present few local divergences. This uniformity can be seen particularly in the ubiquity of the lithographs throughout the country (even among the poorer folk) that represent her personae. Wherever such a lithograph appears (in Vodouisants' homes, for example), a flower vase generally sits on a nearby table. Although these lithographs, used by the church in the past primarily for the purpose of religious instruction, ostensibly represent the Virgin Mary in her various roles as these are depicted in the New Testament, in Catholic hagiology, and in Catholic oral tradition, they are nevertheless interpreted by Vodouisants as representations of the various personae of Ezili. In this way the *Mater salvatoris* becomes Ezili Dantò, the *Virgen de los dolores* corresponds to Metrès Ezili,

The Mater salvatoris or Ezili Dantò

Virgen de los dolores or Metrès Ezili

and the *Maria dolorosa del Monte Calvario* corresponds to Ezili Freda, another of her many personae (but this is purely an outsider's perception, for Vodouisants associate these lithographs with the Virgin, not under her Latin or her Spanish names, but solely under her Vodou names).[3]

The lithographs of the *Mater salvatoris* depict her as a black Virgin, holding on her left arm the black child dressed in pink. Around her head is a halo resembling the sun, and on her head is a golden crown decorated with jewels. Her robe and veil are of blue satin, bordered by golden fringes which match the color of her crown. On her right cheek are two parallel scars. The *Virgen de los dolores* is depicted as a white-skinned Virgin wearing a blue mantle and a veil with golden fringes. Her face is bent slightly forward and turned to her left just enough to reveal a tear flowing from her right eye. Finally, *Maria dolorosa del Monte Calvario* is depicted in a blue robe, with a golden crown, earrings, necklaces, and bracelets—all elaborately carved and decorated with jewels. Her arms are folded across her chest, in which is implanted a jeweled dagger. Her fingers are adorned with wedding rings of various styles. On a table before her, and on the walls behind her, are large golden and pearl heart-shaped medallions engraved with crosses, flowers, and the letter M. On each side of the table are golden vases containing flowers and plants.

Like all other religious symbols in the church, these representations of the Virgin, as well as the objects connected with her envisaged personae, have emblematic significance; some of these interpretations have never officially been part of the doctrinal teachings of the church, but they are part of the traditional beliefs, rituals, and folklore of Haitians, as well as of Catholics in many other parts of the world. There is a tradition in Catholic hagiology (Ferguson 1954, 75–76) that after the crucifixion of Christ, Mary visited many of the places associated with her son's life. In a moment of intense suffering, she prayed to be delivered from life. Soon after, an angel visited her and told her that her son had heard her prayer and that within three days it would be answered. The angel presented her with a palm branch, which she in turn gave to Saint John with the request that it be placed on her coffin. Mary also asked that all the apostles be present at her death; that wish was also granted. This account further states that at the moment of her death, Jesus appeared and carried her soul like a babe into heaven. Mary's body remained on earth and the apostles buried it soon after. The Assumption of Mary occurred three days after her death, when Jesus declared that her body should be reunited with her soul. He sent angels to her grave to carry her body into heaven where he crowned her "Queen of Heaven." He placed a golden crown decorated with many jewels on her head, and invited her to

Maria dolorosa del Monte Calvario or Ezili Freda

sit at his right hand. Hence, in the lithographs the crown and other jewelry are symbols of Mary's royalty.

In Catholic iconography, Mary's rings and circlets are universally accepted as a symbol of eternity. They also symbolize the eternal union that priests and sisters contract with the church. Thus, the ring of a bishop suggests his permanent "marriage" with his diocese, and the bridal ring worn by Catholic sisters is understood as a symbol of commitment to a religious life. The color of Mary's robe is that of the sky, and symbolizes heaven and heavenly love. Blue is the color of truth, because it always appears in the sky after the clouds have dissipated. Thus, blue has traditionally been associated with the Virgin, and in medieval paintings she is usually depicted as wearing a mantle of blue.[4] The tears and the scars on her face symbolize the suffering and loneliness that she experienced during and after her son's crucifixion. The image of the heart symbolizes understanding, courage, devotion, and love; when it is pierced with a dagger or an arrow, it symbolizes contrition, suffering, sorrow, repentance, and devotion under conditions of extreme trial.[5] In these lithographs the heart of Mary, pierced by a dagger, signifies sorrow as well as her devotion to her supplicants (Ferguson 1954, 151, 179).

Ezili in Haiti derives from diverse African ethnic religious traditions, the most notable of which are the Mami Water spirits found in various regions along the western coast of the continent (Brown 1991, 223–24). But most striking are the resemblances between the personae of Ezili in Haiti and those of Oshun in Nigeria and Ezili in Whydah, Benin. In comparing the personae of Oshun and Mary, one notes extraordinary similarities both in the symbols employed and in the significance of those symbols (Idowu 1973, 14, 73, 150; Bascom 1969, 90). These resemblances can be seen in the color blue and in the symbolic significance of jewelry—necklaces, bracelets, earrings, and crown—for both the Fon's Ezili and Yoruba's Oshun. The dagger, too, occurs in the depiction of both Oshun and Mary, although its symbolic significance differs.[6] It is these similarities between the Catholic symbols connected with Mary and those of Oshun and Ezili that have caused Vodouisants to identify Mary with Ezili.

It seems logical to assume that when the missionaries evangelized the slaves during the colonial period, they related the stories of the Virgin's life and made instructional use of the Catholic symbols connected with her, but that the slaves responded to such instruction by transfiguring these symbols in African terms. Although Catholic stories relating to the Virgin's life are no longer part of Vodou iconology, the Catholic symbols that were similar to Nigerian and Whydahian symbols, as related by the mythologies and oral traditions of the Yoruba and Fon, have been retained in Haiti. Thus, for example, although Vodouisants do not know the actual significance of Assumption Day (except that it is dedicated to Mary), Vodou ceremonies are held in Ezili's honor on that day in most ounfòs throughout the country. The Vodouisants come to invoke Ezili in matters related to marital problems or to childbirth, but, as in Nigeria or Whydah, Ezili's crown as depicted in the lithographs is a symbol of her royalty as the only female lwa who governs the universe among all the other cosmic lwas. Her necklaces, earrings, bracelets, jewels, and satin robe represent gifts from her lovers, the lwas and her male devotees. Her wedding rings symbolize her numerous love affairs. The scar and the dagger that appear in two of these lithographs (the *Mater salvatoris* and the *Maria dolorosa del Monte Calvario*) symbolize her occasional Petro anger when she is said to tear the flesh of recalcitrant devotees. The blue color of her robe becomes, as in Yoruba mythology, a symbol of her devotion and her love for her devotees (Bascom 1969). The Christ-child held by the black *Mater salvatoris* is not Jesus but one of Ezili's children born out of her relationship with one of the lwas. The halo around her head, Vodouisants say, is a symbol of her transcendent power and of her radiating beauty.

In the description of these symbols, one can note differences that are perhaps creole additions to the personae of the African deities. Among these is the identification of Ezili with the symbol of the heart, which appears in her vèvè. The heart may well have been borrowed by Vodou from Roman Catholicism, but it has also been transfigured and given new meaning: it is not a symbol of her love, but represents her womb—both the macrocosmic womb from which humankind and the world derive, and the microcosmic womb of woman in which the individual is conceived and from which it is born. A similar observation can be made about the letter M engraved on the heart medallions. According to Vodou iconography, it does not stand for Mary but for Metrès, the familiar form in which they speak of her or invoke her. In her vèvès, where a stylized form of the letter is superimposed on the figure of the heart, it symbolizes her feminine sexuality and her promiscuity (Deren 1972, 121).

In short, symbiosis by identification can be seen from two points of view. First, the efforts of Catholic missionaries gave the slaves a basis for identifying Mary with Ezili, whose envisaged mythological personae derive from both Nigeria and Whydah. Such identification, or rather such transfiguration of the African models, stemmed from the similarity between the symbols in European Catholic iconology and African traditional symbolism. Second, the Vodou use of the Catholic symbol of the heart and the letter M are clearly

Vèvè for Damballah and Metrès painted on a peristil wall

creole inventions, variations stemming from the personae of the West African Mami Water spirits and the Fon and Yoruba religious traditions. In Haiti, the heart and the M have become the symbols of femininity and sex. Such creole phenomena can also be seen in the personae of Metrès and Je-Rouge as depicted in Vodou mythology and as they are manifested in the peristil. In addition, symbiosis by ecology can be seen in the spatial juxtaposition of the performance of the rituals of each religion, in the separation in the use of ritual paraphernalia in two distinct locations, and finally in the use of the names of the saints and lwas by the devotees in different places.

Ogou: The Suffering General

Ogou came to Haiti from Nigeria during the colonial period. The Yoruba's Ogun is lord of fire, and by extension is the patron of all those, such as ironsmiths and welders, whose professions occasion its use. He is also the protector of all artists and workers who use fire to smelt metal, to fashion tools and weapons used in wars or in the hunt.

If Nigerians associate Ogun with hunting, it is because Yoruba mythology makes use of that image extensively in stories told about him. According to a Yoruba myth, before Olodumarè (the Godhead) shaped the world, Ogun came to earth frequently to hunt in the primordial, marshy wastes by descending from heaven on a spider's thread. When Olodumarè finally shaped the earth and arranged its contents, Ogun and the other gods came down to it from heaven to assume the offices assigned to them by Olodumarè. As they traveled the footpath that led to earth, they came to a place of "no-road," where the forest became so dense with trees, vines, and thistles that the deities could not cut a path, for the edges of their machetes were too dull; only Ogun possessed an instrument sharp enough to accomplish the task. Hence, the gods asked Ogun to make a way for them. He accepted this responsibility under the condition that he receive a worthy reward when they all arrived at Ilè-Ifè, their assigned headquarters. After a unanimous agreement among the gods, Ogun cut the way for them. When they arrived at Ilè-Ifè, the gods conferred upon Ogun the title of Osin-Imalè (Chief of All Deities). But, untamed hunter that he was, Ogun found it difficult to live in the city, and so he went to live in solitude at a place called Ori-Oké (Top-of-the-Hill). From there, he still undertakes his hunting expeditions and his wars on behalf of other gods or to fulfill his own needs.

Ogun's symbol is the machete. The Yoruba say that he is the one who goes "before the deities to prepare a road for them." This metaphor establishes his function as the one who makes the way smooth in the gods' spiritual encounter with humans. In this connection he is related to Elegbara (or Legba) who in Nigeria is the keeper of the gates, because he is said to open the way to human destiny for material and spiritual prosperity. Because Ogun is so well armed, the Yoruba also believe him to be the guardian of the entrances to temples and sacred groves throughout Nigeria. And, as at the temples, he also protects the celestial abode of the gods by stationing himself at the gates. For this reason, the Yoruba know Ogun as the "owner of wealthy houses, the owner of numerous houses of heaven." His eyeballs are said to be like flames of fire which project in all directions as he protects the possessions of the deities.

Haitians have not forgotten many of the Nigerian characterizations of Ogun. In Nigeria as well as in Haiti, he is characterized as having two personae: the one beneficent, and the other maleficent. As a beneficent god, he is the one to whom iron and steel are dedicated, as well as any implements made from them. He is also the patron deity of the farmers who use the hoe and the machete to clear the fields for planting. He takes charge of the work of surgeons, and in more recent times he has become a patron of barbers, locomotive crews, automobile drivers, and all who have to do with machines made from metal. The Yoruba and Haitians say that without him, people could not clear their fields or dig water holes to irrigate them, and animals could not be butchered or hunted. They also say that Ogun (or Ogou) is the master of smithing: he inspires the tool-makers in designing their wares. All those who use tools made out of steel or iron depend on him and owe him tribute. They become his devotees and make frequent offerings to him.

The Nigerian Ogun has been creolized extensively in Haiti, as Vodouisants have adapted his African persona to the country's history and national life. Just as his beneficent persona is characterized by constructiveness, his fierce nature is one of violence and destruction. In this role, he is identified with wars. He is said to march columns of warriors into battle, and to infuse their swords, arrows, spears, and machetes with his destructive power (Laguerre 1980b, 131–32). He symbolizes power, authority, and triumph in wars. Power and authority are identified with a person's political office, and Ogou is a political figure in Haiti. He has earned his rank by engaging in guerilla warfare against his people's enemies during both the Haitian Revolution and the American Occupation. He is sometimes depicted on the walls of peristils as a mortally wounded warrior who is unable to stay on his feet, upheld by his devotees on each side; his outstretched arms are thrown loosely over the shoulders of his supporters, while tears roll down his cheeks. On his left sleeve is a spot of blood symbolizing a wound acquired during his many battles. His drooping head, the profound expression of fatigue on his face, and the weight of his weakened body as it is supported by his devotees closely resemble the image of Christ at the deposition (Deren 1972, 132). Depicted thus in the body of a devotee in Vodou ceremonies, Ogou's broken body begs his devotees to sing:

> Ogou, I am wounded
> I am wounded, Ogou Papa
> I cannot see my blood is red
> I am wounded, Ogou Papa.

The affirmation in the third line of the song that he cannot see his own blood refers to his battle fatigue, and presumably to his near-comatose state caused by the excessive loss of blood.

But like the other lwas, Ogou in Haiti has many personae. As a member of the Rada nanchon, he is beneficent. Like the Yoruba, Vodouisants believe Ogou to be the guardian of the gates to the ounfò. In this function, he is depicted as brandishing a machete (or a sword) as if to strike thieves who would try to enter the sacred domiciles of the lwas. The iron armor that he wears makes his body secure, impregnable to his attackers' bullets. His fiery eyes are said to face the four quarters of space, allowing him to watch the four sides of the ounfò simultaneously. As Ogou Batala (or Obatala), he becomes the healer and is the patron lwa of surgeons and doctors. He is often depicted as preparing an herbal concoction into which he infuses the flames from his fiery eyes. In the body of a possessed devotee, Ogou Batala heals those devotees he thinks worthy by cleansing his hands over a flame and touching the parts of their bodies that he believes are affected by disease. Often Ogou becomes Ogou Badagri, who is related to the oungan's benevolent magic; in this persona, he assists oungans with the preparation of potions used to exorcise evil spirits that might cause disease in the bodies of members of the community.

As Petro's Ogou Feray, Ogou is the national hero, the general whom the devotees greet with military salute. Throughout Haiti he is symbolized by Haiti's coat of arms, which is depicted on the walls of many ounfòs. In the body of his devotees, this national hero is an impressive figure, for he presents himself as the general whose agitated pacing to and fro on the floor of the peristil conveys the pressures of battle, or grave conflict and urgency in a moment of crisis in the life of the nation. In such manifestations, he is said to reenact the pressures of war placed on the shoulders of Toussaint, Dessalines, and Christophe during the Haitian Revolution. Intense and ready to fight, he often brandishes his machete and cries out "Forward!" as if leading an entire battalion into the heat of battle.

As already noted in Chapter 1, in moments of brutal oppression, religious millenarianism can threaten a country's political stability by instilling a vivid picture of humanity liberated from its frustrations and stresses in situations of culture contact. This metahistorical dream of a happy future no longer tainted by oppression often inspires the members of such religious movements to see themselves as God's elect, whose violence can bring about the advent of the millennium. By the manifestations of his revolutionary spirit, Ogou Feray recaptures the early millenarian spirit of the slaves during the Haitian colonial period. As a national hero, he is a political leader who is said to have generated the violent spirit of the maroon raids on the plantations preceding the final stages of the Haitian Revolution. These raids did not entail the movement of massed troops led by a hero, but the tempestuous guerilla activities of the slaves whose overt passion to end slavery terrorized the planters. As a warrior, Ogou Feray is also a political figure. His leadership recalls the strict administration of Dessalines and Christophe. In any

Saint Jacques or Ogou

Vèvè for Saint Jacques painted on a peristil wall

country, politicians depend upon skilled oratory to gain the commitment of their followers. But the Haitian well understands that mere oratory does not denote an ability to lead. Like Dessalines, Ogou Feray is not merely a man of words. His power is revealed in Haiti's motto, "Liberty, Equality, Fraternity." To Vodouisants, these are not words that arouse a purely sentimental patriotism for God and country. Rather, they are calls to action. They must lead every Haitian citizen into actual battle. As in the days of the Haitian Revolution, devotees must conduct this battle with unreserved passion, secrecy, and intrigue in their efforts to throw off the power that restricts them.

Because Petro's Ogou Feray symbolizes the spirit of battle, he is identified with Saint Jacques (Saint James). Popular Catholic lithographs depict this saint as riding a horse, brandishing a sabre in the midst of battle, wearing a medieval French cap and a blue robe with a white collar decorated with golden crosses. On the ground are wounded bodies. Behind him is a medieval knight in armor carrying a white banner in the center of which is a red cross. In the background are lowering black clouds. This depiction derives from Spain, where Saint Jacques is known as Santiago. According to Catholic hagiology, Santiago (or Saint James the Great) is the military patron of Spain, who is said to have fought for the liberation of Spanish Christians from the Moors. Hence, the lithographs found in Haiti portray him in much the same way as do many Spanish paintings.

Although many of the Catholic symbols associated with Saint Jacques have been appropriated by Vodou's iconography, they have been given African and creole meanings. Santiago's sword is no longer a symbol of courage in his efforts to introduce Christianity among the Spanish Moors: first, it is seen not as a sword, but as a machete; and second, it has become a symbol of revolution in Haitian political life. Symbiosis by identification can be seen in this use of Catholic iconographic symbols to establish a parallel between the saint and the Vodou lwa.

The personification of Ogou has remained largely Nigerian, but there are nevertheless creole aspects of his personae that reveal themselves in the ceremonial and national lives of Haitians. These include ritual ceremonies offered in his honor in the peristil, and those that relate to such calendrical observances as Independence Day and Flag Day. Ogou Feray in Vodou is the patron lwa of those who are now serving in the military, and of those ancestors who, in the history of the country, have given their lives in revolutions against political and religious oppression. In this role, he is analogous to the Nigerian Ogun, who is also the patron lwa of war. But his persona also reveals certain creole developments. First, Vodouisants have fitted his function as patron lwa of war into the context of Haitian history. Unlike the Nigerian deity, Ogou Feray is not identified so much with warriors as with the envisaged personae of the black generals and leaders who fought during the Haitian Revolution, in the Caco revolts against the American Occupation, and in the Vodouisants' resistance against the church's Anti-superstitious Campaigns. In this context, he is not only the lwa who inspired the leaders of these revolts, but also the hero who reembodies the bravery of Haiti's national heroes. Second, in Haiti his persona has acquired a millenarian aspect. It has already been noted that in some millenarian movements, the re-creation of the remembered past has a symbolic value that lends new meaning to the present: the members of such movements not only see certain past events as admirable, but deem the re-creation of them as "magical formulae" designed to release them from the frustrations of their oppression. The character of such formulae is explicable on the basis of the devotees' psychological association with the past—"psychological," in the sense that they feel that by behaving as their ancestors did, they will in some undefined fashion be able to retrieve the more desirable aspects of their ancestors' situation. In Ogou Feray's persona, Vodou is differentiated from African religious traditions in that it manifests this millenarian character by re-creating the past ritualistically in the peristil.

As already noted, just as Vodou ceremonies can be seen as the reliving of the first act of creation when Bondye fashioned the world, so the manifestations of Ogou Feray in the body of his devotees represent the re-creation of the Haitian Revolution. Such re-creation is confirmed by the mention of the names of Boukman, Dessalines, or Christophe by those who harbor Ogou's spirit within them; the ancestral spirits of these national heroes are thus manifested in the bodies of possessed devotees. A Vodou ceremony in honor of Ogou Feray is therefore an archetypal ritual, a reenactment of the beginnings of a nation. The experiences of the revolution must be relived, the sounds of battle must be heard once more, and the blood of the sacrificial pig at Bois Caïman must again seal the lips of those devotees who were present at the ceremony.

In short, from the point of view of symbiosis by identification, the study of Ogou's personae in Vodou mythology can be seen as the religious adaptation of Catholic and African symbols. These adaptations have two aspects. On the one hand, Vodouisants adopted the Christian symbols in the lithographs that were parallel to Nigerian mythology, and translated them into African terms. On the other hand, these adaptations also mean that the personae of Ogou, particularly that of Ogou Feray, were extracted from their African mythological context and were fitted within the framework of Haitian history. This creole addition to Ogou's personae became clothed with a dormant millenarianism in an African people whose initial contact with Europeans during the colonial period engendered in them a desire for freedom from political and religious suppression. In this sense, Ogou becomes the symbolic embodiment of a struggle to attain a higher ideological, nationalistic order which is a perfected Haiti. Every participant in a ceremony in honor of Ogou, then, participates with the nation's heroes in their sufferings, their struggles, and the deeds that save the life of a nation.

But such gradual creolization—that is, the religious adaptation of Christian and African symbols to Haitian history—derives from Haitians' (and the slaves') disengagement of Christian millenarianism from its theological context and their adaptation of it to their own personal longings and national goals. Indeed, if African religion had not come into contact with European Christianity during the colonial period, it is doubtful that Vodou would have manifested such a millenarian character at all, for by and large, most African traditional religions have developed their millenarianism only recently as a result of their contact with Christianity. To Vodouisants (as perhaps to the slaves), the millenarian dreams taught by the Catholic priests in Haiti provide a reason for living.

Just as the millenarian character of Christianity has a practical use, so too does the persona of Christ. It is interesting that there exist some poignant parallels between Christ and Ogou (Deren 1972, 132). Aside from their reputations as physical and spiritual healers, both have been sufferers and martyrs for a cause that they believed would save their people. Just as Christ's death and resurrection served to save humankind, so too Ogou's manifestations as Boukman, Dessalines, and Christophe represent the death and resurrection of his devotees at every Vodou ceremony in his honor. Nevertheless, while a student of religion can easily see parallels between Christ and Ogou, Vodouisants are, doubtless, unconscious of them. While the depictions of Ogou on the walls of the peristil recall, to a European observer, the paintings of Christ at the deposition, Vodouisants establish no conscious parallels between Christ and Ogou, for most have probably never encountered that Christian image. And even if they had, or if these depictions of Ogou were unconscious imitations of it, it would only testify to their reinterpretation of Christ in terms of their mythological representations of Ogou.

Rather than being identified with Ogou, or with any other lwa for that matter, Christ represents Haiti herself. His sufferings and crucifixion resemble the struggles and eventual death of the national heroes who gave their lives for the liberation of Haiti, and his resurrection suggests the political rebirth of a people whose millenarian dream is to be free from political and religious oppression, not only historically but currently. Today, ceremonies in honor of Ogou Feray symbolize not only martyrdom and death, but the resurrection as well, for possession symbolizes the revivification and the re-creation of the lives of the national heroes. Moreover, for present-day Vodouisants, as was probably the case for the slaves, Christ's promise of heaven has been replaced by a more tangible ideal—a new order that includes their political and religious freedom as they envisage them. And Christ's promise of victory over the miseries and frustrations of their existence, and over death itself, is symbolized in the continuing struggles against political oppression.

Agoue: The Powerful Marine Creature

If spiritually the body is made of the same elements out of which the cosmos is fashioned, physically it encompasses the fabric from which the ocean derives. For, according to Vodou mythology, the blood, like the cosmos and the sea, has motion deriving from an inherent force originating from the Creator. Likewise, the salty perspiration on a person's face contains in it the chemistry of the sea. Just as Vodouisants are in harmony with the universe, so too are they and the sea "old acquaintances": as residents of a mountainous island, they not only see it from wherever they stand, but receive their very subsistence from it. This fact adds to their sense of physical affinity with the sea and reinforces their conviction that their bodies derive from it. Because the sea is so important to Haitians, it holds a unique place in their mythology, and is characterized by a persona. The sea is under the jurisdiction of a lwa who serves a vital function in Haitian ceremonial life: the Haitian Neptune, Agoue Taroyo, whose wife is La Sirènn.

Agoue is a powerful lwa in Haiti, but unlike the other Rada lwas, his power is limited. Just as the fish can live only in water, so is Agoue's power limited to the sea that he rules—to the sea, its creatures, its flora, and the fishermen's sailboats that cleave its waters. And the rituals in his honor, unlike those for the other Rada lwas, are performed almost entirely at sea. The preparations for these rituals involve the entire community and begin several days before the ceremony. They are extremely elaborate and usually expensive to the devotees.

Several days before the ceremony, the community gathers food offerings and selects a sacrificial ram for Agoue. A raft is constructed and stored in the local ounfò, to represent Agoue's banquet "table." Flags and tablecloths in blue and white, Agoue's symbolic colors, are washed and ironed. They are placed around the banquet table where Agoue's divine guests are envisaged to sit. The drums too are made ready: they are painted white and blue for the occasion, and their skins are tightened so that their resonance will awake the deity from the depths of the sea. The sacrificial ram (*dogwe*) is fattened for several days with a special diet; it is well bathed and cleansed with a fusion of purifying leaves steeped in water and indigo so that its color is blue. On the banquet table the oungan (or mambo) arranges the bottles of imported wine and champagne, plates of cooked chicken, rice and beans, hot cornmeal, and vegetables and fruits of all sorts; the ram's feet are tied and it is laid in the middle of the raft to one side.

Agoue's invited guests at the banquet include his wife, La Sirènn, the sea aspect of Ezili; Ogou; the Wèdos; Azaka; Damballah and his wife Ayida; and Ezili, with whom he is said to have had many love affairs. The presence of these lwas, which enhances the importance of the ritual ceremony to Agoue, is usually symbolized by flags bearing the vèvès of each lwa. These flags and vèvès are arranged in the order in which the lwas are envisaged to sit around Agoue's banquet table. At the foot of the table is drawn a crab or fish for Agasou, Agoue's lieutenant, and at the head is drawn a fish for Agoue himself.

The elaborate arrangement of the table takes an entire day. The ounfò and its courtyard are filled with devotees and guests who have come prepared to stay the whole day. Like the raft, the peristil too is beautifully adorned for the occasion. Strips of blue and white paper are plaited over the potomitan (center pole) in a pattern similar to that found in the maypole ceremonies performed in many communities across the United States. Other strips are strung around the potomitan, and hung from the ceiling to form inverted arcades that appear to radiate from the potomitan itself. In one corner, some devotees arrange a makeshift altar: a straw bed (nates), at the head of which they place two pillows for Ezili and her consort Agoue. In the center of this bed, where the hearts of the bodies would lie, they place a bouquet of roses, and a conch shell to symbolize the nuptial bed. Flower vases, food offerings, and Catholic lithographs of Agoue and Ezili are also placed at the head of this nuptial bed.

As for the responsibilities of the oungan or mambo, they must convene the community on the appointed day, and arrange for the rental of trucks to carry the devotees, the raft, and the ritual paraphernalia to the shore— as well as managing hundreds of other details of a secular nature. In addition, they must attend to their clerical duties in making sure that the rituals are performed correctly, for to lead a people in the service of a lwa is to teach them the importance of making him happy by revering him both with sacred words and with objects appropriate to his personae and tastes. Hence, the oungan or mambo must inspire interest and devotion among the people, attending to the needs of some who are discouraged, while keeping the enthusiasm of others within manageable limits.

On the appointed day of the ceremony at sea, the devotees make the final preparations. They load the raft with all its contents on the bed of one truck, along with all the ritual accoutrements: a blue-and-white wedding cake prepared for the occasion, ason, lambi (conch shell), drums, ceremonial flags, banners, baskets of food, and the sacrificial ram. The devotees then climb onto another truck, and the convoy proceeds toward the sea. As the devotees sing, the trucks arrive at the end of the road near the shoreline, where the raft and all the ritual paraphernalia are loaded onto a small sailboat. After a relatively long voyage on the open sea, and standing near the mast which serves as the ambulant potomitan, one of the devotees sounds the lambi to announce their solemn arrival at their destination. Called Zile, it is an island below the sea where the sky and land are believed to meet. It is there also that Agoue is said to reside and where the cosmic banquet is to take place. After some ritual preparations, including the singing of various songs and incantations to the lwas, the men aboard gather around the raft and push it overboard into the sea. There, Agoue is said to rise from the depth of the ocean to carry the food offerings to his banquet table on the sea floor.

Because the fish is often identified with Agoue, it has become an important symbol in Vodou art. Vodouisants draw it wherever special objects are baptized in Agoue's name: in the ounfòs, in their homes, and on fishermen's boats. The fish is also an important symbol in Christian art, for it is the symbol of Christ, the five letters of the Greek word for fish (*ichthus*) being an acronym for the Greek words for "Jesus Christ, Son of God, Savior." The Vodou symbol of the fish was not borrowed from Christianity, however; rather, it derives from Fon mythology. Agoue's name corresponds to that of the Fon sea deity, Agbê, who is also identified as a fish. According to Fon traditional beliefs, Agbê is a member of the sky pantheon. He is said to have taken the shape of a fish soon after creation when Sogbo, the head of the sky pantheon, sent him down to establish himself in the sea. His responsibility is to preserve life "below and above the waters of the sea" (Herskovits 1963, 2:151). The Fon believe that Agbê not only protects fishermen when they are at sea, but also protects all the marine creatures. As Sogbo's son, Agbê is related to many other deities of the sky pantheon, including Gbadè (Badè in Haiti), the wind, who is said to be astute, capricious, and intractable; he is the most headstrong and undisciplined of all the deities of the sky pantheon (Herskovits 1963, 2:153).

In Fon mythology, Sogbo is believed to watch over the earth. Among her many responsibilities, she is above all the guarantor of the rain that waters the fields. Although she gave control of the sea to her son, she did not instruct him to cause the rain to fall, but to send water to the skies whenever she needed it. Gbadè, the wind, is her messenger. The Fon and the Haitians believe that the deity of the wind descends to the waters of the ocean where the sea and the sky meet at the horizon; after gathering the waters, he ascends to the sky, where the cosmic deities later pour them onto the earth. Although Sogbo has been forgotten in Haiti, Vodouisants say that Agoue is

intimately related to all the cosmic deities. He is related to Legba in his personae as sun and moon, for both of these plunge into the sea, travel across
the cosmic waters of the abyss below the earth, and rise into the sky. Agoue
not only shares his dominion over the water with Damballah, but also serves
as a support for Damballah's body as it arches itself across the sky to provide
a path for the sun.

From these details, one can infer that Agoue is Fon in origin. His name,
persona, and function in the universe, and the myths and symbol connected
with his persona, are all essentially Fon. Because Agoue's symbol is the fish,
Vodouisants have identified him with Saint Ulrich. This identification derives from lithographs that depict Saint Ulrich as holding a fish in his left
hand. Seated on a wall outside a church, Saint Ulrich wears a priest's robe—
a symbol of his devotion and humility. He is surrounded by poor people
whom he instructs in the Christian faith. This depiction derives from the
legends in Catholic hagiology in which he is said to have ministered to the
poor and downtrodden. As bishop of Augsburg, he is said to have spent his
life among the disadvantaged, comforting the sick, consoling the downtrodden, preaching, and undertaking the task of a vigilant pastor. After a long
life, he died of illness in 973. His sanctity was attested by so many miracles
during the twenty years following his death that Pope John XV canonized
him in 993 (Butler 1956, 3:27–30).

Although the symbols in the lithographs of Saint Ulrich are intended to
signify his sanctity and humility, his devotion to Christ, and his service to the
poor, Vodouisants have interpreted them in African terms. This observation
can be supported in several ways. First, Vodouisants do not know the story
of Saint Ulrich's life and make no mention of it in their rituals to Agoue; the
saint's robe, which ought to symbolize his poverty, has been interpreted as
a symbol of Agoue's royalty as a cosmic lwa. Second, the fish is no longer a
symbol of Ulrich's Christian evangelism, or that of Christ as Savior, but has
become the symbol of Agoue's domain. Third, although Vodouisants use
the lithograph in their ritual to Agoue, at no time do they mention Saint
Ulrich's name; rather, they see in that image the depiction of a lwa whose
persona recalls that of Agbê among the Fon. Fourth, the entire Vodou ritual
is essentially non-Christian.

Although Agoue's name derives from the Fon, much of the mythology
associated with him derives from Nigeria. The Vodou word Zile itself derives
from the name of the Yoruba mythological city Ilè-Ifè, the headquarters of
the deities, the entrance of which is believed to be a cave or grotto that
leads directly to the royal city. Ilè-Ifè is thought to be the "original home

of all things" in the universe, "the place from which the day dawns," "the enchanted holy city," and the home of divinities and mysterious spirits. According to Yoruba oral tradition, the gates leading to Ilè-Ifè today are open to no one; in mythological times, however, when men and women were allowed to visit the city, the deities treated their visitors royally with food and drink. In return for the deities' hospitality, visitors brought offerings of food, wine, and flowers with them which were placed at banquet tables specially arranged for their visits; humans were then allowed to participate in the festivities and to share the food with the gods (Idowu 1973, 13). Although the different cosmic deities are said to reside in various places throughout the universe, they often gather in the city for banquets and other festive occasions. These striking similarities between Zile and Ilè-Ifè establish a parallel between Haiti and Nigeria, which is seen not only in the mythology of both countries but in some of the rituals that derive from this myth as well. According to Bolaji Idowu, the Yoruba consider many caves to be important shrines in Nigeria (1973, 126–27); when they visit these shrines they bring large quantities of food and other offerings, which they place as presents to the deities at the entrances of the grottoes. This would explain why the ritual to Agoue is so elaborate, and why it involves such a large amount of food—for in their ritual to Agoue, Vodouisants believe that they are providing food for the cosmic lwas' banquet held in Agoue's cave beneath the sea.

From these various details about Agoue, several conclusions can be drawn. First, Agoue's persona and the fish that symbolizes him derive from Benin. Second, Agoue's identification with Saint Ulrich is based neither upon the saint's life nor upon the symbolic Christian significance of the fish, but upon purely pictorial details; once again, symbiosis by identification can be seen in the reinterpretation of Catholic hagiology in African terms. Third, although Agoue and the fish are Fon in origin, the forms of the Vodou ritual to Agoue resemble those in Nigeria. Like the Yoruba, Vodouisants say that their mythological city is the place from which humankind derives. In Vodou, humanity's beginning is symbolized by La Sirènn's womb, in which the body acquires the chemistry of the sea. The entrance to both Zile and Ilè-Ifè is said to be like that of a cave. The numerous offerings that Vodouisants bring to Zile are parallel to those which the Yoruba bring to their sacred caves, and the banquet of the lwas in Zile is also similar to the festive meals held in honor of the deities in Yoruba mythology.

In the Vodou ritual, symbiosis by ecology is also evident in the spatial juxtaposition of Catholic and Vodou paraphernalia. The arrangement of the altar near the nuptial bed in the peristil resembles that of the altars in many Catholic churches in Haiti. But the mosaic quality of this symbiosis is most particularly seen in the spatial juxtaposition of Catholic lithographs of the saints, palms, vases, flowers, and the white tablecloth, to the conch shell, to Ezili and Agoue's nuptial bed, and to the numerous vèvès painted on the flags for each lwa believed to be present at the ritual.

Finally, the spatial juxtaposition of Catholic and African ritual symbols and the incorporation of Yoruba and Fon mythological details into Vodou myths about Agoue are creole phenomena unique to Haiti. As already noted, the ethnic diversity of the maroon republics during the colonial period would have permitted the blending of religious traditions from both regions of West Africa. On the other hand, the occasional contacts between Catholicism and African traditions caused by the infiltration of runaway slaves from the plantations would equally account for the incorporation of Catholic symbols into Vodou's theology. Hence, the simultaneous use of Vodou and Catholic ritual paraphernalia in the same Vodou ritual can be explained by the frequent contacts between the religious traditions, both during the colonial period and in Haiti today.

Bondye: The Old Man in the Sky

Although Vodouisants use the Christian name for God when they speak of their deity, many of their concepts of him recall those of the Godhead in Africa. As do many West Africans, Vodouisants conceive of Bondye anthropomorphically: he is venerable, just, and aged but not aging. His gray hair commands awe and reverence. Like the president of the country, he is the chief administrator, the executive, the politician, who provides for the welfare and the liberty of his people. This is why Vodouisants say that like the president, Bondye commands, rules, speaks, and judges his subjects.

Bondye is the creator of the universe. He is the great architect and the carver of the universe. Just as the potter forms his work with his hand, so too Bondye fashioned the universe, giving it the shape that it has today. As creator, he manifests his power in every part of the universe. He is the guarantor of motion: the motion of the astral bodies, the wind, and the waters of the sea and rivers; the motion seen in the growth of the vegetation; and the motion implicit in the passing of human generations and the determination of existent things. In the lwas, he manifests his power in their roles as the chiefs of the universe; as Bondye's children, the lwas are representations of the many aspects of his personality. In humankind, Bondye manifests himself as the vital force that animates the body. He infuses his power into the gwo-bon-anj, the divine element that ensures the movements of the thoracic cavity in breathing. He is the guarantor of the continuity of life.

Bondye is also the king of the universe. He is above all humans and all the lwas. He dwells above the heavens; his majesty is unique because it surpasses all. He is the *Gran Mèt* (Grand Master) whose resplendent majesty, like the Yoruba concept of God, is so great that it is said to fill the entire sky that arches itself over the earth. In this omnipotence, Bondye has full hegemony over the universe. His will is absolute. Like Olodumarè among the Yoruba, he is seen as the enabler who can achieve all ends. Events in the world occur because he ordains them; without his aid, nothing in the world can happen.

Bondye is all-wise, all-knowing. Like that of the Fon's Mawu, Bondye's wisdom is perfect and infallible. Because the lwas, like humans, can make mistakes, Bondye calls them to his heavenly tribunal to account for their deeds. But Bondye can never make mistakes. Since Vodouisants believe that his power pervades the cosmos, they say that a part of Bondye's perfection is instilled in the world. He is said to have more than one thousand eyes which face the four cardinal points of the universe. He can therefore face all cosmic directions simultaneously. This is why Vodouisants claim that their supreme deity is the discerner of hearts who can see both "the inside and the outside." He sees humankind's hidden secrets—the crafty designs as well as the good intentions.

Unlike humankind with its changing intentions and emotions, Bondye never changes. Vodouisants say that he is constant, even if he manifests himself in the midst of the changes that humans and things undergo in the world. Indeed, humans can grow old, things can decay, the appearance of a hillside can change because of the never-ending erosion of its soil, but deterioration is not part of Bondye's persona. His "ever-living-ness" is like a formidable mountain whose age cannot be counted by any conceivable mathematical system and whose "physiognomy" never alters.

Bondye is also the source of all benefits. Through the lwas, he is the giver of all good things: children, wealth, good living, good character, and everything else that exists for the good of human beings. Vodouisants believe that even the lwas draw their sustenance from Bondye. As the Haitian proverb puts it, "Bondye wills, Bondye takes"—meaning that as the ultimate source of all good things, Bondye exercises his free will in giving or in taking away every good gift. Although this proverb is repeated often by Haitians, it does not express a mere rationalization for the loss of wealth; for in poverty there is indeed little that can be lost. Rather, these words denote the Haitians' sense of fatalism caused by their vision of a destiny that, they feel, can surely crush them. Such fatalism is revealed in the language that they often use in responding to questions related to their general welfare: to the question, "How are you?" (*Kòman sa?*), the conventional answer is, "One is observing" (*Nap gade*), meaning that one has little control over one's destiny, but can merely observe passively the successive events of life.

These phrases are not the theatrical exaggerations of a people given to complaint. On the contrary, the Haitian has a sense of the comic. For although these answers are conventional, they are always followed by concrete exemplifications—descriptions that incite laughter from both parties. Moreover, these colloquial statements express a life in which the present conditions are indeed difficult to endure. Despite the frustrations and anxieties of life, however, Vodouisants can also smile as they prepare to leave a companion by saying "We'll talk again" (*Na pale ankò*), or "We'll see each other again" (*Na wè ankò*), and prudently adding, "if the Good Lord wills it" (*si Bondye vlé*)—for their belief in Bondye always assures them of his continuing protection against life's misfortunes.

If Vodouisants see Bondye as the main force in their future, it is because they also see him as the author and the disposer of their destiny. As in most West African religions, Bondye is the controller of human life; he punishes and rewards his devotees. A Haitian proverb states that "the justice of God, it is like a cart pulled by bulls!" (*jistis Bondye, se kabwèt bèf!*)—meaning that Bondye, like the sluggish motion of a cart pulled by mighty bulls, is slow to anger, and that at times his punishment, like the strength of bulls, falls severely on humankind. Although Vodouisants apply this proverb in a variety of ways, they often cite it to indicate that Bondye's punishment of the strong and wealthy, though slow in coming, is certain. For it is the wealthy and mighty who often occasion the sufferings of the poor. It is also those in high places who often prevent the poor from participating fully in Haiti's national life, or, as Jean-Bertrand Aristide noted, who will not allow the downtrodden to "sit at the table" with them as guests and to partake of the same meal (Aristide 1990).

Bondye's authority is such that it can be questioned neither by humans nor by the lwas. Vodouisants recognize his supremacy by paying special tribute to him on one day each year. On that day, the lwas are said to rise to the "highest realms" of the sky, where they meet in council in Bondye's court above and express their gratitude for his sustaining them. But such a recognition must also be an example for humankind, for although humans cannot enter Bondye's abode they must, as in Africa, observe ritual libations, which the oungan or mambo performs at the beginning of each ceremony. As among the Yoruba, Vodouisants must also recognize Bondye as the first and the last. They give him ultimate preeminence in their lives.

Although these Vodou concepts of Bondye's personae would be shared by most Christians and by non-Christian Africans, there are two main concepts not yet mentioned that contribute to Bondye's Africanness. First, unlike the Christian God, Bondye is not the only supernatural power ruling the universe: as in Africa, he is at the head of large nanchons of lwas who govern the universe. But the enormous nanchons of lwas are, as variations upon a theme, manifestations of one Principle who is Bondye. Each is a facet of the same Principle; each manifests the grandeur of that Principle; each incorporates various aspects of the universe—life-force or fecundity, the protective or paternal, some aspect of the chthonic, the telluric and subtelluric realms (Ginen), some of the positive as well as the negative aspects of the Principle that they represent. Because the lwas symbolize various facets of Bondye, when Vodouisants speak of him, they do not refer to one deity only but to the *vodou*, meaning the entire community of lwas. Second, unlike the Christian God, the idea of Bondye's holiness implies his profound separateness and aloofness from the world. Vodouisants' conception of Bondye's transcendence is so dominant that they give scant attention to the possibility of his immanence. Although they believe that he participates in their lives and that he is good, they say that he is so transcendent that he cannot be bothered with petty human problems.[7] Because Bondye is so remote from the earth, Vodouisants do not pray to him directly; they offer no ceremonies in his honor, nor do they believe that he can possess anyone during rituals— as the Haitian proverb notes, "Big lwas do not mount little horses" (*Gwo lwa pa monte ti chwal*), meaning that Bondye is too powerful to manifest himself in a devotee's body. Although, much as in Africa, the oungan pours a libation to Bondye at the start of each ceremony, it is a formal gesture, symbolic merely of Vodouisants' recognition of the omniscience of Bondye. Hence, Rudolf Otto's idea of the holiness of God in the sense of the active, the swift, the consuming numinous does not describe the Vodouisants' concept of Bondye (1928). Vodouisants have applied these ideas to the lwas to whom they pray and sing, and to whom they offer their sacrifices and offerings.

Bondye's aloofness from the world can be seen in many Haitian folktales, which depict him as being at times so remote from the activities of the lwas and of humans that not only is he fooled by them but his power is often placed in competition with that of the lwas—a competition in which he is

often the loser. One such story tells of a ceremony given in honor of the
lwas and presided over by one of the most powerful oungans in the country.[8] This ceremony was to be held for seven weeks without interruption.
Devotees came from all corners of the island, bringing with them hundreds
of rams, chickens, and pigs as sacrifices. Because there were so many attending the ceremony, a large battery of the finest drummers in the country
were brought to the enormous peristil erected specially for the occasion.
Everyone danced and sang; the celebration continued day and night without
pause. The ceremony was so well attended and so successful that it made
the earth a pandemonium. The noise was deafening, and Bondye heard it—
indeed, the noise was such that he could neither sleep nor concentrate on
the administration of the affairs of the universe.

After a week or so, the patient Bondye decided to put an end to the
noise. He sought the assistance of some of the more adept lwas to conduct the investigation for him. First, he sent the crafty Legba, who upon
his entry into the peristil was met by the possessed oungan. After the customary handshake in the form of a cross and the pouring of libations at the
four corners of the universe, the power of the lwas in the oungan's body
spun Legba counterclockwise; he became possessed and disappeared into
the darkness, as he wandered away from the place of the ceremony. When
a week had passed and Legba did not return, Bondye became angry. The
noise of the drumming and the singing was becoming increasingly disturbing. Bondye sent Damballah. When Damballah approached the peristil, the
oungan shook his hand and twirled him around. Damballah poured libations at the four corners of the universe, for a lwa had entered his body. He
too was sent away, wandering in the darkness. Another week passed, and
Bondye sent the bold Gede, the shy Zaka, the chivalrous Ogou—but they did
not return. Finally, Bondye decided to investigate the matter himself. After
searching a day or so for the peristil, he arrived at the gate of the ounfò. The
oungan greeted him with the customary handshake and spun him around,
after which Bondye poured libations on the ground and went staggering
aimlessly into the courtyard of the ounfò, for he too was mounted by a lwa.[9]

Although this tale relishes the superiority of the lwas over Bondye and
presents him as having been tricked by the oungan, it must not be thought
of as sacrilegious. Like the Fon's concept of God, it expresses Vodouisants'
concept of Bondye as the master of the world, the head of the nanchons
who reserves the right to command the lwas, sending them to earth as his
emissaries. But the tale also reveals Vodouisants' concept of him as a benevolent, patient deity who, in spite of his anger, is slow in interfering in

human affairs. More importantly, it expresses the remoteness of Bondye; as a supreme ruler of the universe, he is unaware of the nature and place of human activities.

Vodouisants express the Africanness of Bondye most poignantly in their interpretation of the lithograph that depicts him. It shows the bust of an aged man, with white hair and a white beard, piercing through gray clouds. His uplifted arms extend over the breadth of the universe. In his right hand, he holds a cross. Directly under the bust, and in the middle of the picture, is an eye from which beams a sunburst, lighting the entire lithograph. Piercing through the clouds on the right side of the picture is a hand holding tipped scales: on the left, lower pan of the scales kneels a penitent, before whom is an angel dressed in pink and holding an open scroll; on the right pan stands a monstrous black creature whose skin is stretched over his bones. Across the bottom of the lithograph are depicted four scenes, of which the two on the left symbolize the beneficent forces in human life, and the two on the right, the maleficent forces. These four depictions may be interpreted as charity, the healing power of God, the ensnaring power of evil, and violence. Charity is symbolized by an old mendicant with a walking stick receiving in his hat alms from a young couple. The healing power of God is symbolized by a young woman lying in bed, with angels of God at the head and foot of the bed who have come to heal her. The ensnaring power of evil is symbolized by a bedridden young man. At the side of his bed, in the foreground of the picture, are two black creatures similar to the one on the scales: one holds the young man's right hand to pull him down to the pit of fire below, while the other pulls on a rope around the young man's neck. In the flames is a black snake, which appears to have just bitten the young man's left arm. In the last of the four scenes, violence is symbolized by two men, one of whom beats the other with a stick and leaves him bleeding on the ground. At the very bottom and in the center of this lithograph, death is depicted by a skull and crossbones.

As in other lithographs, these symbols invoke several themes connected with both scriptural imagery and Christian hagiology: the omniscience of a just God, the Last Judgment, and the victory of the beneficence of God over the maleficence of Satan. According to Catholic iconography, the black clouds symbolize the day of judgment at the end of the world. This image derives from the book of Revelation, where the angel of God "came and stood next to the altar with a golden censer; . . . the smoke of the incense rose . . . before God. Then the angel took the censer and filled it with fire from the altar and threw it on the earth; and there were peals of thunder, loud noises,

Bondye

flashes of lightning, and an earthquake" (8:1–5). The omniscience of God is symbolized by his place above the clouds and the eye in the center of the picture. The eye derives from several scriptural passages, among which is 1 Peter 3:12, which states that "the eyes of the Lord are over the righteous, and his ears are open to their prayers." In Catholic iconography, the eye in combination with the golden rays of light symbolizes God as the light of the world.

The hand holding the scale is that of Saint Michael, the archangel of God who is traditionally said to be the "general-captain of the hosts of heaven, the protector of the church militant in Christendom" (Ferguson 1954, 97–98). It is Saint Michael who will sound the last trumpet to announce the final judgment of humankind at the end of the world. It is also his "office" to receive the immortal spirits of human beings; he will weigh them on the scales separating the good from the bad. As "protector of the Hebrew nation," Saint Michael is the guardian of the redeemed against the temptations of the adversary of God, the prince of hell, who in the lithograph is represented by the black creature on the other side of the scales. The scales tipped by the penitent symbolize the Christian concept that true penitence always outweighs evil. The angel holding the scroll before the penitent represents the unveiling of his deeds on the day of judgment.

In Catholic iconography, the snake represents Satan. This image does not derive from the book of Genesis, but from later biblical and extrabiblical interpretations, such as the book of Revelation where Satan is vividly portrayed as the enemy of God (chapter 16). From this Christian use of the snake to portray Satan, it would seem logical that in the depiction of the ensnaring power of evil, the snake rises from the fiery pit of hell under the young man's bed and bites him as Satan pulls him down to hell.

Although these symbols may have explicit meanings in Catholic tradition, Vodouisants have interpreted them in terms of their own tradition. In this lithograph, Bondye is no longer the Christian God, who on the last day commissions Saint Michael to separate the good from the bad; indeed, as already noted in Chapter 3, since Vodouisants have only a vague concept of heaven or paradise and an equally vague concept of hell, it would seem logical that they would not see them depicted here. Moreover, since Vodouisants, like the Fon, believe that the body at death is always reshaped by Bondye (or Mawu), they cannot conceptualize the Christian idea of the end of the world. Rather, to Vodouisants this lithograph comes to represent Bondye as they perceive him in the personae of the major cosmic lwas. The omniscience of Bondye is symbolized by his image in the sky: his extended arms recall the Vodou and Yoruba concepts of God whose body shapes the vault of heaven. The eye and the golden rays are given a double significance. On the one hand, the eye symbolizes Bondye's omnipresence; although it has the same meaning among Christians, Vodouisants' interpretation of it recalls that of the Yoruba: it is one of Bondye's thousand eyes with which he watches over the universe. On the other hand, the same Vodouisants say that the eye with its golden rays symbolizes the sun, or Legba, who watches over the destiny of humankind. As described above in Chapter 4, the cross that Bondye holds in his right hand represents the four cardinal points of the universe (over which he rules and which he sees simultaneously), in both a macrocosmic and a microcosmic sense. The scales below the eye no longer symbolize God's justice but have come to represent man's destiny as planned by Legba. Hence, the kneeling penitent becomes a male devotee, and the pink angel, Ezili.

In the first of the four images at the bottom of the lithograph, the old mendicant becomes Gede or Zaka; the stick, their symbolic phallus; and the hat, the "plate" from which Zaka receives the food that he eats rapaciously when he invades the body of a devotee. In the second scene Ezili is being helped by emissaries of Bondye in the delivery of one of her newborn; the snake becomes Damballah who is thrown out of Ezili's bed during delivery. The bedridden young man in the third scene becomes a devotee who is being eaten by two of Kafou Legba's bakas; in that same picture the snake becomes Simbi, who has been sent to harm the young man. Finally, the fourth depiction shows the violence of Ogou Feray who strikes his enemy during times of war; his stick becomes a machete, and the bleeding man the oppressor. The bones and skull are symbols of Baron Sanmdi.

Thus, Vodouisants see this lithograph as depicting the numerous personalities of Bondye. The Christian themes dealing with the omniscience and justice of God, the Last Judgment, and the power of good over evil are displaced by the omniscience of Bondye (as understood in the African sense); the destiny of man as planned by Legba and Kafou Legba; Bondye's persona as the guarantor of the continuation of human generations, as symbolized by Legba, Ezili, and Damballah; the effectiveness of Bondye's power in magic and sorcery, as represented by the bakas and Simbi; violence as symbolized by Ogou Feray; and death as represented by Baron Sanmdi. The Africanness of Bondye can be further seen in his remoteness as symbolized by the clouds, in his immortality as seen in the grayness of his hair and beard, in his omnipresence as represented by the eye, and in Vodouisants' interpretation of the cross.

There is no doubt that in the Vodou concept of Bondye one finds symbiosis in two ways: in the adoption of the Christian name "Bondye" to designate the Godhead, and in the translation of his persona (as well as the symbols that describe that persona) into African terms. The causes for this translation can be found in Haitian history, both during Vodou's formative period in the eighteenth century and during the early years following independence. As already noted, slaves came to the island from different parts of Africa, and during the repression of the colonial period and the difficult years that followed they could well have forgotten the various African names for the Godhead. That they adopted the Christian name "Bondye" can be explained by several observations.

First, the need for Africans (and those after them) to communicate verbally with the missionaries would have required them to use "Bondye," which (as already mentioned) is the creole derivative of the French "Bon Dieu" for God. The numerous police rulings as well as the later prohibitions concerning Vodou would have necessitated the use of "Bondye" for God rather than the African names in order to conceal their commitment, and hence to avoid their arrest by local authorities. Moreover, the loss of the various ethnic African designations for the Godhead would have been further occasioned by the infrequent use of those names in Vodou ceremonies; as we have seen, the name would have been seldom mentioned, save for the pouring of the customary libation at the beginning of each ceremony. In contrast, and as Roger Bastide noted, the clandestine practice of Vodou throughout Haitian history would have fostered the recollection of the names of many of the African minor gods as well as the mythological depictions and rituals associated with them (Bastide 1971, 69).

Second, the diversity of African ethnic traditions represented on the island during Vodou's formative years would have encouraged adoption of "Bondye" as a generic name for God. Thus, "Bondye" would have become a symbol of ethnic and linguistic unity. Moreover, although the maroon republics were isolated in the mountains of Saint-Domingue, and indeed maintained virtually no contact with colonial settlements or with the church, the infiltration of newly arrived slaves from the plantations into these republics would have reinforced the adoption of the name "Bondye," since the new arrivals undoubtedly would have brought it with them.

In short, an analysis of Bondye's persona suggests several conclusions. First, symbiosis by identification can be seen in Vodouisants' rendition of the persona of the Christian God and the symbols that depict it in terms of African concepts of God. Second, the pressures of contact between European and African cultures, as well as the diversity of African traditions on the island, would have necessitated the selection of a linguistically intelligible and generic name for God. While the Christian name "Bondye" was adopted, African concepts were poured into Vodou's theological mold.

In addition, symbiosis by ecology can be seen in Vodouisants' religious attitudes toward Bondye. Just as, in the peristil, Vodouisants never pray directly to Bondye, so too in the Catholic churches, the devotees rarely address their invocations to the Christian God, but invoke the saints (or the lwas) as their intermediaries. Although Vodouisants (who call themselves Catholics) believe that God is the ruler of the universe, they do not accept him as a personal one. We thus find a mosaic juxtaposition in the priest's celebration of a Mass to his Christian God before a congregation whose God is essentially African.

....

CONCLUSION

....

In light of the foregoing analysis of the personae of the Vodou lwas, we can draw several conclusions about symbiosis, as well as about the current and future relationship between Vodou and Roman Catholicism in Haiti.

(1) We noted in Chapter 1 that in a situation of culture contact in which a dominant society threatens the religious beliefs of the dominated by exerting political and social pressures upon them, the members of the dominated culture may feel the need to emphasize cultural elements that have fallen into desuetude, stressing their own distinctiveness in order to reduce the stress created by the situation of contact. In such cases, the dominated society may form contra-acculturative movements whereby it attempts to emphasize the values of its original way of life, to move aggressively to restore those values, and, even in the face of apparent impotence, to throw off the restrictive power of the dominant culture. In order to emphasize their own values the members of the dominated society need to revive their ancestral traditions. This re-creation of a remembered past is never identical to the real past, since it is a selective process based on "collective memory." A society may choose to emphasize those elements of its past that can be given a symbolic value to lend new meaning to the present and to the future; such a vision of the past may be seen as a formula for present and future salvation. In short, the members of the dominated society may feel that by selectively reviving their past, and by behaving as their ancestors did, they will, in some undefined fashion, help to re-create a desirable mode of life in the manner of their ancestors, both in the present and in the future.

Such revivification of the past was characteristic of the slave religion during Haiti's colonial period and can be seen in many ways. First, as already noted in Chapter 2, the isolation of the maroon republics from European cultural influences allowed the preservation of whole enclaves of African traditions in Vodou. Second, the shape of the religious beliefs and rituals in each of these republics depended upon a number of variables: the "blending" of ethnic traditions represented, the particular religious traditions of the leaders, and the uneven demographic distribution of ethnic groups.

Together, these factors would not only cause some ethnic traditions to dominate over others, but would also account for the regional divergences that existed among the different maroon republics during the colonial period and that still exist in the various ounfòs throughout Haiti today.

Despite these divergences, however, the names of many African gods (or variations on them) remain more or less ubiquitous in Haiti today, and the personae ascribed to them resemble those of Africa. Thus, as we have seen, Damballah derives from Dã and symbolizes, both in Haiti and in Benin, cosmic motion; Agoue, the marine lwa, who is Agbê in Benin, is associated with the sea in both countries; and Badè, the wind, derives from the Beninois Gbadè. The prominence of any of these lwas in the theology of any one ounfò depends upon the dominant tradition in that region or the particular proclivity of the oungan or mambo.

Other lwas have creole names in Haiti, but their envisaged personae and the symbols and rituals associated with them derive from many parts of Africa. Hence Bondye, whose name comes from Christianity, has retained many of the characteristics of West Africans concepts of the Godhead. Zaka, whose name probably derives from the religion of the indigenous Indians of Haiti, takes his envisaged personae from Benin's Yalóde. Moreover, although Vodou beliefs and rituals are not identical to their African counterparts, they continue nevertheless to be stamped with the mark of West Africa. Indeed, Vodouisants' beliefs about the compartments of the human soul, the burial and reclamation rites, and the significance of names given to persons initiated to the lwas in Vodou recall many of the religious traditions of the Old World from which they derive.

In Chapter 1 we also noted that the re-creation of a remembered past by a dominated society can take on millenarian and apocalyptic aspects if the pressures resulting from the situation of contact are not alleviated. The idea of the millennium symbolizes a metahistorical future, based upon the past, in which the world will be inhabited by a humanity liberated from the oppressions and stresses of the present. The members of the dominated society construct an image of a new social order that will in time replace the present one. This image may be a vivid one, and they may believe that its advent will be heralded by brutal means, including wars and cataclysms in which the supernatural will participate. As the bearers of good tidings and the elect of the gods, they may move aggressively to accelerate the advent of the new order, which they see as an abrupt jump onto another level of existence. This explains why millenarian dreams can be threatening to any government. The outcome of millenarianism in the dominated culture is dependent upon the intensity of the contact situation between the two cultures: the threat of disruption may weaken if the conditions of extreme frustration and hardship lessen, but if suffering and frustrations become more intense, it may well revive.

During the Haitian colonial period, slave revolts were led by such prophets as Macandal and Boukman, who envisioned the new order to be their eventual return to their fatherlands and who taught their followers that the gods would reappear to take them there. In the postcolonial period, Ogou took on a new persona, and was integrated into the framework of Haitian history. He became identified with the heroes of the revolution, the symbolic embodiers of Vodouisants' national ideal, the bringers of a higher order which was to be a perfected Haiti. Vodou's millenarianism reappeared during the American Occupation, the Antisuperstitious Campaigns, and more recently in 1986, in 1990, and again in 1991, during weeks of *dechoukaj* (reprisals) in which the masses took to the streets throughout the country to avenge the murders, the theft, and the civil rights abuses of the tontons macoutes during the twenty-nine years of the Duvalier oligarchy. Thus, Ogou Feray has inspired Haitians to resist political and religious suppression many times in their history. His persona reflects Vodou's ability to re-create the past, for in every ceremony in his honor, Vodouisants relive the political and religious traditions of their national past—a symbolic reenactment of the Haitian Revolution.

In short, we can safely say that the large extent to which the names (or variations upon them) and the personae of the African gods are remembered in Haiti implies that Vodou is a religion that is continuous with African religious traditions. By this I mean that Vodou could not be classified as an African religion, but as an African-*derived* religion whose theological development has allowed its adherents not only to rekindle many of their African ethnic traditions, but to transform these traditions according to their environmental, sociocultural, and economic situations.

(2) We have seen that the continued contact between Roman Catholicism and diverse African religious traditions on the island has caused Vodouisants to incorporate the names or personae ascribed to the saints as well as the symbols associated with them into an already existing divergent core of African ethnic traditions. The choice of a particular saint to correspond to a specific African and Vodou lwa is based on the similarity of symbols between Catholic and African iconographies. Legba, for example, whose symbol is the rooster, becomes Saint Peter; Damballah, the gentle snake, be-

comes Saint Patrick; Mary's beauty as depicted in the lithographs causes her identification with Ezili; Saint Ulrich's association with the fish leads to his identification with Agoue; and so on. Similarly, the maroons' contact with the religious traditions indigenous to the island caused them to incorporate those traditions into their theology as well. Thus Zaka, the Haitian Pan lwa whose name derives from Amerindian religions, becomes Saint John the Baptist, but his persona corresponds to that of Yalóde in Benin. We thus have a clear situation of symbiosis by identification.

Symbiosis by ecology can be seen both in the mosaic juxtaposition of Catholic and Vodou objects on the same pe or altar, and in the temporal separation of Catholic and Vodou rituals. Mosaic juxtaposition was observed on the makeshift altars erected at the wakes, and at the ceremonies in honor of Agoue. The temporal separation of the two religions was seen in the funeral cycle of observances where the Catholic ceremonies were performed at the church or at the home of the deceased and those of Vodou at the ounfò, and in the distinct locations of the Vodou and Catholic rituals accompanying the pilgrimage to the waterfalls for Ezili and Damballah.

Just as tiny pieces of a stained glass window are juxtaposed to each other to make a whole, so too fragments of the Catholic ritual performed by the prèt savann and those performed by the oungan coexist in the same location to make the whole of the Vodou ritual. Such is the case, for example, in Vodou baptisms, which, as we recall, entail ritual performances by both the prèt savann and the oungan. Moreover, the presence of both prèt savann and oungan in the hierarchy of the ounfò illustrates the coexistence of the two religious traditions in symbolic form. And finally, symbiosis by ecology can also be seen in Vodou's adaptation of the Catholic liturgical calendar to the religious observances in honor of many of the lwas. We observed in Chapter 5, for example, that the Catholic holy day reserved for the Virgin in Haiti was adopted for ceremonies in honor of Ezili and Damballah.

(3) We further noted that Vodou was a tertium quid, a creole phenomenon deriving from the historical, socioeconomic, and political contexts of Haitian history. Hence, many of its traditions bear little or no resemblance to those of Africa or Europe. Such is the case with most of the Petro lwas, especially with the persona of Ogou Feray whom Vodouisants have identified with insurrections and political revolutions. The indigenous nature of Vodou can also be seen in the names ascribed to many of the lwas: while Zaka's persona recalls that of Yalóde, his name is Amerindian.

Moreover, we may recall other observations made about the creole nature of Vodouisants' religious lives, whose traditional practices are dissimilar to those of both Africans and Europeans. These include: the identification of the lwas with the saints, the separate sites of the Catholic and Vodou rites, the coexistence of Vodou and Catholic ritual paraphernalia on the same pe, and the temporal juxtaposition in the ritual manipulation of each of these objects in the same Vodou ceremonies. Finally, Vodouisants' simultaneous practice of Catholicism and Vodou, as well as the correspondences in the liturgical calendars of the two religions, achieve the creole character of Vodou.

....

VODOU AND CATHOLICISM

Vodou is thus an amalgam of religious traditions from three widely separated regions, all of which have persisted throughout Haitian history and have proven essential to the people's cultural and religious life. The Vodou lwas and the imagined mythological personae or faces associated with them have been shaped by the events in Haitian history. The lwas provide the mythological links that permit every Haitian to identify with Africa as well as with Europe. At the same time, the creativity with which Vodouisants have assimilated New World beliefs to pour them into a European and African mold clearly shows their cultural and religious identity with Haiti's indigenous cultures as well.

But a glance at Vodou beliefs, as discussed in the preceding pages of this book, reveals that perhaps one of the most striking features of Haitian society has been the tenacity with which Haitians have held to their Vodou lwas, and the multifaceted ways in which these lwas have ordered Haitians' religious lives, both in the past and in the present. The ubiquity of Vodou in Haitian life has been the underlying theme of this study, and has also been the principal thesis of much of the ethnographic research about Haitian culture cited throughout this book. But, as Janheinz Jahn noted, perhaps the most effective vehicle to characterize the persistence of Vodou in Haitian life is Haitian literature (1961, 56–57). Such is the case with Jacques Stephen Alexis's novel *Les arbres musiciens*, which recounts the story of a wealthy family living in the small village of Fonds-Parisien during the time of the last Antisuperstitious Campaign in 1941.

In this novel, Léonie Osmin was a mother who worked very hard to rear her three sons and to ensure their formal education. Edgar became an army officer; Diogène, a Catholic priest; and Carles, a lawyer. As the story unfolds, the church influenced the state to acquire some land to build a church in the village. The state sent functionaries to Fonds-Parisien to study the matter. During that same period, Edgar was named commandant of the district, while Diogène was appointed the local curate. When the functionaries arrived, they found that Vodou was practiced openly in the district. Under pressure from the state, and in the spirit of the Antisuperstitious Campaign, Edgar and Diogène began their crusade against Vodou. They sought out every ounfò in the vicinity, to destroy its altars and force its devotees to renounce their religion. By their crusade, the Osmin brothers made a powerful enemy: namely, Bois d'Ormes Létiro, a famous Vodou papalwa (high priest) who had inherited the leadership of an old ancestral shrine from an African patriarch who came to Haiti as a slave during the colonial period. Bois d'Ormes realized that the church and the state were united against him, and that they wanted to eradicate from the community the legacy that he had inherited from his ancestors, which he had worked so hard to maintain.

In a moment of despair, Bois d'Ormes wondered why his ancestors had fought for Haiti's independence: "Why did Dessalines live, if the whites [European priests leading the campaign] come to take our land again?" He asked Carles, "How is it that the city police have now called whites to give our land to them when they had not dared to take it themselves? If the whites give you an order and you obey, the one who gives you the order reserves the right to do so. But what if the order is wrong?" He reminded Carles that he was a lawyer, and therefore an educated man, and asked why it was that the whites suddenly wanted to destroy Vodou: "What have we done to them? I am old, my hair is white and my head trembles, my steps are not as decisive as they once were, I thought that I had learned a great deal through the years, I don't understand." Carles was ashamed of his two brothers' beastly treatment of the old man. He noted that he was young, and hence had no answer to Bois d'Ormes's question, except to say that behind his brothers' endeavors to destroy the shrine and its contents were "powerful men, foreigners, whites. . . ." Carles affirmed that his brothers' behavior posed a far greater threat to the lwas than to the state or to the church. He confessed that he believed in neither God nor the devil, but trusted only the land, and respected all that came from the earth. Like the banana, the manioc, and the maize of Haiti, the lwas came from the earth. Vodou was like the maize: it survived the devastating fury of the hurricanes, and the dry, torrid heat of the tropical summer. "Why does the maize grow here, and not wheat?" he asked. "Our sun is hot, and the maize grows despite the heat, despite the use of our hands and the unsophisticated tools with which we cultivate the land. . . . The whites want Haitians to renounce their religion for that of the whites, but Vodou is like the maize of Haiti; the religion of the whites is like the wheat. It cannot grow in Haiti" (Alexis 1957, 269–70).

A few days later, Bois d'Ormes wandered by a lake with Gonaïbo, a young woman living in Fonds-Parisien. He told her that he was old, and felt death's terror looming about him. "All my life," he said, "I have suffered and struggled to maintain the legacy of my African ancestors who founded this shrine. I have cultivated the land that they left me, helped their descendants and their children, and tendered the offerings to their altars. . . . Now it is time to rest my old, tired body in the earth," the place where the lwas reside. "A voice cries within me, and it tells me that it is you that the lwas will choose [to continue my work]. . . . Alone, you will struggle to gain knowledge [of the lwas and the ancestors], but the lwas will give you the clairvoyance" to understand the mysteries of the earth. "You will suffer Gonaïbo. Didn't I suffer? Suffering saves, Gonaïbo, you will never be unhappy, never . . . you will have peace in your heart. . . . Promise me not to search the sound of thunder and lightening so as not to heed the call [of the lwas]" (Alexis 1957, 356).

Like Carles, Bois d'Ormes could have been distressed about the future of the lwas in Fonds-Parisien. But he did not discuss his fears about the disappearance of the lwas with Gonaïbo. Instead, he drew from his pocket a golden chain. Balancing it on his thumb, he said to the girl, "Do you see this, child?" Then he lifted it; mustering as much strength as he could draw from his old, gnarled body, he cast it into the water as far as he could. Bois d'Ormes then walked toward the water, entered it, and sank deeper and deeper into it as Gonaïbo watched him disappear completely from sight. She wondered if the old man had drowned. Had he committed suicide? Was he performing a final death ritual? Extraordinary stories were told in the community about his magical powers, such as his ability to move rocks from a distance; no one understood his behavior, and Gonaïbo thought that he might never return. But as she looked over the horizon in search of the old man, she saw his twisted body rise slowly out of the water and come closer and closer to her. Between his teeth, he held a large gray fish. Kneeling, he dropped the fish onto the ground, opened its belly with his teeth, searched its entrails, and found the golden chain. Then he rose and walked toward Gonaïbo, placed the chain around her neck, and said, "Go Gonaïbo, go, let me be" (Alexis 1957, 358).

Because several acts of terrorism against the church were committed by members of the community in response to the campaign against Vodou, the Osmin brothers perceived Bois d'Ormes's presence as a serious threat to the welfare of the inhabitants of Fonds-Parisien. Accompanied by soldiers, Diogène, the curate, went to the site of the shrine with the intention of overturning its altars and burning it in keeping with the spirit of the campaign. When they arrived, they found that Bois d'Ormes had burned it himself, preventing its desecration by profane hands. Standing before the blaze, Bois d'Ormes addressed Diogène. He told him that the lwas were "immortal like the gods of eternal Africa," and that they would never allow the state or the church to raise their iniquitous hands against the shrine. He added that although it had been destroyed, one day it would rise again "in the same spot, greater and higher, more beautiful, like the lwas of eternal Africa" (Alexis 1957, 359).

Bois d'Ormes had depicted his sentiments about his religion; he had described the immortality of the lwas. In the face of persecution Vodou, as symbolized by the chain, may seem to disappear, but one day, several generations later, it will rise again. The wisdom of old sages like Bois d'Ormes may die today, merely to reappear in the future in a young child like Gonaïbo. For below the water, in the navel of the earth, is Vilokan, the mythological city of the lwas. These lwas will rise again and again, as Bois d'Ormes rose out of the water, to make themselves known to their devotees' progeny. The fragile wheat, like European culture, can never withstand the torrid sun of the tropics, nor can it achieve the stature of the banana tree. The lwas, like bananas, are rooted in the earth and grow on the land. Just as the cultivation of fruit requires the grower's full attention, so too devotion to the lwas requires the devotees' abiding service. Or as Carles seems to suggest, like the maize, which is cultivated with primitive tools like the hoe, Vodou appears to many as unsophisticated, but it will resist the most determined and tenacious efforts to eradicate it.

But if, as the characters of the novel seem to suggest, Vodou is such an integral part of Vodouisants' religious lives, so too is Catholicism. Manuel, a character in Jacques Roumain's novel Gouverneur de la Rosée, describes the distinction between the two religions, as well as their pervasiveness in Vodouisants' lives. Manuel says, "There are the affairs of heaven and the affairs of the earth; that makes two and they are not the same thing. Heaven is the pasture of the angels; they are happy; they do not have to attend to eating and drinking" (Roumain 1944, 14). But the earth is a daily battle with the complex problems of life: "Life's resignation is treacherous; it is discouragement. It breaks your arms; one waits for a miracle from Providence, with rosary in hand, doing nothing. One prays for rain, for harvest, one recites orisons. But Providence is the good will of the Negro not to accept misfortune" (56).

Later, he affirms: "When the drums beat, it affects the pit of my stomach. I feel an itching in my loins and a current in my legs, I feel I must enter the circle" (56).

If Catholicism is identified with heaven, Vodou is associated with the earth. And if Haitian writers say that the lwas "have to do with the earth," and hence cannot be uprooted from Haitian life, it is because Vodou fulfills important functions in Haitian society that are distinct from those of Catholicism. Aside from its healing power through magic, it maintains the vision and the hope of the lwas' assistance in enabling its devotees to cope with the poverty and famine caused by the incessant erosion of arable soil by the torrential rainfall of the tropics. Moreover, the oungans and mambos are powerful individuals in Haitian society, for they do not merely officiate at Vodou ceremonies, but fulfill important civic as well as political functions which the Catholic priests cannot perform. Often, local authorities will call upon Vodou priests to furnish character references on behalf of members of the community.

But Catholicism too is integral to Vodouisants' lives. Apart from the social services provided by its schools and hospitals, its rituals offer a means through which its communicants can participate in Haiti's official culture. Their children's baptisms, confirmations, and first communions, their marriages and funeral masses, provide occasions for social intercourse. And it serves, as it did in the formative years of the republic, as a means by which Haiti maintains contact with the outside, providing opportunities to participate with other nations in common international ventures.

Because of the importance of both Vodou and Catholicism to Haitians, it is doubtful that either of them will ever disappear from the country—but the continued contact between them may produce changes in both. As mentioned in Chapter 2, if Haitian society remains stable, and if the country's political life is free of revolutions, it is possible that syncretism may develop between the two religions in the future. This possibility is strengthened by the ecumenical spirit of Vatican II, and by the overwhelming support given to the Salesian Father Jean-Bertrand Aristide ("Titid") by voters during the December 1990 presidential election.[1] Aristide's government lasted merely nine months; it was toppled on September 30, 1991, by a military coup. But the complex issues that initiated the coup did not change the fact that, since 1986, the Haitian clergy has had to acknowledge Vodou as a vital force in Haitian political and social life, and its oungans and mambos as powerful and influential figures in Haitian religious life. Haiti's March 1987 Constitution guarantees religious freedom to all its citizens, and hence legally grants to Vodou a status equal to that of the church.

The provisions of the new constitution have helped to foster an atmosphere of religious openness throughout the country in recent years—an openness in which Vodouisants have enjoyed a religious freedom reminiscent of the days of Faustin Soulouque. On a recent trip to Haiti, I heard what was perhaps one of the rare moments in Haitian history: the radio and television programs broadcasting general news about religion included events, not only in the life of the church (both Catholic and Protestant), but those of Vodou as well.[2] Moreover, a significant change in the church and among its clergy has occurred in the domain of the arts. The church has recognized the talents of Haitian artists, even though many of them are Vodouisants. Many parishes have allowed local artists to paint biblical scenes on the walls of church sanctuaries. These murals are colorful representations of Haitian life. Christ, the saints, and the apostles are black; they are depicted amidst the towns and cities of the country, even near what appear to be ounfòs.

In the domain of ritual, the church has been swift in assimilating Vodou elements into its liturgy. In many rural parishes, Vodou songs with new Christian words are used as church canticles. While attending Mass at one prominent provincial parish, I observed an event that heretofore would have been unthinkable: like the oungan in the ounfò who pours rum libations at the four corners of the peristil floor at the start of a ceremony to recognize Bondye and all the lwas, the curate poured libations of water at the four cardinal points before the celebration of the Eucharist, as if to acknowledge the presence of God, the saints, and all the lwas in the cosmos. Also, for the first time in Haitian history, drums have been allowed in the rituals of some rural parishes; locally produced woodcarvings have begun to replace the European statues of the saints in the sanctuaries; and Sunday morning sermons inveighing against Vodou are seldom heard.

If the current efforts at indigenizing the church continue, the sanctuary may one day replace the peristil; sacred rattles and other Vodou ceremonial paraphernalia may be assimilated into the church's rituals; and the Vodou lwas and the myths associated with them may well replace the saints and Christian hagiology. In short, the recent efforts on the part of many Haitian clergy to creolize the church have brought it closer to Vodou. At the same time, Vodouisants as well as Christians have been granted the right to practice their religion according to their culture and conscience.

Despite the recent, steady growth of evangelical Protestantism (which has traditionally opposed both Catholicism and Vodou), and the religious freedom enjoyed by Vodouisants since the Duvalier oligarchy, the status of Catholicism in Haitian society differs from that of both Protestantism and Vodou. It continues to enjoy special privileges accorded to it by Haitian law, for it receives financial support from the government; priests' salaries and travel fees are subsidized partially by public funds; and the repair of many church buildings, parochial schools, and hospitals is also partially funded by the Haitian government. In contrast, Vodou and Protestantism enjoy no such privileges and obtain no official subsidy from the government. Although Protestant sects and denominations are sustained by local and foreign contributions, local oungans and mambos are supported entirely by their devotees, a growing number of whom are members of the upper classes; Vodou edifices are erected and repaired using whatever funds their oungans or mambos can expropriate from the devotees.

An examination of the relations between Vodou and Catholicism indicates that the future of Catholicism in Haiti rests upon a number of considerations. There is no possibility, as the novels by Alexis and Roumain suggest, that Vodou will ever be eradicated from Haitian society, because, as noted throughout this book, it is interwoven so completely within the fabric of Haitian life. Indeed, its resilience in the face of the Antisuperstitious Campaigns, as well as in the face of the intransigent hostility of the clergy attempting to destroy it in the past, attests to the steadfastness that Vodouisants have demonstrated toward their lwas. Although both religions have changed significantly in the past and will continue to do so in the future, Vodou's adaptation to Haitian culture far exceeds that of the church. Such adaptation has been possible precisely because of Vodou's flexible structure in the hierarchy of the local ounfòs, and its inherent ability to incorporate, as in the religion of the maroon republics of the colonial period, divergent local folk traditions into its theology and practice. This same ability to incorporate local beliefs and practices—to give local "flavor" to its religious traditions, as it were—has resulted in the heterogeneous nature of Vodou today. Catholicism, in contrast, has not been as flexible, at least until recently. Its clergy have sought to preserve the church's *depositum fidei* in order to safeguard those religious traditions which, in the eyes of many Catholics, have maintained and enhanced the church's prominence in Haitian social and political life. But if the church is to survive in Haiti in the future, its clergy will need to concede to more changes than those mentioned earlier in an effort to adapt Catholicism to the country's changing culture. They will need to reevaluate the church's mission as well as its function in Haitian society.

This reevaluation should entail the continued cognizance that Vodou is an integral spiritual reality in Haitian cultural life, and that to oppose it means in effect to oppose the culture of the very people whom the church is claiming to serve. Moreover, like Vodou, the Haitian church will need to become doctrinally more flexible, and to make provision for its parishes to assimilate the local indigenous traditions of the people whom they serve. In short, if Catholicism is to survive in Haiti, it will have to become genuinely Haitian, both in doctrine and in practice. It will have to "de-Europeanize" (or "demythologize") itself, free itself from its cultural and historical contexts, accelerate its eventual "Haitianization" (or "remythologization") in its direct engagement with Haitian culture. It must allow Haitians the opportunity to exercise their own resourcefulness in their religious practices, to take their destiny into their own hands, and to determine once and for all the fundamental choices necessary to ensure the formulation of, and adherence to, their own genuine religious traditions—whether these be purely Vodou, or a Vodounized Catholicism.

....

GLOSSARY

....

(This glossary contains terms used in this book as well as others that are frequently used in theological and ritualistic contexts in Vodou.)

Ago A ritual exclamation used in the sense of "Amen."

Angajan A pact between a lwa and a person; a business transaction in which a person seeks the help of a lwa in malevolent magic in exchange for his confirmed service to the deity.

Anj A lwa—usually used to refer to a mèt tèt or a guardian lwa.

Arada (Rada) *See* Rada.

Ason The sacred Vodou rattle, the property of a oungan, a mambo, or a oungenikon. It is made of a small calabash that has a handle-growth. After the calabash has been dried, a small hole is made in the handle into which are inserted small pebbles, beads, and animal vertebrae. Tied to the handle is a bell; both are used to call forth the lwa at ritual ceremonies. It is usually decorated with several strings of beads of various colors.

Asòtò A very large drum used at ritual ceremonies. Some measure as much as five to six feet in length.

Axyon degras A prayer which is usually pronounced by the prèt savann before every Vodou ceremony.

Ayibobo *See* Ago.

Ayida Wèdo The wife of Damballah.

Bagi A room containing an altar dedicated to a lwa. A ounfò may have as many as three to four bagis, depending on the financial resources of the surrounding community.

Baka An evil spirit which roams at night and which takes the form of an animal.

Baron Sanmdi A member of the Gede family.

Basen A pool usually constructed or dug in the ground in the courtyard of the ounfò in which Simbi, Agoue, or Damballah may reside.

Batèm A baptismal ceremony at which numerous objects used in the ounfò are consecrated to the lwas.

Bato Agoue A specially constructed raft on which offerings are placed for Agoue, the spirit of the sea.

Baton A long stick or a crutch used by Legba.

Batri The Vodou orchestra, composed of drums (usually three) and ogan.

Batri maconik A special rhythmic beat produced by clapping the hands and beating the drums to symbolize the rapping on the door of the underworld, the abyss of the dead, or the world of the lwas.

Benyè The one who bathes the body of the deceased.

Bizango Vodou secret society, reportedly known for its practice of zombification.

Boa A phallus—often used to refer to Legba's or Gede's penis.

Bòkò A sorcerer. He is to be distinguished from a oungan in that a bòkò deals solely with malevolent magic.

Bondye The all-powerful deity who is at the head of all the Vodou pantheons. The Demiurge who rules the universe. (From the French "Bon Dieu.")

Bosal A Vodou adherent who has not been initiated. One whose lwa is untamed and uncontrolled. The term originates from the colonial period, when it meant a newly arrived slave.

Boucan (Boukan) A bonfire lighted at a Vodou ceremony. The term is related to the *boucaniers*, or buccaneers, who often dried their meat by lighting a fire in the courtyard of their settlement.

Boula The small Rada drum.

Boule zen A ceremony involving the burning of a jar believed to contain the gwo-bon-anj of the deceased. Performed several days after the person's death in some communities in Haiti, the ceremony has the purpose of dispatching the spirit to its abode.

Case kanari Part of the cycle of death rituals in which a large clay jar is broken in a ceremony in the ounfò to symbolize the death of a person.

Ceremoni A Vodou ceremony.

Ceremoni kay An elaborate ceremony performed to encourage the lwas to favor their place of residence.

Chay A magical power deriving from the lwas enabling a person to change the course of events.

Chwal A horse. A person who is possessed or "mounted" by the lwa.

Còk mò The person who digs the grave and buries the deceased.

Dahomey The name of a kingdom in West Africa. In Vodou it refers to the residence of the lwas, thought sometimes to be in Africa, and at other times on an island in the water under the earth.

Dechoukaj Street reprisals against the tonton macoute and Duvalierists during and after the revolution that toppled the presidency of Jean-Claude Duvalier, in which they were burned in the streets of cities and towns.

Dènyè priyè The final prayer for the dead said by the prèt savann at the cemetery.

Desounen The part of the death rituals that separates the gwo-bon-anj from the body of the deceased.

Dogwe Sacrificial ram for Agoue.

Espri The spirit. Also used as a generic term to designate the spirit of the living-dead.

Farin The cornmeal used to trace the ritual vèvès.
Farin Ginen Powdered ashes from charcoal, used to trace the ritual vèvès.

Gangan *See* Oungan.
Ganmel A large wooden vessel carved from the trunk of a tree. It is used to hold grain, to wash clothes, and to prepare food to be offered to the lwas.
Ginen The abyss, the world of the dead, which is said to be under the water below the earth.
Gouyad A movement associated with Gede's gait. It is similar to the movements of sexual intercourse.
Govi A clay jar containing the spirit of the dead. It is to be distinguished from the kanari, which is used to hold water.
Gran Mèt The name of the deity; Bondye, the head of the pantheon.
Gwo-bon-anj Literally, "big-good-angel"; the metaphysical double or the spirit of a person, which derives from Bondye, the Godhead.

Hoholi The sesame seeds (*Sesamum indicum*) placed in the coffin of the deceased to prevent the machinations of sorcerers.

Ibo Originally the name of a Dahomean tribe. In Haiti it is the name of a pantheon of deities. The Ibo pantheon of lwas has generally been absorbed into the Rada pantheon.
Imaj A lithograph of a saint.

Kafou The crossroads. The term is used often to refer to Legba's Petro designation.
Kalbas A calabash. The term originates from the Carib *calabazza*.
Kanari A large clay pot, measuring approximately two and one-half feet in height and three feet in diameter, used to hold water. It is never used to carry water.
Kanzo A trial or an "ordeal" by fire administered as a symbol of purification to those who are initiated into Vodou.
Kleren A strong drink made from the sap of the sugar cane; raw rum. A favorite drink of Gede.
Kola A sweet nonalcoholic drink served at parties, and sometimes at special Vodou ceremonies.
Konbit A team of men gathered to do road work, or to work in the fields.
Konesans Knowledge of the lwas and Vodou rites.
Kongo A nation or pantheon of lwas having its own rites. These originate from West Africa, as the name indicates. Many of them have been absorbed by Petro.
Kouzen Cousin, an affectionate appellation for Azaka.
Kwasiyen To trace a cross with farin in the vèvès or on a person.

Lakou A compound or courtyard in which various families live communally. The lakou has the shape of a horseshoe and resembles the Dahomean compound.

Lambi A conch shell used as a horn. It is usually associated with maroons of the colonial period. It is often used in ceremonies, particularly those connected with Agoue, the lwa of the sea.

Langay A sacred language spoken during possession. The words are mostly of African origin and are unintelligible to most Vodouisants.

Laplas A oungan's assistant.

La Sirènn The sea aspect of Ezili, Agoue's consort.

Lespri A person's spirit, associated with the ti-bon-anj.

Lougawou A small supernatural creature that is said to wander in some places at night.

Lwa A Vodou deity.

Lwa rasin *See* Rasin.

Maji Magic.

Makout A sack used largely by peasants to transport their crops. Women carry it on their heads, and men wear it around the neck or the shoulder. It usually has a long woven handle. According to Vodou mythology, Legba, Gede, and Azaka carry such a sack.

Mamalwa A high priestess.

Mambo A female priest. In Haiti, mambos are extremely powerful individuals, both socially and spiritually.

Manje djo An offering used during the rites of consecration. It consists of yams, sweet potatoes, cornmeal, cassavas, manioc, roasted peanuts, and *akasan* (porridge made of cornmeal).

Manje Ginen A ritual offering to the spirit of the dead.

Manje lwa An offering to the lwas.

Manje mò *See* Manje Ginen.

Manje sek A dry offering of uncooked vegetables.

Manman The largest of the Rada drums.

Manman Brijit The wife of Baron Sanmdi, a member of the Gede family of lwas.

Marasa The Divine Twins.

Mazanga *See* Baka.

Mèt ounfò The guardian lwa of a ounfò.

Metrès Mistress, the name used for Ezili Freda.

Mèt tèt Master of the head, a person's guardian lwa.

Mistè The lwas. They are distinct from the living-dead. The term is also used to refer to certain ritual ceremonies.

Monte To mount; used in possession when a lwa is said to mount his horse. *See* Chwal.

Nanchon Nation, a Vodou pantheon of lwas.

Nanm The soul of a person.

Novena A nine-day death ritual for the soul of a recently deceased person. It is done during the period in which the ti-bon-anj is believed to hover over the body.

Ogan A musical instrument used at Vodou ceremonies. It consists of the blade of a hoe which is struck rhythmically—with a stone, a large nail, or any other piece of metal—in time with the drums.

Ogantie The ogan player.

Ouanga A magical charm used in malevolent magic or sorcery.

Ouete mò nan ba dlo Ceremony by which the soul of the living-dead is reclaimed from Ginen and placed in a govi.

Ounfò A Vodou temple, including the peristil, the numerous bagis, the courtyard, and the repozwas. The designation often includes also the ritual paraphernalia and the oungan's house, which generally adjoins the temple proper.

Oungan (Gangan) The Vodou priest; from the Fon *oun*, "spirits," and *gan*, "chief."

Oungenikon The ounfò official who leads the socyete in singing.

Ounzi A member of the socyete. There are several stages of elevation. *See* Bosal; Ounzi kanzo.

Ounzi bosal *See* Bosal.

Ounzi kanzo An initiated person in the Vodou religion who has passed the fire test; the first level attained in the local ounfò.

Papalwa A high priest.

Pe The Vodou altar.

Peristil The roofed structure supported by four poles in which ceremonies are held. *See* Ounfò.

Petro A pantheon of lwas which are said to be creole, originating on Haitian soil.

Pitit fèy An initiated member of a socyete.

Plasay A mating relationship in which two persons of opposite sex enter into common-law marriage.

Plase A person who is in plasay with another.

Plate marasa Plates of red clay especially designed to contain offerings for the Twins. They consist of two red bowls joined together at the top.

Poto Legba *See* Potomitan.

Potomitan The central pole in the peristil, which functions as the major avenue to the world of the lwas.

Prèt savann A "bush priest," an official of the ounfò who reads the Catholic prayers before the Vodou ceremonies. Although his role is generally perfunctory, he is important at funerals and at baptisms.

Rada A pantheon of cosmic lwas. The name derives from the Dahomean kingdom of Arada.

Range A magical rite in which an object is charged with the power of the lwas.

Rara A large number of people who gather to dance in the streets, especially during the Mardi Gras period.

Rasin Root, as the root of a tree. Used in connection with "lwa" ("rasin lwa" or "lwa rasin"), it refers to the root lwa or the spirit from whom a community believes it descends.

Rèd Stern, strong, reticent. Used in connection with Petro lwas.

Rèl The ritualistic mourning of the dead.

Repozwa A rectangular area in the courtyard of a ounfò containing the lwas.

Revnan *See* Zombi.

Sen A saint of the Catholic Church. It is sometimes used to designate a lwa.

Sèvitè One who serves the lwas, a devotee.

Simidò A singer of songs in the konbit.

Siyale A ritual movement performed by the oungan or mambo in recognition of the lwas at the four cardinal points of the universe.

Sobagi *See* Bagi.

Socyete The assembled members of the local ounfò.

Syèl The sky. It also refers to the place where the ti-bon-anj goes after the death of an individual.

Ti-bon-anj Literally, "little-good-angel"; the part of the human soul identified with personality.

Tonton macoute Literally, "bogeyman"; the name was applied to the Duvaliers' much feared secret police because they conducted many of their operations at night.

Vantaye A ritualistic movement "airing" the fire under a sacrifice.

Vèvès The geometric figures that symbolize the lwas. At a Vodou ceremony, they are usually traced with cornmeal or ashes (farin or farin Ginen).

Veye The wake in the cycle of death rituals.

Vilokan The mythological city of the lwas.

Wèdo Name designating the place of origin of certain lwas from the Dahomean kingdom of Whydah.

Yanm A root vegetable widely consumed by Haitians.

Yanvalò (Yanvalou) A ritual Rada dance form.

Zen Ceremonial pots used to cook food for the lwas.

Zen Men Fò *See* Ginen.

Zepòl The shoulder. The Rada shoulder dance.

Zile The island below the waters. *See* Dahomey.

Zombi A soulless body. A person whose soul is believed to have been removed, whose body has been interred and raised again. The body is used for slave work in garden plots, in households, and in the building of houses.

NOTES

CHAPTER 1

1. As seen in movies such as *The Serpent and the Rainbow*, and the film made for television, *The Believers*.

2. In the Creole language of Haiti, Vodouisants use "Bondye" to designate the Christian and Vodou Godhead. It derives from the French "Bon Dieu," meaning "Good Lord."

3. Métraux uses the term *symbiosis* fleetingly in his description of the relationships between Vodou and Roman Catholicism in Haiti. He defines it as a "narrow parallelism" between the liturgical calendars of the two religions—that is, the religious observances performed on the days reserved for the Vodou lwas correspond to those performed on the days dedicated to the saints of the church that represent those lwas (1958, 292).

4. Because Vodouisants regard the prèt savann as the representative of the church, and more precisely of the local Catholic priest, prèt savanns are usually male rather than female.

5. There is evidence that the millenarian spirit of the revolution recurred during the early period of the "Duvalierist Revolution" in the 1960s. Many Haitian supporters saw François Duvalier not only as a political leader, but as a spiritual leader, a reborn spirit of an ancestor who had come to deliver the oppressed masses from brutal oppression. Duvalier often drew parallels between his revolution and that of 1804, and saw his role as analogous to that of the leaders of the war of independence (Duvalier 1969, 324–35).

CHAPTER 2

1. Bartolomé de las Casas went to Hispañola with his father, Pedro de las Casas, in 1493. Pedro had been invited by Columbus to join him on his second voyage to the New World; he was a wealthy entrepreneur who was later reported to have "acquired profitable interests in the island of Hispañola" (Helps 1868, 4). When the governor of the island undertook the campaign to subjugate Cuba, young Bartolomé accompanied Diego Velasquez to seize land for the Spanish crown and to begin "the pacification of the [Indian] population" there. Las Casas was converted to Christianity shortly after his arrival in Cuba in 1514, joined the Dominican order, and spent the rest of his life pleading the cause of the Indians (MacNutt 1909, 99).

2. Several days before Las Casas's death in 1566, and after a long illness, he recog-

nized that slavery was wrong, that war was unjustifiable, and that the annexing of Amerindian land by Europeans was unscrupulous and unethical, and he condemned all the European governments that transported slaves from Africa. He also beseeched God's forgiveness for having recommended the importation of Africans to the New World (MacNutt 1909, 305–7).

3. Rotberg reports that already in 1788, Saint-Domingue was exporting about 3.7 million francs' worth of goods to the United States (Rotberg 1971, 27).

4. The slaves' deportment is not surprising, for it mirrored that of their masters. According to Girod-Chantrans, the masters went to church as if they "came to participate in a casual assembly or a profane spectacle. They entertained each other, laughed and joked, and used God's name in their discourse with each other in a manner that I found intolerable" (1785, 8).

5. It has been estimated that the deplorable conditions on the plantations and the mistreatment of slaves resulted in the death of about 17,000 annually between 1790 and 1804, while the birth rate among them remained at 1 percent annually. Moreover, the working life expectancy of slaves around 1790 averaged about 15 years.

6. In this connection Brutus notes that Leclerc "falsely blamed yellow fever for the death of his troops" (Brutus [n.d.], 2:381).

7. Between 1760 and 1793, marronnage increased significantly. Statistics for that short period show that there were some 48,000 cases of marronnage. Of the 10,573 slaves brought from Africa to Saint-Domingue in 1788 alone, 2,000 ran away from their plantations (Fouchard 1981; Debien 1966b).

8. A fact infrequently mentioned by historians is the maroons' knowledge and efficient use of the surrounding fauna and flora to mix poisons to kill white masters. Poison as a "weapon" was often as destructive as armed rebellion (Davis 1988, 221–23).

9. While it is generally true that Vodouisants regard the Petro lwas as maleficent and the Rada as beneficent, these distinctions are not absolute. The Petro lwas can protect a person from danger, while the Rada can inflict disease on a recalcitrant devotee. In short, in both its Rada and Petro characterizations, a lwa is both beneficent and maleficent. In their ritual characterizations, the Petro lwas are associated with the sound of gunpowder and the cracking of the whip, sounds that echo the masters' treatment of their slaves and the spirit of revolution and nationalism.

10. Two French navy frigates appeared in Port-au-Prince harbor to impose this settlement.

11. Two things might explain Boyer's concern that France recognize an independent Haiti. First, Haiti maintained diplomatic relations with few nations after her independence, and Boyer thought that France's recognition would lead other nations to follow suit; in time, these nations would open up vast markets that would enhance Haiti's economy. Second, like Christophe before him, Boyer probably wanted to lend dignity to his government by seeking Rome's recognition. These points are discussed in more detail in the following section of this chapter.

12. In this connection, Pluchon seems to suggest that Toussaint also gave nominal reverence to the Christian God. Shortly before his capture, Toussaint is reported to have said to the curé of Gonaïves, while holding a crucifix in his hand, that "he no longer wanted to serve the Christian God. Then crushing this crucifix under his feet, he began to set fire to the church with his sacrilegious hands" (Pluchon 1987, 103). As for Dessalines, in early 1803 he is said to have entered the old cathedral Notre-Dame in Port-au-Prince wearing a red robe; he was dressed like Ogou, the lwa of war, whom he served and who he believed was his protector (Beauvoir-Dominique 1991, 59).

13. It was during this period that sizable numbers of Lebanese and other immigrants from Middle Eastern countries, all of whom are commonly referred to by Haitians as "Syrians," settled in Haiti. A fairly substantial Chinese community also came to Haiti.

14. By 1915, Haiti's international debts had risen to 22,574,316 dollars in toto (Delbeau 1990, 38).

15. The most notable such incidents include the anchoring of a Spanish armada that appeared in Port-au-Prince harbor to collect debts due to the Spanish government on February 6, 1861; the appearance of two German frigates on June 11, 1872, to collect 3,000 pounds sterling, and again on December 6, 1897, to claim 20,000 dollars on behalf of German investors in Haiti allegedly victimized by financial losses. English ships were present in 1877 to collect 682,000 dollars plus interest which Haiti owed to the British government (Delbeau 1990, 38–39).

16. It was also during this period that Papa Doc admitted openly to being a Vodou high priest (papalwa), a fact that has never been substantiated historically. There are no records of his Vodou initiation. Papa Doc's frequent public admission of his adherence to Vodou during this period of his administration might have been more a political tactic than an expression of religious commitment.

It is interesting to note that the government's tolerance of Vodou represented a complete reversal from its earlier policies. The Penal Code 409 signed by president Sténio Vincent on September 5, 1935, forbade Vodou practices. The Code was to be strictly enforced by the police and the military; it stated that anyone caught "performing rituals considered superstitious, ceremonies, rites, dances, and meetings during which offerings or sacrifices consisting of cattle or fowl are used" would be arrested and sentenced to "a six-month jail term, and . . . required to pay the sum of 400 gourdes [$80 U.S.]"; a similar sentence would be applied to all those persons who "exploited others, making them believe that, by occult means, it was possible to change their situation, or who claimed to be able to heal diseases by procedures unknown to medical science" (ANH: Code Pénal 409, 1935).

17. McAlister notes that the raras have traditionally been part of the Mardi Gras festivities in Haiti. They are large bands of people (sometimes numbering into the thousands) who dance in the streets of major towns and cities to the rhythmic music of an ensemble. They are similar to street groups at the New Orleans Mardi Gras, except for several important differences. First, they are strongly inspired by Vodou, and

particularly the Petro lwas. Second, they possess a highly structured hierarchy, not unlike those found in the ounfòs; there are various levels of authority and specialization involving a whole assortment of responsibilities assigned to individuals dancing in the raras by those in charge. The master of a rara (or *mèt*) is often a ougan or a prominent member of a secret Vodou society, such as the bizango. Third, raras fulfill a double function in Haitian society: on the one hand, they provide an opportunity for the participants to affirm a sense of religious and social *communitas* by reinforcing the African "roots" and the common "heart values" of Haitians; and on the other, they serve as media for social and political protest. McAlister's study suggests that from the days of the colony, these roving bands of dancers have been particularly active in crucial periods in Haitian life. That is why she sees the function of the raras as essentially liminal—that is, they provide passage from one sociopolitical phase to another, and are thus facilitators of sociopolitical change in Haiti (McAlister 1991).

18. Washington was aware of Duvalier's departure well in advance of its occurrence. The State Department mistakenly announced Baby Doc's departure at a press conference twenty-four hours before the event took place.

19. *Pile pie'm, pa di'm padon, sa padon ou a fè pou mwin?*

20. *Foumi pa janm mouri anba barik sik.*

21. *Rosh nan dlo pa konnen doulè rosh nan soley.*

CHAPTER 3

1. These stories are quickly being forgotten in Haiti, particularly by city dwellers. Traditionally, their plots resemble those of Br'er Rabbit in the Southern part of the United States, or the *anansi* tales of Jamaica. They relate the tensions between two characters: the strong (Ti Malice or Jan Lespri), and the weak (Bouki or Jan Sote). These tensions are resolved when the weak figure successfully outwits the strong one by tricking him.

2. Like kindred tales everywhere, in many parts of West Africa as well as in other parts of the world, these stories begin with standard phrases. In Haiti, the beginning of a story takes the form of a dialogue between storyteller and listeners. It has no significance other than to put the audience in the proper frame of mind to hear the story. The origin of the introductory phrases is not clear. Diane Wolkstein thinks that the phrase "cric, crac" may have been brought into Haiti by Breton sailors in the seventeenth century (1978, 2). The stories often end with standard phrases as well. For instance, the storyteller will say: "I was there and saw it. They gave me a great big kick and sent me all the way over here to tell you about it"; or again, "They gave me a blow, and I flew over the house to tell you this story." The formulistic endings often provide a dramatic punch. There are a number of scholarly works that analyze and record Haitian myths (Telchid 1985; Wolkstein 1978; Courlander 1960; Paul 1962).

3. A portion of this creed is based upon that mentioned by Leyburn (1972, 143).

4. The head of the lakou is often the *chèf sekcion*, the chief of one of the sections

within a department. Haiti's constitutional structure provides that the country be divided into departments equivalent to states or provinces. These provinces in turn are subdivided into sections. Each section has its chief, who may serve as a local oungan, a patriarch to one of the lakous in a department, and/or chief of the konbits. The konbits traditionally have been made up of members of several lakous. They are work groups hired to work in the fields or on public works, especially during the time of the American Occupation. For more details, see Chapter 2.

5. For more information about the house system in New York, see *The Legacy of the Spirit*, a one-hour documentary film about Vodou written and produced by Karen Kramer.

6. The ason is a ritual rattle made of a small calabash in which are inserted stones, and around which are strung multicolored glass beads. Its purpose is to awaken the lwas and to summon them to attend the Vodou rituals.

7. Vodouisants believe that sorcerers often raise bodies from the grave, a practice related to zombification. Zombis are believed to be soulless creatures who are usually incapable of moral judgment, but are presumed to be under the powerful direction of the sorcerers who have raised them. Vodouisants claim that zombis are used for housework, field labor, or other tasks (Hurston 1938). They are not usually used for malevolent purposes, although the raising of them is thought to be a malevolent act. Vodouisants fear the possibility of being turned into zombis, and dread their possible encounter with one, not because they are afraid of hard work, but because they value their state of consciousness and their capacity for moral judgment. The zombi is therefore thought to be a living symbol of Vodouisants' disdain for the lack of individual self-control (Deren 1972, 42).

Controversy about zombification has recently arisen among ethnobiologists. According to a number of sources, zombification is a part of the religious and pharmacological practices of the bizango secret society of sorcerers. According to Davis and others, small doses of pharmacological concoctions, made of tetrodotoxin derived partly from the backbone of the puffer fish, create states of profound lethargy in which an individual may be pronounced dead, buried, and then raised from the grave within a few hours. The controlled administration of small doses of the chemical to an individual after he or she has been raised will maintain this state of lethargy indefinitely. For further discussion of zombification and the controversy surrounding it, please see Davis 1988; L. Douyon 1980; Kao 1983.

It is interesting that the Haitian Penal Code takes cognizance of zombis. Article 249 reads: "Also shall be qualified as attempted murder the use against any person of substances that, without causing actual death, produce a more or less prolonged lethargic coma. If after the administering of such substances, the person has been buried, the act shall be considered murder no matter what result follows" (ANH: Code Pénal).

CHAPTER 4

1. An exclamation often heard in Vodou songs which "seals" the supplications of the devotees. In a sense, it may be compared to the Judaic and Christian *Amen*.

2. As the Godhead, Mawu Lisa is said to be sexually complete; Mawu is the female, and Lisa the male. The Fon usually refer to the Godhead by her female designation.

3. The reference to welding here relates to one of the Fon's most sacred activities: iron smelting, an art form that is also important in Haiti.

4. Mawu therefore does not create the world ex nihilo, but is essentially the arranger of the universe.

5. These concepts of the emergence and maintenance of the cosmos are not unique to the Bambara, but are shared by a number of cultures around the world. In Africa, the Dogon (of Mali) traditional story of creation is that the world derives from the vibration of a primordial seed inside an egg from which all of creation flowed (Griaule and Dieterlen 1955). Similarly, the Vaisheshika school of philosophy in early Hinduism taught the eternal motion of small "factors" which coalesce continually to create the emergence of things in the world (Hiriyanna 1973, 225–66). Among the Bambara, silence is the sacred principle that lies at the core of the universe and symbolizes harmony; noise (yo), which fills the world, derives from harmony but militates against it, disrupting that sacred order. This is why elders teach the young the profound spiritual value of silence in order to restore that order (Zuesse 1979, 154).

6. Translated as "the inherent forward movement of the universe." This game involves the tracing of a cross with millet (*Penincillaria spicata*).

7. Scholars disagree about the origin of the vèvès. Métraux states that they originated in Dahomey, but gives no explanation of their specific transmission (1958, 148). Maximilien writes that they date back to pre-Columbian Aztec culture, but likewise provides no explanation as to how these Aztec symbols come to be found in Haiti (1945, 41–59). Thompson notes that the term *vèvè* derives from the archaic Dahomean Fon term for the palm oil used in drawing geometric symbols on the ground; their cruciform cosmograms derive from Congo and neighboring regions of West Africa (1983, 188). While it may be correct to assume that in their use of the cross, the vèvès are essentially African, it is also possible that parts of their symbolic configurations may well have derived from Arawakan-Taino cultures, originating on the northern coast of South America. It is possible that the Tainos migrated from the northern coast of South America to the Lesser Antilles, the Greater Antilles, and Meso-America (Rouse 1964, 140–44). This hypothesis is supported by evidence of similar drawings among the Bororo of Brazil. If it is correct, it would support the thesis of symbiosis—that is, the juxtaposition of religious traditions in the spatial arrangement of symbols from two different continents. It would also confirm the thesis that vèvès are creole phenomena, that the combinations of various symbols (as well as the meanings ascribed to them) are New World inventions. It is possible that these symbolic images were adopted by the maroons who, in the colonial period, came into contact with

Amerindian Arawak republics in the interior of the island. Future archaeological excavations will determine the relations between African, European, and New World cultures in the composition of the vèvès.

8. Like Mawu Lisa among the Fon, Bondye is thought to be sexually complete. In parts of Haiti, he is invoked as "Mother" (Bondye Manman moin).

9. Bòkò derives from the Fon word for sorcerer, *bocono*.

10. *Ceiba pentendra*, belonging to the same family as the baobab tree in West Africa.

11. In parts of Haiti, Legba is also identified with Saint Anthony.

12. Bastide also notes the adaptation of the traditional African calendar to the Roman one in the case of Brazilian Candomblé (see Bastide 1978, 198).

13. See Chapter 3.

14. Deren lists at least ten of these (1972, 304), and most of them are mentioned in works by other scholars (Herskovits 1972; Courlander 1960; Maximilien 1945).

15. Literally translated as "three shovels full" (of excrement, presumably), "filth," or "fart."

16. This story is recorded by Herskovits and a number of others (Herskovits 1963, 1:64; Paul 1962, 278–79). Hazoumé also records another version of the story: Da Sousa visited Brazil, "the Antilles, possibly Haiti and Havana," and did not find Ghezo's mother (Hazoumé 1957, 27–32).

17. Guédévis is a minor spirit in some sects of Bahian Candomblé in Brazil. It was brought to Bahia, suggests Bastide, by the Ketu priests captured by the Dahomean soldiers and sold into slavery (Bastide 1978, 197).

18. Herskovits identifies Gede with the Ghédéonsu (about whom he does not comment), powerful ancestral spirits in ancient Dahomey (1972, 247).

19. It is interesting that "Dahomey" should derive from "Dā," meaning "the womb of Dā." Dahomey is thus the child of Dā. By logical extension, it is comparable to *glā* among the Bambara. As motion, Dā is the eternal resurrection of things. The future of Dahomey as a nation is assured by the remolding of bodies by Mawu and the gods (Paul 1962, 271).

20. The complete name for Damballah is Dā Ayida Wèdo. "Wèdo" is reminiscent of Whydah in Dahomey, the ancient city, the seat of the kingdom of Whydah, the lwa's place of origin.

21. Sogbo was believed to be the head of the sky pantheon in ancient Dahomean mythology (Mercier 1968, 220).

CHAPTER 5

1. Deren also mentions that Vodou mythology does not share with European mythologies the connection of the principle of fecundity with agrarian activities; such agrarian connections are made, however, with the Marinette family in the Petro nanchon (1972, 137). Ezili's spiritual beauty can be compared to the virtue of womanhood extolled in some of the well-known poems in Western cultures.

2. As will be discussed later, Ezili has some connections with the sea, especially in the persona of La Sirenn, Agoue's consort. Agoue is the lwa of the sea; Ezili is therefore the link between the lwas associated with the land and those of the sea.

3. These lithographs, like all the others, are printed in Mexico and in the Dominican Republic. They are imported into Haiti and can be bought at local markets at a minimal cost. They are distributed widely.

4. Among other examples of medieval and Renaissance paintings showing Mary in a blue robe are Raphael's *Madonna and the Fish* and Hans Memling's *Adoration of the Magi*.

5. This image in Catholic iconography derives from the Epiphany—that is, the presentation of Jesus to Simeon the prophet in the temple at Jerusalem. Simeon predicted that Jesus was a sign which humanity would reject and that Mary's heart would be pierced, meaning that she would experience suffering in the future (see Luke 2:35).

6. The Yoruba say that Oshun's dagger is the instrument with which she inflicts punishment upon her devotees (Bascom 1969, 90–91).

7. There is an unresolved contradiction here. Although Vodouisants see Bondye's separateness from the universe, they also say that he is omniscient and sees all human actions. But because Bondye is remote, they do not regard him as a lwa.

8. A similar version of this story is told by Courlander (1960).

9. This story is somewhat similar to the Ashanti stories about Nyankonpon who is duped into dancing to the drum of the trickster (Ananse).

CHAPTER 6

1. Popular support for Aristide derived overwhelming from the masses. *Lavalas*—meaning the outpouring of social justice for the poor and downtrodden, national and racial pride, religious and political liberation—were the principal themes of his political campaign. He also promised religious freedom to all Haitian citizens, in accordance with the country's new constitution.

2. That there is religious openness in the country may seem incongruous with the country's history, for the religious freedom that Haitians have enjoyed since Aristide's assumption of power was guaranteed to them by a president who was a Catholic priest. Aristide and members of his administration have made their peace with Vodou, but for political rather than religious reasons. But they have had to recognize that the future of political democracy, which they have espoused and which they hope to establish in Haitian society, depends upon their acknowledgment of Vodou as a powerful agent for social and political change.

....

BIBLIOGRAPHY

....

ARCHIVAL SOURCES

Paris

ANP (Archives Nationales de Paris)

File C9: Collection of sundry letters written by colonists in Saint-Domingue.

File F3: Collection Moreau de St.-Méry, M. L. E.—Assorted letters and notes from residents of Saint-Domingue about colonial life.

File F5: Notes relating impressions of colonial life and Catholic missions in Saint-Domingue.

File F52: Documents relating the missionary work of the Catholic church in Saint-Domingue.

File F90: Ordinances and assorted Police Rulings regarding the slaves and masters in the French colonies.

File F246: Assortment of notes about the religious lives of the slaves in Saint-Domingue.

Port-au-Prince

ABFI (Archives de la Bibliothèque des Frères de l'Institution Chrétienne Saint Louis de Gonzague). Contains various unpublished reports and statistics concerning the work of the Roman Catholic Church in Haiti. The archives also contain *The Report of the Forbes Commission to Haiti.*

ANH (Archives Nationales d'Haïti). Official documents of state.

Department of Cults. "Statistical Reports on the Work to the Roman Catholic Church in Haiti." Also unpublished reports of the department containing statistics for 1972–80.

UNPUBLISHED DOCUMENTS

"Addresse à l'assemblée nationale par les hommes de couleurs libres de Saint-Domingue." ANP, Records of the Assemblée Nationale in Saint-Domingue, 1789.

Forbes, W. "Report Covering Haiti Prepared in the Division of Latin American Affairs." Unpublished transcript, Washington, D.C., Library of Congress, 1954.

(Additional materials about colonial Saint-Domingue, and materials about the Anti-superstitious Campaigns and the work of the Catholic church up to 1935, can be found at the Archives du Petit Séminaire Collège Saint Martial and the Archives de Saint Louis de Gonzague, both in Port-au-Prince.)

PUBLISHED WORKS

Aberle, D. 1962. "A Note on Relative Deprivation Theory as Applied to Millenarian and Other Cult Movements." In *Reader in Comparative Religion: An Anthropological Approach*, edited by William A. Lessa and Evon Z. Vogt, 537–41. New York: Harper and Row.

Adresse de la société des amis des noirs. Reedited by E. Clasnière. Paris: Desenne, 1791.

Alexis, J. S. 1957. *Les arbres musiciens*. Paris: Gallimard.

Aristide, J.-B. 1990. *In the Parish of the Poor: Writings from Haiti*. New York: Orbis Books.

d'Auberteuil, H. 1782. *Considérations sur l'état présent de la colonie française de Saint-Domingue*. 2 vols. Paris.

Balandier, G. 1963. *Sociologie actuelle de l'Afrique noire*. Paris: Presses Universitaires de France.

Barkun, M. 1986. *Disaster and the Millennium*. Syracuse, N.Y.: Syracuse University Press.

Barrett, L. 1974. *Soul-Force: African Heritage in Afro-American Religion*. Garden City, N.Y.: Doubleday.

——— . 1976. *The Sun and the Drum: African Roots in Jamaican Folk Tradition*. London: Heinemann.

Bascom, W. 1969. *The Yoruba of Southwestern Nigeria*. New York: Holt, Rinehart and Winston.

Bastide, R. 1970. *Le prochain et le lointain*. Paris: Editions Cujas.

——— . 1971. *African Civilisations in the New World*. New York: Harper and Row.

——— . 1978. *African Religions in Brazil*. Baltimore, Md.: Johns Hopkins University Press.

Bastien, R. 1951. *La familia rural haitiana*. Mexico City: Libra.

Beauvoir-Dominique, R. 1991. *L'ancienne cathédrale de Port-au-Prince: Perspectives d'un vestige de Carrefours*. Port-au-Prince: Editions Henri Deschamps.

Bellegarde, D. 1938. *La nation haïtienne*. Paris: J. de Gigord.

Bendix, R. 1964. *Nation-Building and Citizenship: Studies of Our Changing Social Order*. New York: John Wiley.

Bergounioux, F., and J. Goetz. 1958. *Les religions des préhistoriques et des primitifs*. Paris: Arthème Fayard.

Bidney, D. 1958. "Myth, Symbolism, and Truth." In *Myth: A Symposium*, edited by Thomas Sebeok, 1–14. Bloomington: Indiana University Press.

Bird, M. 1869. *The Black Man; or, Haytian Independence, Deduced from Historical Notes, and Dedicated to the Government and People of Hayti*. Freeport, N.Y.: Books for Libraries Press.

Bonneau, A. 1862. *Haïti: Ses progrès, son avenir*. Paris: Armand-Colin.

Booth, W. 1988. "Voodoo Science." *Science* 240 (no. 4850): 274–77.

Bourguignon, E. 1973. *Religion, Altered States of Consciousness and Social Change*. Columbus: Ohio State University Press.

——— . 1974. *Culture and the Varieties of Consciousness*. Menlo Park, Calif.: Cummings Publishing Co.

———. 1975. "Importante papel de las mujeres en los cultos afroamericanos." *Montalban* 4:423–28.

Brown, K. McC. 1976. "The Vèvès in Haitian Vodou: A Structural Analysis of Visual Imagery." Ph.D. diss., Temple University.

———. 1989a. "Mama Lola and the Ezilis: Themes of Mothering and Loving in Haitian Vodou." In *Unspoken Worlds: Women's Religious Lives*, edited by Nancy A. Falk and Rita M. Gross, 235–45. Belmont, Calif.: Wadsworth Publishing Co.

———. 1989b. "Systematic Remembering, Systematic Forgetting: Ogou in Haiti." In *Africa's Ogou: Old World and New*, edited by Sandra T. Barnes, 65–89. Bloomington: Indiana University Press.

———. 1991. *Mama Lola: A Vodou Priestess in Brooklyn*. Berkeley: University of California Press.

Brutus, E. [n.d.] *Révolutions dans Saint-Domingue*. Brussels: Les Editions du Panthéon.

Butler, A. 1956. *Lives of the Saints*. 4 vols. London: Burnes and Oates.

Cabon, P. A. 1929. *Mgr Alexis Jean-Marie Guilloux, deuxième archevêque de Port-au-Prince (Haïti)*. Port-au-Prince: Grand Séminaire Théologique d'Haïti Saint Jacques, Archevêché de Port-au-Prince.

———. 1930. *Notes sur l'histoire religieuse d'Haïti, de la révolution au concordat 1789–1860*. Port-au-Prince: Imprimerie de Compiègne.

Campbell, J. 1972. *The Hero with a Thousand Faces*. Princeton: Princeton University Press.

Campbell, M. 1988. *The Maroons of Jamaica 1655–1796: A History of Resistance, Collaboration, and Betrayal*. South Hadley, Mass.: Bergin and Garvey.

Candler, J. 1842. *Brief Notices of Haiti*. London: Th. Ward and Co.

Cassirer, E. 1960. "Galileo: A New Science and a New Spirit." In *Science and Society: Selected Essays*, edited by Alexander Valvoulis and Wayne Colver. San Francisco: Holden Day.

Césaire, A. 1981. *Toussaint Louverture: La révolution française et le problème coloniale*. Paris: Présence Africaine.

Charlevoix, X. de. 1733. *Histoire de l'île espagnole ou de S. Domingue*. 4 vols. Paris: Hippolyte Louis Guérin.

Chiara, C. E. di. 1988. *Le dossier Haïti: Un pays en péril*. Paris: Tallandier.

Cohn, N. 1961. *The Pursuit of the Millennium*. New York: Schocken Books.

Comhaire-Sylvain, S. 1958. "Courtship, Marriage and Plasaj at Kenscoff." *Social and Economic Studies* 7:210–33.

———. 1961. "The Household at Kenscoff, Haiti." *Social and Economic Studies* 10 (no. 1): 192–222.

Courlander, H. 1960. *The Drum and the Hoe*. Berkeley: University of California Press.

Courlander, H., and R. Bastien. 1966. *Religion and Politics in Haiti*. Washington, D.C.: Institute for Cross-Cultural Research.

Craan, A. 1988. "Toxicologic Aspects of Voodoo in Haiti." *Biomedical and Environmental Sciences* 1 (no. 1): 372–81.

Curtin, P. 1969. *The Atlantic Slave Trade: A Census*. Madison: University of Wisconsin Press.

Dalencourt, F. 1923. *Le sauvetage national par le retour à la terre*. Port-au-Prince: Imprimerie Le Matin.

Dardel, E. 1954. "The Mythie." *Diogenes* 7 (Summer): 33–51.

Davis, W. 1988. *Passage of Darkness: The Ethnobiology of the Haitian Zombie*. Chapel Hill: University of North Carolina Press.

Debbasch, Y. 1964. "Le marronnage, essai sur la désertion de l'esclavage antillais." *Année sociologique* 1961–1962, 2–112. Paris: Presses Universitaires de France.

Debien, G. 1966a. "Les esclaves marrons à Saint-Domingue en 1764." *Jamaican Historical Review* 61 (no. 124): 9–20.

———. 1966b. "Le marronnage aux Antilles françaises au XVIIIe siècle." *Caribbean Studies* 6 (no. 3): 3–44.

Delbeau, J. C. 1990. *Société, culture et médecine populaire traditionnelle, étude sur le terrain d'un cas: Haïti*. Port-au-Prince: Imprimerie Henri Deschamps.

Deren, M. 1972. *The Divine Horsemen: The Voodoo Gods of Haiti*. New York: Delta Publishing Co.

Descourtilz, M. 1809. *Voyages d'un naturaliste*. 3 vols. Paris: Defart.

Desmangles, L. G. 1977a. "African Interpretations of the Christian Cross in Haitian Vodun." *Sociological Analysis* 38:13–24.

———. 1977b. "Baptismal Rites, Religious Symbiosis of Vodun and Catholicism in Haiti." In *Liturgy and Cultural Religious Traditions*, edited by Hermann Schmidt and David Powers, 51–61. New York: Seabury Press.

———. 1977c. "Roman Catholicism and Vodoun in Haiti: What of the Future?" *Freeing the Spirit* 4 (no. 2): 28–35.

———. 1980. "The Vodun Way of Death: Symbiosis of Vodun and Roman Catholicism in Haiti." *Journal of Religious Thought* 36 (no. 1): 5–20.

———. 1990. "The Maroon Republics and Religious Diversity in Colonial Haiti." *Anthropos* 85:474–82.

Dieterlen, G. 1951. *Essai sur la religion Bambara*. Paris: Presses Universitaires de France.

———. 1971. *La notion de personne en Afrique noire*. Paris: Editions CNRS, no. 544.

Dorsainvil, J. C. 1975. *Vodou et névrose*. Port-au-Prince: Imprimerie de la Presse.

Douyon, E. 1965. "La crise de possession dans le Vaudou haïtien." Ph.D. diss., University of Montreal.

Douyon, L. 1980. "Les zombis dans le contexte vodou haïtien." *Haïti Santé* 2 (no. 1): 19–23.

Du Morier à l'assemblée nationale, contre la motion faite par Gaudet, relative à l'état politique des gens de couleurs, et contre toute autre motion tendant à faire évoquer ou altérer le décret du 24 Septembre 1793. Paris: Didet Jeune, 1791.

Dupuy, A. 1988. *Haiti in the World Economy: Class, Race, and Underdevelopment since 1700*. Boulder, Colo.: Westview Press.

Duvalier, F. 1969. *Mémoires d'un leader du Tiers Monde*. Paris: Librairie Hachette.

Eliade, M. 1959. *Cosmos and History: The Myth of the Eternal Return.* New York: Harper Torchbooks.

Ferguson, G. W. 1954. *Signs and Symbols in Christian Art.* New York: Oxford University Press.

Ferguson, J. 1989. *Papa Doc, Baby Doc: Haiti and the Duvaliers.* Cambridge: Basil Blackwell.

Foisset, J. 1942. "Quelques considérations générales sur la campagne anti-superstitieuse." *La Phalange,* February 25.

Fouchard, J. 1981. *The Haitian Maroons.* New York: Edward W. Blyden Press.

Franklin, J. 1828. *The Present State of Hayti.* Westport, Conn.: Negro Universities Press.

————. 1830. *Notes on Haiti.* London: H. Colburn and R. Bentley.

Frazer, J. G. 1927. *The Golden Bough.* New York: Macmillan.

Frostin, C. 1975. *Les révoltes blanches à Saint-Domingue aux XVIIème et XVIIIème siècles.* Paris: L'Ecole.

Gayot, G. 1956. *Clergé indigène.* Montreal: Imprimatur Gayot.

Geggus, D. 1989. "The Haitian Revolution." In *The Modern Caribbean,* edited by Franklin W. Knight and Colin A. Palmer, 21–50. Chapel Hill: University of North Carolina Press.

Genovese, E. 1967. *The Political Economy of Slavery: Studies in the Economy and Society of the Slave South.* New York: Random House.

Gerlach, L., and V. Hine. 1970. *People, Power, and Change.* New York: Bobbs Merrill Co.

Girod-Chantrans, F. 1785. *Voyage d'un suisse dans différentes colonies d'Amérique.* Neuchâtel.

Gisler, A. 1965. *L'esclavage aux Antilles françaises (XVIIe–XIXe siècles).* Fribourg: Editions Universitaires Fribourg Suisse.

————. 1988. "L'église et l'esclavage aux Antilles françaises." In *Le phénomène religieux dans la Caraïbe, Guadeloupe, Martinique, Guyanne, Haïti,* edited by Laënnec Hurbon, 41–56. Montreal: Les Editions du CIDIHCA.

Glazier, S. 1980. "Religion and Contemporary Religious Movements in the Caribbean: A Report." *Sociological Analysis* 41:181–83.

————. 1983. *Marchin' the Pilgrims Home: Leadership and Decision-Making in an Afro-Caribbean Religion.* Westport, Conn.: Greenwood Press.

Gloch, C. 1959. *The Sociology of Religion in Sociology Today.* New York: Basic Books.

Gray, Richard. 1990. *Black Christians and White Missionaries.* New Haven, Conn.: Yale University Press.

Griaule, M., and G. Dieterlen. 1955. "The Dogon." In *African Worlds,* edited by Daryll Forde, 83–110. New York: Oxford University Press.

Gurvitch, G. 1958. "Sociologie en profondeur." In *Traité de Sociologie,* edited by Georges Gurvitch, 148–57. Paris: Presses Universitaires de France.

Halbwachs, M. 1975. *Les cadres sociaux de la mémoire.* Paris: Presses Universitaires de France.

Hazoumé, P. 1957. "Le pacte du sang au Dahomé." *Mémoires de l'Institut d'Ethnologie* 25 (no. 3): 37–52.

Helps, A. 1868. *Life of Las Casas: The Apostle of the Indies.* London: Bell and Daldy.

Herskovits, M. 1963. *Dahomey: An Ancient West African Kingdom.* 2 vols. New York: J. J. Augustin.

———. 1972. *Life in a Haitian Valley.* New York: Doubleday.

Hiriyanna, M. 1973. *Outlines of Indian Philosophy.* Bombay: George Allen and Unwin.

Hoffmann, L. F. 1990. *Haïti: Couleurs, croyances, créoles.* Port-au-Prince: Imprimerie Henri Deschamps.

Howard, T. P. 1985. *The Haitian Journal of Lieutenant Howard, York Hussars 1796–1798.* Knoxville: University of Tennessee Press.

Hurbon, L. 1972. *Dieu dans le vodou haïtien.* Paris: Payot.

———. 1989a. "En jeu politique de la crise actuelle de l'église." *Chemins Critiques* 1 (no. 1): 13–22.

———. 1989b. *Le phénomène religieux dans la Caraïbe.* Montreal: Les Editions du CIDI-HCA.

Hurston, Z. 1938. *Tell My Horse.* Philadelphia: Lippincott.

———. 1939. *Voodoo Gods.* London: J. M. Dent.

Idowu, E. 1973. *Olodumarè: God in Yoruba Belief.* New York: Friederich A. Praeger Publisher.

Jacobs, C., and A. Kaslow. 1991. *Spiritual Churches of New Orleans: Origins, Beliefs, and Rituals of an African-American Religion.* Knoxville: University of Tennessee Press.

Jahn, J. 1961. *Muntu: An Outline of the New African Culture.* New York: Grove Press.

James, P. I. R. 1949. *Les jacobins noirs.* Paris: Gallimard.

Kao, C. Y. 1983. "New Perspectives on the Interaction of Tetrodotoxin and Saxitoxin with Excitable Membrane." *Toxicon* suppl. 3:211–19.

Kao, C. Y., and T. Yasomuto. 1990. "Tetrodotoxin in 'Zombie Powder.'" *Toxicon* 28 (no. 2): 129–32.

Korngold, Ralph. 1965. *Citizen Toussaint: A Biography.* New York: Hill and Wang.

Labat, J.-B. 1722. *Nouveaux voyages aux isles d'Amérique.* 8 vols. Paris: Cavelier.

Lacroix, P. 1819. *Mémoires pour servir à l'histoire de la révolution de Saint-Domingue.* 2 vols. Paris: Pillet Aîné.

Laguerre, M. 1973. "The Place of Voodoo in the Social Structure of Haiti." *Caribbean Quarterly* 19 (no. 3): 10–24.

———. 1974a. "Ecological Approach to Voodoo." *Freeing the Spirit* 3 (no. 1): 4–12.

———. 1974b. "Voodoo as Religion and Political Ideology." *Freeing the Spirit* 3 (no. 1): 23–28.

———. 1980a. "Bizango: A Voodoo Secret Society in Haiti." In *Secrecy,* edited by S. K. Tefft, 15–28. New York: Human Science Press.

———. 1980b. *Voodoo Heritage.* Beverly Hills: Sage Library of Social Research.

———. 1986. "Politics and Voodoo Still a Potent Combination in Haiti." *Wall Street Journal,* April 18, 19.

———. 1989. *Voodoo and Politics in Haiti.* New York: St. Martin's Press.

Las Casas, B. de. 1699. *An Account of the First Voyages and Discoveries Made by Spaniards in America.* London: J. Darby and D. Brown.

Leclerc's Letter to Bonaparte. Paris: Archives du Ministère de la Guerre, 1802.

Leirus, M. 1953. "Notes sur l'usage de chromolithographies par les vaudouisants." *Mémoires de l'Institut Français d'Afrique Noire* 27:201–7.

Lemoine, M. 1981. *Bitter Sugar.* London: Zed Press.

Le Ruzic, Msgr. I. 1912. *Documents sur la mission des frères-prêcheurs à Saint-Domingue.* Lorient: Le Baron-Royet.

Lewis, G. 1983. *Main Currents in Caribbean Thought: The Historical Evolution of Caribbean Society in Its Ideological Aspects 1492–1900.* Baltimore, Md.: Johns Hopkins University Press.

Lewis, I. 1971. *Ecstatic Religion: An Anthropological Study of Spirit Possession and Shamanism.* Middlesex, England: Penguin.

Leyburn, J. 1972. *The Haitian People.* New Haven, Conn.: Yale University Press.

Linton, R. 1979. "Nativistic Movements." In *Reader in Comparative Religion: An Anthropological Approach,* 4th ed., edited by William A. Lessa and Evon Z. Vogt, 415–21. New York: Harper and Row.

Lundhal, M. 1979. *Peasants and Poverty: A Study of Haiti.* London: Croom Helm.

McAlister, E. 1991. "The Celebration of Raras in Haiti and Brooklyn: Spiritual and Political Warfare." Paper delivered at the Haitian Studies Association, Boston (quotes used by permission from the author).

Macaulay, Z. 1835. *Haïti, ou renseignements authentiques sur l'abolition de l'esclavage à Saint-Domingue et la Guadeloupe.* Paris.

McKenzie, C. 1967. *Secret Societies.* New York: Collier Books.

MacNutt, F. 1909. *Bartholomew De Las Casas: His Life, His Apostolate, and His Writings.* New York: G. P. Putnam.

Madiou, T. 1922. *Histoire d'Haïti.* 2d ed. Port-au-Prince: Imprimerie Chenêt.

Marcelin, M. 1949. *Mythologie vodou.* Port-au-Prince: Les Editions Haïtiennes.

———. 1952. "Les fêtes en Haïti." *Optique* 16 (no. 12): 33–45.

Margrat, P. 1781. *Les lettres édifiantes et curieuses écrites des missions étrangères, mémoires d'Amérique.* Paris: Mérigot.

Marrett, R. 1920. *Psychology of Folklore.* London: Methuen and Co.

———. 1955. *La crise de possession, essai de psychiatrie comparée.* Port-au-Prince: Imprimerie de l'Etat.

Maximilien, L. 1945. *Le Vaudou haïtien.* Port-au-Prince: Imprimerie de l'Etat.

Mbiti, J. S. 1970. *African Religions and Philosophy.* Garden City, N.Y.: Doubleday.

Mercier, P. 1968. "The Fon of Dahomey." In *African Worlds: Studies in Cosmological Ideas and Social Values of African Peoples,* edited by Daryll Forde, 210–34. New York: Oxford University Press.

Métraux, A. 1954–55. "Les rites d'initiation dans le Vodou haïtien." *Tribus* (Linden Museum, Stuttgart), n.s., 4/5:177–98.

———. 1958. *Le Vaudou haïtien.* Paris: Gallimard.

Midy, F. 1989a. "L'affaire Aristide en perspective: Histoire de la formation et du rejet d'une vocation prophétique." *Chemins Critiques* 1 (no. 1): 45–57.

———. 1989b. "Haïti, la religion sur les chemins de la démocratie." *Chemins Critiques* 1 (no. 1): 23–43.

Mintz, S. 1971a. "The Caribbean as a Socio-Cultural Area." In *Peoples and Cultures of the Caribbean: An Anthropological Reader*, edited by Michael M. Horowitz, 17–46. New York: Natural History Press.

———. 1971b. "Toward an Afro-American History." *Cahier d'histoire mondiale* 13:317–32.

———. 1972. Introduction to *Voodoo in Haiti*, by A. Métraux. 2d ed. New York: Schocken Books.

———. 1974. *Caribbean Transformations*. Baltimore, Md.: Johns Hopkins University Press.

———. 1975a. *Slavery, Colonialism, and Racism*. New York: Norton Press.

———. 1975b. *Working Papers in Haitian Society and Culture*. New Haven, Conn.: Antilles Research Program, Yale University.

———. 1985. *Sweetness and Power: The Place of Sugar in Modern History*. New York: Viking Press.

Montilus, G. 1968. *Les repas sacrés haïtiens: Essai d'interprétation théologique*. Paris: Mémoire de Théologie.

Moral, P. 1978. *Le paysan haïtien*. Port-au-Prince: G. P. Maisonneuve and Larose.

Moreau de Saint-Méry, M. L. E. 1784–90. *Loix et constitutions des colonies françaises de l'Amérique sous le vent, de 1550 à 1779*. 6 vols. Paris.

———. [1797] 1958. *Description topographique, physique, civile, politique et historique de la partie française de l'isle de Saint-Domingue*. 3 vols. Paris: Société de l'Histoire des Colonies Françaises. (Originally published in Philadelphia.)

Mugambi, J. N. K. 1989. *African Religions and Christianity*. Nairobi: Longman Kenya.

Mulira, J. G. 1991. "The Case of Voodoo in New Orleans." In *Africanisms in American Culture*, edited by Joseph E. Holloway, 34–68. Bloomington: University of Indiana Press.

Murphy, J. 1990. *Santeria*. Boston: Beacon Press.

Murray, G. F. 1976. "Women in Perdition: Ritual Fertility Control in Haiti." In *Culture, Natality, and Family Planning*, edited by John F. Marshall and Steven Polgar, 59–78. Chapel Hill: University of North Carolina Press.

———. 1977. "The Evolution of Haitian Peasant Land Tenure: A Case Study in Agrarian Adaptation to Population Growth." Ph.D. diss., Columbia University.

Nicholls, D. 1979. *From Dessalines to Duvalier: Race, Colour, and National Independence*. Cambridge: Cambridge University Press.

———. 1985. *Haiti in Caribbean Context: Ethnicity, Economy, and Revolt*. New York: St. Martin's Press.

Oexquemelin, A. O. [1674] 1681. *Pirates de la America*. Colonia Agrippina: Lorenzo Struikaman. (Published originally in Dutch.)

Ott, T. 1973. *The Haitian Revolution (1789–1804)*. Nashville: University of Tennessee Press.

Ottenberg, S. 1971. *Leadership and Authority in an African Society.* Seattle: University of Washington Press.

Otto, R. 1928. *The Idea of the Holy: An Inquiry into the Non-Rational Factor in the Idea of the Divine and Its Relation to the Rational.* London: Oxford University Press.

Paul, E. 1962. *Panorama du folklore haïtien.* Port-au-Prince: Imprimerie de l'Etat.

Peters, C. E. 1960. *La croix contre l'asson.* Port-au-Prince: Imprimerie Telhomme.

Peytraux, L. 1897. *L'esclavage aux Antilles françaises avant 1789.* Paris: Hachette.

Pierrard, P. 1974. *Dictionnaire des prénoms et des saints.* Paris: Larousse, 1974.

Plauson, C. 1974. *Un initié parle.* Paris: Collection Dieu.

Pluchon, P. 1987. *Vaudou, sorciers, empoisonneurs: De Saint-Domingue à Haïti.* Paris: Karthala.

Plummer, B. G. 1989. *Haiti and the Great Powers.* Baton Rouge: Louisiana State University Press.

Pressoir, C. 1945. *Le protestantisme haïtien.* Port-au-Prince: Imprimerie de la Société Biblique et des Livres Religieux d'Haïti.

Price, R. 1973. *Maroon Societies.* New York: Doubleday.

Price-Mars, J. 1928. *Ainsi parla l'oncle.* Port-au-Prince: Imprimerie de Compiègne.

Prince, R. 1988. *Haiti: Family Business.* London: Latin American Bureau.

Réflexions et documents pour servir au ministère apostolique. Port-au-Prince: Imprimerie La Phalange, 1950.

Richman, K. 1991. "Discovering the African Traditions." Paper delivered at the Haitian Studies Association, Boston, Mass. (quotes used by permission of the author).

Rigaud, M. 1953. *La tradition Vaudou et Vaudou haïtien: Son temple, ses mystères, sa magie.* Paris: Editions Niclaus.

———. 1974. *Ve-Ve.* New York: French and European Publications.

Ritzenthaler, P. 1966. *The Fon of Bafu.* New York: Thomas Y. Crowell Co.

Romain, C. P. 1986. *Le protestantisme dans la société haïtienne: Contribution à l'étude sociologique d'une religion.* Port-au-Prince: Imprimerie Henri Deschamps.

Rotberg, R. 1971. *Haiti: The Politics of Squalor.* Boston: Houghton Mifflin.

Roumain, J. S. 1940. "The Southeast and the West Indies." In *Prehistoric Patterns in the New World,* edited by Gordon R. Wiley, 165–72. New York: Viking Fund Publications in Anthropology.

———. 1942. *A propos de la campagne anti-superstitieuse.* Port-au-Prince: Imprimerie de l'Etat.

———. 1946. *Gouverneurs de la rosée.* Paris: Les Editeurs Français Réunis.

Rouse, I. 1955. "The Circum-Caribbean Theory: An Archeological Test." *American Anthropologist* 55 (no. 2): 188–200.

———. 1964. "Prehistory of the West Indies." *Science* 144 (no. 3618): 140–52.

Ruben, V., ed. 1960. *Caribbean Studies: A Symposium.* Seattle: University of Washington Press for American Ethnological Society.

St. John, S. 1884. *Haiti and the Black Republic.* London: Smith, Elder and Co.

Saint-Rémy, L. de. 1854–57. *Pétion et Haïti: Essai monographique et historique.* 2 vols. Paris: Moquet.

Sala-Molins, J. 1987. *Le code noir ou le calvaire de Canaan*. Paris: Presses Universitaires de France.

Salgado, J.-M. 1963. *Le culte africain du Vodou et les baptisés en Haïti*. Rome: Université Pontificale de Propagande Fide.

Schmidt, H. 1971. *The United States Occupation of Haiti, 1915–1934*. New Brunswick, N.J.: Rutgers University Press.

Schoelcher, V. 1843. *Colonies étrangères et Haïti: Résultats de l'émancipation anglaise*. 2 vols. Pointe-à-Pitre, Guadeloupe: Emile Désormaux.

Shanin, T. 1971. "Peasantry as a Political Factor." In *Peasants and Peasant Societies*, edited by Teodor Shanin, 238–63. New York: Penguin Books.

Simpson, G. E. 1945. "The Belief System of Haitian Vodoun." *American Anthropologist* 47 (no. 1): 37–59.

———. 1948. "Two Vodun Related Ceremonies." *Journal of American Folklore* 61 (no. 239): 49–53.

———. 1978. *Black Religions in the New World*. New York: Columbia University Press.

———. 1980. *Religious Cults of the Caribbean: Trinidad, Jamaica, and Haiti*. Caribbean Monograph Series, 15. San Juan: Institute of Caribbean Studies, University of Puerto Rico.

Smith, E. 1950. *African Ideas of God*. London: Edinburgh House Press.

Smith, M. G. 1965. *The Plural Society in the Caribbean*. Berkeley: University of California Press.

Soboul, A. 1989. *La révolution française*. Paris: Gallimard.

La société des amis des noirs à Arthur Dillon. Paris: Imprimerie du Patriote Français, 1791.

Solasge, A. 1967. *A la recherche d'une pastorale haïtienne*. Port-au-Prince: Imprimerie de l'Etat.

Sterlin, P. 1954. *Vèvès Vodou*. Series 1 and 2. Port-au-Prince: Edition Sterlin.

Talmon, Y. 1965. "The Pursuit of the Millennium." In *Reader in Comparative Religion: An Anthropological Approach*, 2d ed., edited by William A. Lessa and Evon Z. Vogt, 517–22. New York: Harper and Row.

Taylor, J. V. 1963. *The Primal Vision*. Philadelphia: Fortress Press.

Telchid, S. 1985. *Ti Chika . . . et d'autres contes antillais*. Paris: Editions Caribéennes.

Tempels, P. 1959. *Bantu Philosophy*. Paris: Présence Africaine.

Thomas, W., and F. Znaniecki. 1971. "A Polish Peasant Family." In *Peasants and Peasant Societies*, edited by Teodor Shanin, 23–36. New York: Penguin Books.

Thompson, R. F. 1983. *Flash of the Spirit*. New York: Vintage Books.

———. 1991. "Kongo Influences on African-American Artistic Culture." In *Africanisms in American Culture*, edited by Joseph E. Holloway, 148–84 . Bloomington: Indiana University Press.

Trouillot, H. 1983. *Introduction à une histoire du Vandou*. Port-au-Prince: Editions Fardin.

Trouillot, M.-R. 1986. *Les racines historiques de l'état duvaliérien*. Port-au-Prince: Imprimerie Deschamps.

Tylor, E. B. [1871] 1970. *Religion in Primitive Society*. 2 vols. Gloucester, Mass.: P. Smith.

de Vaissière, P. 1909. *Saint-Domingue: La société et la vie des créoles sous l'ancien régime*. 2 vols. Paris: Perrin.

Verschueren, J. 1948. *La république d'Haïti: Le culte Vaudou*. Paris: Lethielleux.

Wach, J. 1944. *Sociology of Religion*. Chicago: University of Chicago Press.

Wallace, A. 1979. "Revitalization Movements." In *Reader in Comparative Religion: An Anthropological Approach*, 4th ed., edited by William A. Lessa and Evon Z. Vogt, 421–30. New York: Harper and Row.

Warner, M. 1989. *Seule entre toutes les femmes: Mythe et culte de la Vierge Marie*. Paris: Rivages/Histoires.

Weber, M. 1964. *Theory of Social and Economic Organization*. Translated by Talcott Parsons. New York: Free Press.

Weinstein, B., and A. Segal. 1984. *Haiti: Political Failures, Cultural Successes*. New York: Praeger Press.

Wilentz, H. 1989. *The Rainy Season: Haiti since Duvalier*. New York: Simon and Schuster.

Wimpffen, Baron de F. A. S. 1911. *Saint-Domingue à la veille de la révolution*. Paris: Albert Savine.

Wingfield, R., and V. Parenton. 1965. "Class Structure and Clan Conflict in Haitian Society." *Social Forces* 43 (no. 3): 338–47.

Wolf, E. 1966. *Peasants*. Englewood Cliffs, N.J.: Prentice-Hall.

Wolkstein, D. 1978. *The Magic Orange Tree and Other Haitian Folk Tales*. New York: Schocken Books.

Zahan, D. 1960. *Société d'initiation Bambara, le N'Domo, le Kore*. Paris: Mouton.

Zuesse, E. M. 1979. *Ritual Cosmos*. Columbus: Ohio State University Press.

INDEX